SMALL BUSINESS

BIG POLITICS

SMALL BUSINESS
BUSINESS

WHAT

ENTREPRENEURS

NEED TO KNOW

TO USE THEIR

GROWING

POLITICAL POWER

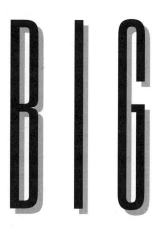

BIG

POLITICS

CHARLES A. RILEY II

PETERSON'S/PACESETTER BOOKS
PRINCETON, NEW JERSEY

95

Small Business, Big Politics is published by Peterson's/Pacesetter Books.

Pacesetter Books, Peterson's/Pacesetter Books, and the Pacesetter horse are trademarks of Peterson's Guides, Inc.

Library of Congress Cataloging-in-Publication Data

Riley, Charles A.
    Small business, big politics : what entrepreneurs need to know to use their growing political power / Charles A. Riley.
     p.   cm.
    "Peterson's/Pacesetter Books."
    Includes index.
    ISBN 1-56079-474-7
    1. Small business—United States—Political activity. 2. Small business—Government policy—United States.
    HD22346.U5R54   1995
    322'.3—dc20   95-13194
                                                                            CIP

Cover design by Susan Newman
Interior design by Greg Wozney Design, Inc.
Cover photograph by Christine Rodin

Printed in the United States of America

10 9 8 7 6 5 4 3 2 1

Visit Peterson's Education Center on the Internet (World Wide Web) at http://www.petersons.com

To Teb Barnard, Brian Eckel, and Paul Iskyan, best of friends and shining examples of the American entrepreneurial spirit, and to our fathers, who showed us the way.

CONTENTS

Preface

Small Business, Big Politics is a book full of surprises. Right off the bat, it will probably be surprising for entrepreneurs and government officials to learn just how powerful the small business lobby already is in Washington and throughout the state legislatures. It may shock many entrepreneurs to know how much political influence they actually wield and how often they will have the chance to use their newfound power in the coming decade as they—the small business owner-managers of this country—reshape the economic and regulatory policies that govern them. They may be astonished to find out how many federal and state employees are specifically charged with playing the role of small business advocate, looking out for their interests on the inside. They may also be surprised at how effective certain largely unknown lobbying groups are in pushing the cause of small business on the national level.

Certain small business owners will be drawn, naturally, to the chapters of this book exploring aspects of government policy that most directly affect their business, such as export laws or environmental regulations. However, I hope the reader will discover what I did in writing this book: that the interconnections among these issues are of fundamental importance in understanding how government works and how small business can work with and within government, because a shift in thinking at the Environmental Protection Agency (EPA) can very rapidly create an echo at the Internal Revenue Service (IRS) or the Justice Department. The sensitivity to these trends, and the knowledge of how to apply pressure at the right points and at the right time, comes from a general knowledge of how the interrelations arise. The appendix provides a directory of names and direct lines to Washington and to lobbying organizations. I hope that entrepreneurs will use this information to make contact and voice their opinions about how government is doing its job and what can be done better.

As a journalist, I maintain my distance from party politics or interest groups. My role is to observe and report, to talk to the policy makers and the small business owner-managers who are affected by what they do. Their stories are related from both sides of the desk in an effort to illuminate the misunderstandings, and potential for collaboration, that characterize the relationship between small business and government in our time. My aim is not to sympathize with the plight of small business and cry foul about the awful burden of regulation.

From inside Washington's corridors of power and various local regulatory offices, the open doors for entrepreneurs as activists can be glimpsed. Working with government is no picnic. For a writer or an entrepreneur, the atmosphere on the inside can be dismal and the complete antithesis to the way we hustle through our day. As I learned when covering big business interests in Washington during my years at *Fortune*, many political appointees are slow, unproductive, and too lazy to get up out of their chairs without an audible groan about the effort it is costing them. The picture of government we see on television is often no less encouraging—chaotic legislative sessions, gales of rhetoric at press conferences, and the steady stream of scandal involving conflict of interest and general incompetence.

But there are signs of life in Washington. In order to create an accurate and nonpartisan representation of the problematic—and promising—relationship between government and small business, this book offers portraits of the individuals involved, including not just entrepreneurs but also the legislative and regulatory officials with whom they too often deal either anonymously or across the distance of official detachment.

Some government officials are far from detached and indifferent to the cause of small business. Among the sources who were of tremendous help in making *Small Business, Big Politics* happen, I must thank Jere Glover, the Small Business Administration's dynamic chief advocate, and his staff, who together are the most important friends in Washington that entrepreneurs have. They are joined by Barbara Jenkins, the small business ombudsman at the IRS, and Karen Brown, the ombudsman at the EPA, along with Bob Hardacre at the EPA, who were also energetic and helpful sources for this book.

The official advocates for small business make up a tough, determined, and smart community that does not always get along. I received a tremendous amount of assistance from the National Federation of Independent Businesses (NFIB) and would like to thank their president, Jack Faris, as well as Terry Hill, the head of public affairs. On the other side of many of the issues, the Small Business Coalition on Health Care Reform, and Phil Schneider in particular, provided insight and information whenever I needed it. Oren Teicher, master strategist of the American Booksellers Association, was a friendly and incisive guide to the role of industry associations in the political process.

But more than any other group, I was utterly enthralled by the enthusiasm and political genius of the members of the National Association of Women Business Owners (NAWBO), who have similarly surprised most of official Washington with their skill and energy. I am indebted in particular to NAWBO's executive director Judith S. Johnson and chief strategist Virginia Littlejohn for the long interviews they endured and helpful pointers they gave me, and I would like to thank as well Debra Lessin and Terri Boekhoff for sharing their personal stories about becoming involved in politics.

The diversity and drama of the entrepreneurs' experiences is endless, of course. There is no standard entrepreneurial "type" that can be summarized in a basic career path. While some are mavericks who have broken away from the corporate world and others scarcely view themselves as business people, preferring to think of what they are doing as a form of self-expression that helps to sustain them not only monetarily but psychologically as well, all of them share a common trait: individuality. Telling their stories, letting them explain what business and government means in their own words, is the only way to fully appreciate their contribution to the policy process. I would like to express my deep gratitude to these heroes of the trenches, including Teb Barnard, Paul Iskyan, Brian Eckel, Josie Natori, Lisa Hahn, Kevin Gallagher, and the dozens of others who gave me their time and wisdom. They have been the greatest source of inspiration for this book.

Among the many minds I have picked in pulling this broad-reaching and ambitious book together, I must thank my agent, Nicholas T. Smith, and my editor, Andrea Pedolsky, for their unfailing support and their help as a constant, generous source of ideas, suggestions, and new information. At Baruch College, I have been blessed with the counsel of fine colleagues, such as Professors S. Prakash Sethi, Terrence Martel, and H. Jack Shapiro, as well as Alvin Puryear, who heads the College's small business lab and development center. My thinking on the importance of seeing political and social change before it has an impact on small business has been shaped by long conversations and collaboration with Andre Alkiewicz, the chairman of Perception International, a think tank in Connecticut, as well as Asher B. Edelman, the chairman of Datapoint Corporation. I first wrote about the small business lobby in Washington in a cover feature for *Owner Manager* magazine, a venture that I helped start up with Vincent Ricasio, who deserves my thanks. Many ideas in the book were honed in debate with Edward Reynolds, a savvy former lobbyist and ardent political observer.

Creating a new magazine was not my only small business experience. The small business genes are in my blood. I have fond memories of the hard work my father and I put into setting up his independent machine tool business, which, ironically enough, was one of the early casualties of government regulations regarding liability insurance. He and I inherited our entrepreneurial and political tendencies from our forebears, including Calvin Coolidge, who still stands as an emblem of the connection between business and politics, and before him from my namesake, Ethan Allen, and his brother Ira, who played their role not only in the Revolutionary War but in the beginning of the American entrepreneurial tradition as it developed in the small manufacturing towns of New England. My father's fiercely critical yet deeply patriotic view of government taught me, more than anything else, the importance of putting up a good, tough, and honest fight—and that spirit, I hope, will come across in these pages.

—Charles Allen Riley II

THE NEW FORCE
What Small Business Has to Gain Politically

At first glance, it looks like a blowout: Big government and big business—the combined resources of the Fortune 500 and Wall Street with their lobbyists, plus the Congress, the White House, the Internal Revenue Service, the Environmental Protection Agency, Customs, and every other regulatory agency—against the little shop on Main Street with five employees. What possible chance could the individual entrepreneur have in a political arena dominated by professional giants? And what could make playing politics worth the effort when the odds are so heavily stacked against the individual?

The conventional wisdom urges us to stay clear of a fight that looks intimidating and confusing. But for small business, which is anything but small in importance under the lens of current political thinking, this is an era of unprecedented political opportunity and a time to assume the role of a giant force for change in the relationship between government and business. Inside Washington and the state capitals, the political experts have already learned how potent the small business cause has become in the minds of lawmakers and policy formulators. They know that the voice of small business is the one credible business interest that legislators want to hear, making it the most sought-after testimony in the regulatory reform process. In this sense, the nation's small business owners compose the most extensive "politically correct" group in policy circles. No party, agency, or division of government, from the White House to the state house, can afford to alienate small business. It may be good politics for the Republican Congress to take away welfare benefits from individuals or the Democrats to whack multinationals with higher corporate tax rates, but any member of Congress or of a state assembly takes a risk by introducing a measure that hurts the chances for enterprises to develop.

STRENGTH IN NUMBERS

Where does the firepower come from that is needed to effect historic change in the relationship between politics and business? And how real is the change for the average small business? Political power arises from economic power. No matter whose figures you use, small business is the single most important economic force in the country today. The economic recovery depends on it. So will the outcome of the elections in 1996 and after. Political careers will be made and broken depending on the degree to which candidates can come through for small business with legislation that spells regulatory relief.

Despite an earnest effort by the Census Bureau and public relations firms representing major corporations to show that the failures of small business mean the elimination of jobs at almost the same rate as their creation, most data show clearly that the small business sector has been the sole engine of growth for the American economy through the lean years from 1988 through the present. Small business accounted for two thirds of the new jobs created during this era, including 45 percent of job creation between 1986 and 1988, and then virtually all new jobs between 1988 and 1990. This amounted to a net of 400,000 new positions provided by businesses with fewer than 500 workers over the course of a decade racked by recession. It coincided with major hemorrhaging at GM, Exxon, IBM, the major investment banks, and other huge corporations—a pattern of job loss at the top of the Fortune 500 that has continued well into what is supposed to have been the recovery of the U.S. economy. After a string of broken promises that left their former employees and stockholders in revolt, these corporate giants lost their credibility with the government, too. When the Republicans swept to victory in the Congress in November 1994, they were led by a number of House and Senate winners who are former small business owners and know, firsthand, how important enterprise is to the economy and how difficult it is to grow a business in an adverse political climate.

By contrast with the poor record of big business, small business as a community has kept its promises. It creates the jobs that bring votes, it pays its taxes (at a disproportionately higher rate), it generates the growth in exports that the government desperately needs, and it holds the door open to women and minorities who still, even after decades of affirmative action, do not get a fair shake in the corporate world.

The small business phenomenon in the United States is as varied as it is healthy, with strength in both service and manufacturing concerns and a track record of racial diversity that far surpasses the giant "corpocracies." According to the latest statistics, nearly 57 percent of all private-sector employees work for firms with fewer than 500 people.

The Small Business Administration (SBA) tracks nearly 6.5 million small businesses in the United States alone. That represents, as any Congressperson or local Assemblyperson can tell you, a hefty power base in voting terms as well as economic terms. The sheer size that makes the small business constituency so attractive to policy makers also makes it nearly impossible to unify. There is no single, monolithic small business point of view. The constituency comprises Democrats and Republicans, environmentally conscious "greens" and archconservatives, and proponents of virtually every side of every issue whose revenues can be helped or hurt by specific decisions or government actions. Blanket statements about the position of small business on any given issue are therefore next to impossible.

This broad spectrum of views can be focused on occasion into a single beam of intense power. All it takes is coordination and activism. Within the last few years, the growth and development of a half dozen small business lobbying groups in Washington have been tremendous, and entrepreneurs now have several choices regarding who should represent their interests. These lobbying organizations are far more professional and technically sophisticated than many of their political rivals, such as lobbying groups for big business or labor, suspect. The best-organized small business lobbying organization can, in a matter of seconds, use its computer database to pinpoint at least 1,000 members in any given Congressional district.

Beyond representing a lot of voters, small business has the added attraction of comprising eminently *successful* members of society. The gains posted by small business look formidable against the backdrop of what is happening elsewhere in the American economy. The total employment among Fortune 500 companies fell from 12.5 million in 1989 to 11.5 million in 1994, according to David Birch, president of Cognetics, an economic research company in Cambridge, Massachusetts. But Birch points out that most of the job growth in the United States over that period has come from companies with sales growing at 20 percent a year and at least $100,000 in annual sales. These "gazelles," as Birch calls the rapidly expanding companies that include up to 2,000 workers, added over four million net jobs to the economy between 1989 and 1993.

The annual growth rate of many of these firms is not just in the triple-digit range; it is solidly in the area above 200 percent per year. Take the example of a firm like Discovery Zone, a family-oriented network of play centers for kids. Its annual growth rate has been 229 percent over the last five years, boosting the company to sales of $85.9 million a year with profits of $5.8 million. Another success story is Callaway Golf, the maker of the most popular driver, Big Bertha, and a favorite of the New York Stock Exchange's golfers, which nearly doubled its stock price within the first year of listing. It has grown at 124 percent per year to $282.6 million in sales. Boston Chicken, a franchise operation selling specially roasted chicken, hopes to add 1,000 stores to its network in the next three years; it is growing at 124 percent a year. These and thousands of other hugely profitable businesses are defying the well-known risks faced by entrepreneurs.

THE DREAM DEMOGRAPHICS OF THE SMALL BUSINESS CONSTITUENCY

The demographics of small business is a remarkable story in and of itself. For both the Republican and Democratic parties, both of which have long sought a way to put together their economic and social agendas, the fit between small business and the "marginalized" communities Washington hopes to serve is perfect for legislators who are loathe to dictate an "industrial policy" (a taboo in Washington today) but want to address the economic and social issues from an integrated perspective. The ideologies involved in this synthesis of policy objectives are varied. On the one hand, conservative Republicans, often with a religious agenda, can throw their now considerable weight behind small business as an emblem of the family values they promote. On the other hand, liberal Democrats see a lot to like in the populist possibilities of minority owner-managers able to gain upward mobility without remaining indebted to the corporate fat cats with whom the Republicans, though they are turning their backs on big business, continue to be identified.

The number of minority-owned small businesses is climbing at a healthy rate. Washington loves small business because it is a bellwether for many trends. As sociologists have noticed, women are the most potent new force in the small business field. According to the SBA, women head 5.5 million proprietorships in the United States, which is about one third of all businesses, and the compound rate at which their number is increasing is about 8.4 percent, nearly double the 4.5 percent growth rate of male-owned proprietorships. Despite extensive press coverage, the growing force of women entrepreneurs is underestimated, except in Washington, where it is gaining powerful allies in both the legislative and executive branches. And many retirees are finding a way back into the workforce through small business.

But it is not enough to talk about these groups in the abstract language of statistics and sociological categories. The small business community in the United States is an endless stream of fascinating, inspiring, and surprising stories of both success and failure, too varied to be lumped together in a few casual generalizations.

On the shores of Lake Minnetonka, in a little village of 2,400 residents called Excelsior in Minnesota, is the Kuempel Chime Clockwork and Studio. A small staff of 17 master craftspeople work at building the company's 300 clocks a year, ranging in price from $525 to $3,500. They hoped to reach $700,000 in sales in 1994. More important than any of these numbers, perhaps, is the fact that the average age of the workers is 69, and many of them are in their eighties. The owners of the business, a pair of Methodist church members in their fifties and two bankers, refuse to have a mandatory retirement age and offer starting pay of $5.50 an hour so Social Security payments are not affected. With the national life expectancy statistics going up every year and inflation threatening to eat up retirement plans, it's easy to see how these grandfathers and grandmothers at work on their clocks are really ahead of their time. They are also an irresistible example for lawmakers to praise when they are in search of support from older voters.

In the Boston suburb of Norwood, Massachusetts, to take another example, the brainchild of a 41-year-old woman with an associate degree from a Florida junior college, is a shoe company that gave Princess Diana her favorite pair of fitness shoes. The company is called Ryka, and it was just bought by L.A. Gear for $65 million from its founder, Sheri Poe. Poe is not just a businesswoman—she is an activist and philanthropist who used her political acumen and ability to read the writing on the wall regarding changes in society to turn a tidy profit. Together with her prospering shoe factory, which brings in about $14 million in sales a year, Poe runs the Ryka Rose Foundation, a nonprofit organization committed to stopping violence against women; it receives 7 percent of Ryka's annual profits and $10,000 a quarter. It took an awareness not only of a fitness trend (the entry of women into the aerobics market) but of the positive effects of political activism on business to make it happen. Multiply the politically conscious and financially prosperous story of Sheri Poe by thousands and you have a sense of the growing strength of women in the small business army.

While only 3 percent of all businesses in the nation are known to be owned by African-Americans, according to the Census Bureau the number of black-owned companies has increased 38 percent over the five years ending in 1987 (a new survey is under way currently). Moreover, sales of black-owned business-service firms have quadrupled over the past four years, according to Timothy Bates, an economist and scholar of African-American businesses.

Three publicly traded companies in the health-care field—United American Health-Care and Caraco Pharmaceutical in Detroit, along with American Shared Hospital Services in San Francisco—were founded by blacks, and health care continues to attract many black entrepreneurs who are interested in manufacturing real estate for facility sites, marketing, and services. A privately owned firm involved in medical and pharmaceutical supplies, Qualiti-Care Medical Services, was started in 1992 in Baltimore with the help of the city authorities, and now has revenues of $17 million and a new 30,000-square-foot warehouse built in part from the $4 million in financing offered by a major supplier. These entrepreneurs and others in a wide range of fields, including banking, media, and fashion, are encouraged by the push in Washington, as well as local governments, toward the use of minority vendors in the bidding process.

TAKING THE MESSAGE TO WASHINGTON AND TOWN HALL

The groundswell of the small business agenda in Washington began more than a decade ago. Its signs are evident in the Capitol. They include:

- Elevation of the Small Business Administration (SBA) administrator to a Cabinet-level post
- Creation of a Congressional small business caucus
- Creation of small business ombudsman positions at major agencies, including the Internal Revenue Service and Environmental Protection Agency, on both the federal and state level
- Strong legislative results from past White House Conferences on Small Business
- Greater attention paid to the Regulatory Flexibility Act examining the impact of regulation on small business
- A rethinking of the SBA that makes it more of a political advocacy organization than a lending institution
- Growth of politically savvy lobbying organizations devoted exclusively to small business interests
- Inclusion of specific small business provisions in major regulatory legislation

The victory of the small business lobby over the original 1994 health-care reform package was one of the most dramatic signs that the wave has arrived. The small business lobby faced down not only the White House, but also the Big Three automakers and other major corporate supporters of the health-care bill. The lesson this triumph is teaching small business political leaders is one that will inevitably filter down to the grassroots level of owner-managers themselves in communities throughout the world: Small business must do something about the policies and regulations that affect it by becoming part of the political process instead of waiting and reacting to its decisions.

Politics is all about momentum and, as in business itself, making the most of an opportunity the moment it arises. Small business has to build upon its new power base in understanding how government works and learning to read the messages coming out of Washington, as well as Tokyo, Moscow, Berlin, Beijing, Brussels, London, Paris, Mexico City, Ottawa, and the other decision-making capitals of the world. The federal level may be the most obvious place to look for signals, but owners of small businesses have to become attuned to political change on all levels, from the international to the local.

As the major corporations learned when setting up their lobbying efforts three decades ago against the threat of consumer and environmental critics, the local arena can be the toughest of all when it comes to the legislative and political changes that shape the future of business. But it is also the home turf for small businesses that are mainstays of a community, where they have a political advantage they do not always exploit. While it can take years, or at least months, to pass a bill through Congress or enact an executive order, a town council or village assembly can put together a ban on packaging materials, chemicals, or an ordinance about emissions controls in an evening. That is why DuPont, Mobil, and other huge corporations have vast, overpaid staffs of public relations and legal specialists putting out the little fires across the country that, when joined, could create an inferno.

Congress has given tremendous regulatory powers to bodies below the state level. Protected by Supreme Court decisions, counties and cities have enacted guidelines of their own in a wide range of areas that are not specifically addressed by federal regulatory agencies, and many of these guidelines have proven to be more and more unfriendly toward small business. By entering the debate on these issues—in fact, by learning to recognize the earliest tremors of anxiety in a region that foretell the coming debate—a more politically active small business constituency will find its voice and get its way.

PAYING THE PRICE FOR OVERREGULATION

Inside the Beltway, they have an acronym for the distrust and disillusionment that characterize the general feeling toward officialdom: FOG, or fear of government. Judging by the recent history of regulatory misery endured by small business, FOG is justified. Going back twenty-five years, the cost of administering federal regulatory programs was already a hefty $4 billion. It topped $13 billion in 1994 and is expected to rise. Economists at the Office of Management and Budget admit that the cost of regulation to the economy is about $392 billion a year, with $100 billion of that going to paperwork alone. The figures come from an estimated five billion hours spent by the private sector to fill out the forms and handle inspections, at an average cost of about $20 an hour. On top of that, fines and compliance expenditures add another $22 billion to the bill, and most agree that a disproportionate amount of the tab falls on the weary shoulders of small businesses.

As the economist Ravi Batra attempted to show in his study of business failures during the late 1980s, there is a direct correlation between the rise in the number of economic laws and the rise in the number of business failures. Since 1986, Congress has enacted 10 major regulatory packages, including the Clean Air Act, the Americans with Disabilities Act, and the Nutrition Labeling and Education Act, all of which passed in 1990. In 1992, when President Bush announced, as a desperate campaign measure, a 90-day moratorium on new regulations and "a top-to-bottom review of all regulations, old and new, to stop the ones that will hurt growth," the very idea of a moratorium on new regulation was considered novel. By March 1995, the House had passed a comprehensive cost analysis bill, the Risk Assessment and Communication Act, that places economic standards ahead of health-based standards for all regulation. And the Republican-controlled 104th Congress is considering a moratorium on regulations and yet another review.

But no matter how sincere the pro-business rhetoric coming out of Washington may sound, small business owner-managers are too smart to buy it until genuine regulatory relief is evident. Tune in to the real voices of small business, and you pick up a stern message of impatience and skepticism.

For manufacturers that stay close to the high-tech edge, like Hitemco in Old Bethpage, Long Island, the regulatory picture is confusing and often bleak. Left to its own devices, Hitemco has been a roaring success in the field of high-temperature coatings for the space shuttle engines, satellite systems for the entire free world, and other aeronautical projects. Within the last two years, the firm moved into the health field, sponsoring research on synthetic bone implants for orthopedics. Since opening up on Long Island in 1974, Hitemco has managed a brilliant compounded growth rate in annual revenues of 20 percent. They have achieved this despite their location. Nassau County, Long Island's richest county, is rapidly earning the reputation for being a regulatory nightmare and a phenomenally expensive region for doing business, thanks in part to local ordinances and the incompetence of the Long Island Lighting Company, the catastrophe-plagued local utility.

Teb Barnard, Hitemco's president, is a committed environmentalist and a skier in the winter and a boating enthusiast in summer. Like many other owner-managers who have inherited a family-run business, he likes to treat his employees like family. But he finds that much of the intense regulatory scrutiny his company endures is not just expensive— it's wasteful:

> We're trying to be good and conscientious neighbors, doing everything that is asked of us, because we live here as well as work here. But I'm afraid that the government is going to end up stifling what is already a hurting economy.

At least one member of Hitemco's staff of 55 is devoted full-time to taking care of regulatory compliance, including the Food and Drug Administration (FDA), Environmental Protection Agency (EPA), and Occupational Safety and Health Act (OSHA), as well as the growing presence of the local air quality board and town inspectors. That's a whole salary and benefits package that would be viewed as a complete write-off in terms of productivity. The accountants watch tax rules change, and because Hitemco has just started a joint venture in France, they have to closely monitor export and import restrictions, as well as trade negotiations involving high-technology standards in Europe.

However, local regulations are every bit as worrisome as complex international developments. The region's air quality regulations will cost Barnard over $120,000 of his capital over the next three years on new systems to clean the particulate out of the new exhaust system his plant uses. Barnard adds this to the cost of outside consultants; the expense of administering hearing tests to his workers on a monthly basis; the cost of removing wastewater in 55-gallon barrels by a special truck; as well as nickel-and-dime annoyances like the $500 fine he had to pay the local government when an inspector noticed dust on the executive dining table, and the $35,000 fine slapped on him by the local fire department, when, during construction, a pair of gas containers were temporarily left too close to the building. "It's nitpicking stuff they get hung up on, little tiny things that cost you money and the nonproductive use of time," Barnard complains.

The picture is similar in the service sector. As the American service economy boomed in the 1980s, it caught the eye of revenue-hungry commissions in Washington. In the case of the banks and savings and loan institutions that brought down whole communities in Texas and New England, it would be hard to argue that the increased attention was unjustified, but for a number of smaller operations struggling to turn the corner on profitability, the effect was often devastating.

Paul Iskyan represents the fourth generation of leadership in his family-owned rug renovating firm, now headquartered in East Orange, New Jersey. The first three generations kept the firm in Queens, just outside of Manhattan. But inefficient public utilities and overly strict New York City regulatory controls drove them across the Hudson River to a more pro-business environment at an estimated savings of 40 percent on government-related costs.

Regulation is still a headache for Iskyan, however. "Administratively, it takes a lot of resources between government forms and compliance with child support for the Bureau of Labor. It's zapped the business," Iskyan says wearily. He sees a four-year downward cycle in his industry that has been accelerated by overregulation. "Business goes down and regulation goes up," he observes, echoing Ravi Batra. Iskyan tries to draw a relationship between the culture of the regulators and his own situation: "They're bureaucrats, and they have to keep their own jobs, but I have to keep about 70 people working too."

Iskyan finds that the government framework doesn't respond to the needs of small business and fails to understand the real economic forces at work in our time. His politics reflect the sort of conservatism that has been identified with the small-business lobby, although in fact the politics of small business is so diverse as to defy most labels. A staunch Reaganite, who blames former President George Bush for diluting the pro-business policies of the nation, Iskyan was at first vehemently opposed to President Clinton. Now he views Clinton's promises to small business with cautious optimism but has his continuing reservations regarding the environmental policies of Vice President Al Gore: "If the Ozone Man goes wild, we've got trouble."

A PRIMER ON POLICY

Three basic types of government policy have a direct impact upon small business: monetary, fiscal, and regulatory. For entrepreneurs, a thorough understanding not only of policy basics but of the divergent forces that are pushing governments to try using them in different ways is essential. To become conversant in these matters is to enter a circle of business thinkers who make the most—financially and politically—of their knowledge through anticipating the next moves of government and influencing them as well.

With the currency markets in a perpetual state of emergency, and the real estate picture so closely linked to interest rates, it is no surprise that monetary policy receives the most press coverage and, with that attention, a certain weight in popular opinion. Monetary policy is the key to softening the effects of volatility in the basic economic cycles traced by overall GDP, discretionary spending, and unemployment.

The Role of Monetary Policy

Monetary policy is the traditional means of controlling inflation. Most pundits blame careless monetary policy for the rampant inflation of the 1970s and give the Federal Reserve credit for using appropriately draconian measures to keep inflation in check during the 1980s. During the relatively tumultuous year of 1994 the Fed raised interest rates seven times—six times between February and June. Yet fear of inflation continued to dog the stock and bond markets into 1995.

If the back-and-forth, tidal forces of change such as fear of inflation seem somewhat remote and abstract to most small business owners, the best way to bring it home is to track the impact the Federal Reserve's moves have on day-to-day operations. Easy credit and the possibility of paying back loans at a lower dollar level are attractive reasons for wanting to see interest rates hit a lower level. The stock market loves it. Should small business? Only to a degree, if the lessons of history serve. Despite a number of promises regarding easier money from both government and major banks, the credit crunch for small business remains a stern reminder that what is good for big business—and possibly personal finance—in the nation at large is not necessarily good for small business owners. Even if interest rates are low, credit remains tight for certain high-risk categories, especially start-ups. What looks like easy money at a low interest rate is still out of reach for most small businesses looking for financing.

One factor in the monetary equation that is often overlooked is the role of the Small Business Administration, which, as the nation's biggest small-business lender, is supposed to take up the slack in the credit markets. But the SBA's role is changing. Despite a Herculean feat of housecleaning done by former head Erskine Bowles during his brief tenure from 1992 into 1993, the organization is under pressure to become something very different from a bank. The Republican-controlled Congress envisions a more politically active SBA that will speak up as an advocacy group for small business interests. As described in Chapter 6, the reasoning behind this provides a revealing window into the new power structure of Washington, which has already shifted toward what trade negotiators might call the trilateral agenda of small business–big business–government from the old bilateral configuration of big business and big government.

Reading Between the Lines of Fiscal Policy

During the 1960s and 1970s, one unsuccessful experiment after another in fiscal management of the economy served to dispel the myth that it could work. For one thing, fiscal attempts to solve ongoing economic crises generally come too late since they have to get Congressional approval. Those measures to stimulate the economy usually come into effect after a recovery begins so they only serve to promote inflation.

The prime mechanisms of fiscal policy are tax cuts or raises, as well as stimulus packages, such as the now-forgotten one President Clinton unsuccessfully promoted in the opening weeks of his presidency. In the 1980s, the attempt to promote spending with tax cuts ended in an exacerbated budget crisis. Similar attempts to curb inflation by raising taxes have never worked. The results of this tinkering: the massive budget deficit and federal debt that eats up more than $300 billion per year.

The realization that neither fiscal nor monetary dipsy-doodling on the part of Washington is going to solve the economic problems of the nation has changed the nature of the White House's pronouncements on policy. A new modesty is coming out of Washington. Listen to Robert D. Reischauer, director of the Congressional Budget Office and one of the silent yeomen of policymaking whose name rarely appears in the press: "We've matured as a political society. We now realize that there are costs and disruptions even when we take actions that appear desirable."

Government spending is not being used, as it once was, as a tool for manipulating key indicators. But small business has to learn to read between the lines of the spending bills to understand the thinking and trends that will affect their business. All business is in some manner touched by what happens on Capitol Hill. Following the paper trail of legislative and government reports, and in particular being able to decode the rhetoric and technical language of government as it is formulated and changed, is a valuable skill. Few-enough corporate leaders really know the process on their own. They hire teams of lawyers, strategic planners, and consultants to do it for them. The owner-manager of a small to mid-sized company can't afford that kind of support work but can't afford not to understand the buzz that comes out of Washington and other capitals of the world. This is not a narrow specialty. In a global age, it is vital for the businessperson to understand the political process of many different countries as well as the intricacies of federal, state, and local governments in the United States.

The Legislative Path

Any fiscal move starts out as a bill in draft form that is "marked up" and revised many times before it reaches the floor of the House or Senate. Similarly, trade agreements and local ordinances begin as documents written in terms that are even perplexing to lawyers. Until government reform reaches the stage, as promised, where these documents are more clearly and accessibly written, an entrepreneur must learn how to decode a bill for signs of change that will directly affect his or her business. Nothing is gained by waiting and watching from the sidelines as these measures progress from one legislative body to another, only to appear "on the books" and have a sudden and seemingly unforeseen impact on the way business is done.

It is not unusual for a fiscally oriented bill to conceal a hidden agenda, such as research projects included in defense spending, and tip off experts to policy decisions involving more than just the Pentagon. When the dust on the Congressional debate over one of these measures clears, industry analysts can pick up the first indications of government support, or tighter regulation, of their own agendas. For instance, the advent of the data superhighway was telegraphed to savvy entrepreneurs long before Al Gore made it part of the headlines. From the mid-1980s to recent legislation, any bill with "telecom" in it moved fast through the appropriations or approval process, just as during the early 1980s any package that involved health care was accorded instant priority.

The shock waves from major fiscal decisions ripple outward from Washington faster than most people think. The stocks of the major defense contractors like Martin Marietta, Northrop Grumman, and General Dynamics register the news within minutes of the announcements from Washington, and their fortunes rise and fall from year to year based on the votes.

But the hidden effects of fiscal legislation go past that. For the hundreds of thousands of independent subcontractors who are also linked in the economic web of the defense industry, the news is also vital. When the Pentagon sneezes, a small parts supplier can be blown into bankruptcy. One right decision on the part of a savvy subcontractor can suddenly increase sales a thousandfold. More importantly, even for those small businesses that do not directly benefit from the specific appropriations set forth in Congressional bills, the ability to read the change in the character of fiscal legislation is a blessing. It can indicate the direction in which the government as a whole is moving with regard to industrial policy, the types of research and development that are likely to be supported by loans or tax incentives, and the future of regulation.

THE CASE FOR REGULATORY RELIEF

The third, and for small business the most important, prong of potential government intervention is regulation. The most massive and publicized regulatory initiative of the Clinton administration—health care reform—was an initial disaster. Its failure, attributed by most Washington insiders to the efforts of the small business lobby, started a snowball of antiregulatory feeling in Washington that was accelerated in November 1994 when the Republicans swept to a majority in Congress. In a Republican-controlled Congress, with the reins tightly held by Speaker of the House Newt Gingrich and Majority Leader Bob Dole, the forces are certainly aligned against initiatives of this kind.

Government agencies have two principal tasks: regulating and planning. The evolution of the current system has been pushed by Congressional promises to the consumer more often than to the producer or worker, although the idea of a level and relatively unrestricted playing field is meant to benefit all three. There is a logical conflict between the two functions of the agencies, which simultaneously must control prices and practices among producers and also promote commerce and economic activity. During the extended recession, more was expected of the government to goose the economy into recovery than to hold the line on price controls, minimum wage laws, and other restrictions.

The details of regulation and planning are supposed to be left to the agencies, so that the Federal Communications Commission (FCC) is meant to sort out the auctioning off of the frequencies on the radio spectrum, while the Securities and Exchange Commission (SEC) works out the rules on insider trading, and so on. The degree of independence is an important issue. Ideally, these agencies are completely autonomous, so that the White House, Congress, and Supreme Court will leave the complexities of different industry issues and cases to specialists.

The proliferation of the agencies from relatively straightforward policing organizations meant to carry out comparatively simple mandates to vast bureaucracies employing thousands of specialists and engaging in industrial policy making and planning is a matter for the history books. The idea that these agencies act on their own without the day-to-day controls of Congressional or Executive policy initiatives is hopelessly naive, and that is why insight into the interaction between the highest levels of government and the foot soldiers meant to carry out the rules they have devised based on broader legislation is so necessary.

But politics is not exclusively the province of specialists. The highest-ranking regulatory officials, like the Supreme Court justices, are appointed by the President. The appointments are approved by both the House and Senate. Moreover, the Congress approves their budget—specifically the Ways and Means Committee. The patronage system of big lobbies and Congressional favors is a major part of the composition of the agencies at the beginning of any presidential term. As in Congress, a number of inconsistencies slip into rulings based on favors owed or political influence, showing that the independence of the fourth division of government is a myth.

Under the original design of the system their power was supposed to stem from their expertise. It does not really work that way, however. Despite the fact that the agencies are technically more related to the legislative branch of government than to either the judicial or executive, they take their style from justice and their orders from the executive. There is, actually, a tremendous resemblance between a regulatory agency and a court. The agencies have big "courtroom" style chambers in each of their headquarters. During hearings, commissioners sit on a dais in very judicial-looking high-backed chairs next to a witness stand and face a group of tables where attorneys and their clients argue their cases before a block of seats reserved for the audience. The regulators even enter the hearing chambers after a gavel is banged and the meeting is called to order. Their rulings are handed down on a case-by-case basis, as in the courts.

By contrast, the dimly lit, uncomfortable offices of most of the agencies are often in a state of turmoil since job security is hardly one of the perks of the job. Since they owe their jobs to the President, the pseudo-legislative status of the regulators is undermined by the need to stick with the program as defined by the White House, although to a lesser degree than the cabinet appointees.

Some agencies are less under the thumb than others. Federal Reserve appointments, for example, are for fourteen years. A perpetual complaint from the business advocacy community is that personnel and jobs are too often mismatched. One famous story that epitomizes this ludicrous state of affairs comes from a Senate confirmation hearing nearly two decades ago when a Federal Communications Commission nominee was asked about his qualifications for the post. He replied, "Senator, I don't know anything about communications. I came to Washington expecting to be appointed to the Federal Power Commission."

The case-by-case nature of the regulatory process is time-consuming, although less than 10 percent of the decisions handed down go through the whole drama of a hearing. Most are handled through "informal adjudications" held in private, generally in Washington, with the attorneys for the business as well as the CEO and in-house counsel facing the agency staffers who have prepared the case. Private meetings among agency experts and industry representatives are also used to work on legislation that could affect an industry or region.

THE ROLE OF SMALL BUSINESS IN REGULATORY REFORM

The commonly held notion of how the regulatory machine operates assumes that the main players are big business and the agencies. But, historically, small business has played a significant role in the development of the nation's regulatory structure and the 1990s are proving a period of great opportunity for small business in the field of regulatory reform. This does not always mean that small business has pushed for *less* regulation, however. In some areas, small business public policy advocates look for tougher enforcement. Most of the fair trade and antitrust laws were developed as watchdog measures to ensure that big business does not exploit or dominate small business. They place the regulatory agency in the position of referee between small business and large corporations. Thanks to a number of high-profile cases— including an antitrust investigation of Microsoft—and strategically adroit lawsuits or complaints brought by small business trade organizations, antitrust and fair trade measures are once again the focus of Congressional and regulatory attention.

The fair trade laws are dear to the heart of small retailers. Chains that offer customers steep discounts and have tighter relationships with the major manufacturers which allow them to secure steep discounts and other preferential treatment from them—such as the major drugstore, bookstore, or supermarket chains that have special relationships with Nabisco or Doubleday or Pfizer—are now the target of small business activism and consumer skepticism. Not only Washington but local governments are hearing from small businesses on these matters. Spurred on by "professional" activists, small businesses across the nation have opposed the expansion of Wal-Mart and other discounters into their communities, winning occasionally in the courts, town council meetings, and state assemblies, and scoring decisively in public opinion.

Their plight is drawing sympathetic attention in Washington, and so is their might, because despite the overall sluggish performance of the major retailers, the small business side of the retail picture shows signs of great vitality. In the fall of 1994, a report prepared by Dun & Bradstreet together with G. A. Wright Inc., a Denver-based retail consulting firm, showed that the economic vitality of small retailers was underestimated. Of the 37 sectors studied, overall sales in 30 were dominated by firms with less than $1 million in sales annually, which created half the job growth in the retail areas considered during the nine-year period of the study. In certain sectors, such as gifts, sports, and jewelry, smaller firms accounted for as much as 70 percent of job growth. These figures translate into political vitality, as well, and fair trade laws that adhere to the principle of a manufacturer's suggested retail price are once again being enforced by civil suits brought by manufacturers against retailers that use steep discounts, or by smaller players who can afford the legal firepower to take on the chains. More action on the federal level is likely to come—while most states have had retail price-fixing laws on the books for decades, no national structure exists.

In fact, the closest Congress has come to a national fair trade law was a bill, the Robinson-Patman Act of 1936, that added on to the existing antitrust law a set of provisions banning manufacturers from discriminating between wholesalers and retailers, echoing the language of the Clayton Act of 1914, an antitrust bill that modernized the Sherman Act of 1890. The modernization of the antitrust laws to include pricing came about as mail-order giants like Sears Roebuck and supermarket chains such as A&P pushed even the mid-sized wholesalers, as well as smaller retailers, out of business.

Antitrust provides another testing ground for the new power of small business in Washington. The boom in mergers and acquisitions from 1987 through 1990, echoed recently by a rise in M&A activity, along with cartel-like movements in air and freight fares, as well as collaborations between entertainment and telecommunications are all interpreted as indicators of the low level of antitrust enforcement. This in turn is read by some experts as a danger signal for small business rather than as a welcome sign that government is turning to a laissez-faire policy on regulation.

The antitrust case against Microsoft has polarized the legal and political advocates of small business along the lines of those who want government regulators actively on the side of entrepreneurs and those who want them to keep their hands off business in general. All of them were watching with keen interest when, one Saturday morning in mid-July 1994, Assistant Attorney General Anne Bingaman issued a consent decree that seemingly ended a wide-ranging antitrust dispute between Microsoft and the Justice Department.

A great deal was made, even in the Justice Department's speeches, of the nearly legendary role Microsoft has played in going from a tiny startup company to a global powerhouse in information technology. During the press conference announcing the consent decree, Bingaman was almost apologetic for going after a symbol of American innovation. "Microsoft is an American success story; there is no excuse for trying to cement its success through unlawful means," she told reporters.

As a guide for how to behave in Washington, most insiders would not recommend following the model of Bill Gates. His strategy was to fight tooth and nail. Gates was public in his vehement refusal to give in to the investigation. There are even reports that in private meetings with FTC commissioners he blasted them in a loud voice about the limits to their jurisdiction. That may be fine for Bill Gates—it won't work for most entrepreneurs who go into government hearings without a squad of corporate lawyers.

Those who said Microsoft actually won the battle spoke too soon. On July 14, 1994, U.S. District Court Judge Stanley Sporkin overturned the settlement. And in turn, the Justice Department said it would appeal that decision. However the case is decided, it is of symbolic importance for small business. Microsoft chairman Bill Gates is both an icon of entrepreneurial success and an icon of corporate America. The message sent by government could be miscontrued as a warning against growing a small business too big. Many regulations, by exempting companies with, for example, 50 or fewer employees, are already perceived as a means of keeping entrepreneurs from expanding past certain officially sanctioned limits. When a symbol of entrepreneurial success, like Gates, is targeted by regulators, it can be a positive and a negative sign. Should small business cheer when he is busted?

The strict enforcement of any regulation is a two-edged sword. The Microsoft case is a reminder that businesses enjoy less freedom under the Constitution than the press, individuals, or even religious institutions. It will be up to the activists in the small business community to put the freedom to own and manage a private concern on a footing with private conduct in the future. The fear that drives legislation limiting commerce is simply the same fear that propels one branch of government to limit the scope of another. It is a fear of power. When Microsoft became too big—as the railroads or AT&T or even IBM once had—the government felt its wings had to be trimmed. The small business advocates who cheered on the Justice Department in its pursuit of Microsoft may at a later date yearn for a less aggressive government regulatory stance—the tables turn quickly.

A CLASH OF CULTURES

The main reason small business and big government have problems getting along is not the obviously adversarial nature of their relationship—this book outlines a number of exceptions to that antagonism—but something more elementary. Let's call it "cultural differences." Since the late 1980s, business journalists and professors, as well as university anthropologists and private consultants with anthropology backgrounds, have made a cottage industry of studying the corporate culture of Fortune 500 firms like General Electric, Motorola, or AT&T. These studies make colorful reading, because they take you inside the doors of the big firms and often convey clever ideas for running any organization more smoothly.

One could only wish for a similar examination shedding real light on the cultural abyss that separates small business from government. It is costing entrepreneurs power and money, and it is costing the country in terms of economic growth. When entrepreneurs and government meet face to face, the differences are dramatized. An owner-manager who sacrifices seven days a week, 16 hours a day, to keep the business going has trouble respecting a government clerk who takes every mandated coffee break and has an eye on the clock long before that magical five o'clock quitting time comes around. For bureaucrats, the entrepreneur's impatient disdain for paperwork and backup records seems bizarre and irresponsible. The secret of success for many an entrepreneur lies in identifying the unique, completely innovative business niche, while government likes to deal with categories, groups, and broad definitions. The list of personality differences goes on and on.

There are already signs that major government institutions and small business are benefiting from the anthropological perspective in ways that will heal the rift between government and small business. For the most part the message that is being delivered to government is that it has to knock off the "high and mighty" arrogance that keeps it from understanding changes in the society it is meant to serve. For example, Al Gore's plan to "re-invent government" was introduced in 1992—basically he was promoting a streamlined approach analogous to the then-hot management idea of "re-engineering" the corporation. At the same time, in a series of changes more symbolic than business-oriented, the Department of the Navy, the Central Intelligence Agency, the New York City Police Department, and other beleaguered government institutions announced their own intentions to redefine their internal culture to break up the fraternity atmosphere and pay attention to critics who found that attitude deeply offensive.

Anthropology points the way to an understanding of why small business and government have drifted so far apart and may reveal potential areas where the gap can be bridged. Talk about a culture usually ends up in generalizations, and inevitably it will become "us" against "them" unless an effort is made to pin the differences down more precisely. But what about the other side of the desk? The government is made up of individuals, too—not machines. Who are these people? How did they get where they are? What educational and business background do they bring to their jobs? What do they think of the entrepreneurs into whose books and offices they peer every day? What, most importantly, is their agenda? By taking a moment in these pages to find out their stories and examine the more subtle indications of where government thinking is going in the coming years, we can take a step past cultural generalities to reveal what really is on the minds of business and government when they face one another.

THE INCENTIVE TO BECOME INVOLVED

Change is the key factor in regulation. Business loses or makes money on rule changes. That is why small business cannot afford to be left out of the process. Whether through trade organizations or directly through their representatives in Congress, small business owner-managers are finding that they must become involved in the policy decisions that shape their own destinies.

Getting involved starts with the very first steps of launching a business, where a tight hand on the regulatory reins hurts small businesses trying to gain entry into industries governed by particular agencies: the SEC and stock exchanges control their membership, the states control bank charters, the FCC controls radio and television, and the Interstate Transport Commission issues permits to truckers. Rather than promoting competition among the optimum number of businesses large and small, these agencies can make it very difficult for a start-up to edge into the field.

Or they can open it up under political pressure. One fascinating new development in this area was the public auction of bandwidths along the radio spectrum by the FCC. Under the most freewheeling, open conditions ever to exist between broadcasters and the FCC, the unprecedented auctions were a huge success for the government, raking in $300 million. Nobody knows yet how important they will prove for small business.

This underscores a very important element in the relationship between small business and government: access to information, technology, resources, and power. The economic significance of the data superhighway is even greater than the rhetorical buzz surrounding it has suggested. When Al Gore promises access to those who for financial reasons may have been disenfranchised in the past, small business ought to be ready to hold him to it. As a way of expanding a company's reach in both the research direction and in international marketing, the realization of fully interactive, desktop-based networks is the key to growth without massive additions to costs, such as travel or manpower.

YOUR BIGGEST CUSTOMER

Small business cannot afford to ignore government because government represents a vast amount of customer power. By the most modest measure, 22 percent of total GDP is attributable to government on one level or another, making it the single biggest entity in the U.S. economy. That makes it a potent factor in the equation of American business. The General Services Administration (GSA) is implementing a new strategy devised in 1994 that is going to direct more government contracts to small companies, including but not limited to minority-owned and women-owned businesses. The new rule says that all bidders on contracts above $500,000 (or $1 million in the case of construction) should offer subcontracting plans that will "aggressively" include small businesses. Currently, that rule only applies to actual bid winners.

The ruling came as a response to White House pressure, and it could involve special considerations for higher price bids that involve small business contractors, along the lines of the provisions for minority contractors already in effect. (Every federal department—such as Energy, Transportation, Commerce—has a special office for small business that is specifically a liaison position to aid small businesses in gaining procurement contracts. The names and phone numbers of these liaison officers are listed in the directory that is the appendix to this book.)

Recognizing the needs and inner tendencies of government as a target market is a first step toward coming to grips with an institution that should look less and less like a monolith and more like a trading partner, which is going to seem an odd notion to those accustomed to the old adversarial image. It would be crazy to wish that 22 percent of the economic buying power in the nation would simply go away.

IT IS WHAT YOU KNOW THAT COUNTS

The business benefits of political activism should not be downplayed. However, they are tough to accurately gauge according to conventional income. While experts have estimated the annual regulatory burden on individual businesses and every owner-manager is well aware of the costs arising from obligations to the local and federal government, it is another matter to turn this around and ask what businesses are really saving by taking on specific issues.

One nonquantitative way to look at what small business owners gain by becoming politically savvy is to relate their activism to the whole notion of intellectual capital. Recognized as the new measure of knowledge-based competitive advantages, it is not just an attribute of top management at major corporations. Intellectual capital is the kind of asset that a small enterprise can lay claim to as well, to the extent that it can enhance the investment potential of a small business. Entrepreneurs already recognize that their own talents and ideas are the major component in the value of their companies. It is time for them to realize that political skills are also part of the package. Not easily quantified, the added market value brought by knowledge is attracting the attention of both the investment and management communities.

The concept of intellectual capital became popular in 1994 through a series of books and feature articles in magazines like *Fortune*, *BusinessWeek*, and *Forbes*. In fact, the phrase was coined about a decade ago at Perception International, a think tank in Ridgefield, Connecticut, where it has been a central message for the consulting firm's large corporate clients such as AT&T and Conrail. In this area, what works for the big businesses will also work for small business. Andre Alkiewicz, Perception International's chairman, observes, "Companies are finding out that knowledge adds value and will have to find ways to attract and to hold on to such intellectual capital. This in many instances will require a change in corporate culture. Corporate restructuring, which more often than not was plain downsizing, will shift gears to intellectual upgrading."

Intellectual capital, in other words, has the potential to redress the political balance between large and small corporations. Even if a small business literally possesses assets that are a fraction of a major multinational in dollar terms, the in-depth understanding of a regulatory or trade issue can put them on a level in terms of intellectual capital.

The owner-manager who knows the ins and outs of local as well as federal government has obviously gained the upper hand on a competitor who may be in all other ways comparable. One who combines that understanding with an even broader scope of political knowledge, taking it to an international level, will rise to a still higher rung on the ladder. Among the identifiable intellectual assets, then, for those who add intellectual capital to the equation of market value will be the capacity to foresee political and social change, to become involved where strategically beneficial, and to steer a company clear of it when that is prudent.

If you win a lawsuit, you know what the settlement is precisely and how much it cost you in legal fees—as well as the time it took from ordinary affairs. If you win a political battle, the full value of your gain usually goes far beyond the usual estimates on how much each year in taxes, penalties, or compliance costs that have been calculated by the number-crunchers. That is because political victories have a kind of resonance that lasts beyond the particular moment when the law is changed or the regulatory burden is lifted. Precedent is such a potent factor in law and politics that a seemingly minor triumph in one area, even among the details or wording of a rule, can produce a ripple effect of further legislative victories in other related situations. It can also act as a powerful deterrent to future policy writers who might be thinking of introducing similar measures.

TAKING THE BULL BY THE HORNS

This is the true hidden benefit of a political victory—its psychological and precedent-setting influence on coming measures. One of the most important steps forward, in this regard, is the set of legislative requirements that entrepreneurs have won regarding the analysis of the potential cost and effect of all different regulatory changes upon small business. The Regulatory Flexibility Act of 1980 stands as a pillar of small business's rights in the federal regulatory process. Once its basic principles were laid down, a series of similar bills and amendments could extend what it set down by stipulating the level of detail and the scope of analyses of the cost and impact imposed on small business by new rules. By building this into the process, entrepreneurs have, at least in part, guaranteed that their interests will be respected by lawmakers even in areas that would not at first seem to have a direct effect upon them.

Coming to grips with the process, learning its secrets and the opportunities to intervene, and finding out how to read the writing on the wall early enough to change course are vital skills. As lobbyists, political activists, and political journalists realized long ago, the opportunities to exert pressure at the right points, taking advantage of the comment process, changing the direction of legislation to accommodate their views, present themselves only to those who understand the way political documents are put together and are moved through the bureaucratic levels. It's like cutting in on the dance floor. You can take the lead deftly if you know the music and the steps.

Small business is going to have to keep its eye on Washington, and its mouth open. "Mind your own business" is an outdated aphorism. It has been replaced by a more heads-up attitude toward what is going on in Washington—and Town Hall—by those who know the positive as well as negative potential of political change. Owner-managers must become attuned to shifts in ideology and the hidden, sometimes personal, agendas that rapidly become public policy. By learning to read trends accurately, small business strategists not only protect themselves against the onslaught of new regulation but can plug into the opportunities created by legislative change. For their part, government officials—whether elected or appointed—are showing signs that they have to learn about the small business agenda or risk losing their jobs in upcoming elections. With all that government and small business stand to gain from a better understanding of one another, there could not be a better time for the message of enterprise to reach government.

CAPITOL PUNISHMENT: WASHINGTON AND SMALL BUSINESS

CLEAN AND MEAN
The Politics of the
Environment

T hat emotions and politics go hand in hand is, perhaps, axiomatic. One branch of the federal government stirs most deeply the passions of small business owners with its overregulation and general unfairness: the Environmental Protection Agency (EPA). Cited time and again by entrepreneurs and the business press as an "antibusiness" bureaucracy that stifles enterprise and economic growth, the EPA is easily the most feared and loathed of all the federal regulatory institutions. Manufacturers in particular view the agency's fines and rigorous inspections as direct assaults on their bottom line, like another form of taxation. What has made this all the more traumatic for small business is the rapid pace of change and growing complexity of new environmental rules that have proliferated since the early 1980s, when a dizzying succession of new forms and standards whirled into effect without any advance notice. Even bureaucrats agree that more than in any other regulatory area, environmental and safety rules are subject to constant change.

For this reason, no matter what your business entails there is an almost obligatory sense in which these continually modified rules force you to be politically aware. Legally responsible for keeping their employees updated regarding these changes, small business owners have to be on top of what is coming out of Washington, the state assembly, or local council meetings. Given the rapid pace of the environmental regulatory process, e-mail and regular informational briefings have supplanted the old, yellowing notice taped on a factory wall or stuck on a bulletin board where it is never read or recalled. Environmentalism is one of the "no excuses" areas of political engagement for owner-managers. Its potentially disastrous financial impact on any company's profits offers a compelling reason for up-to-the-minute knowledge and interaction with the people who implement the rules as well as those who make them.

With a basic understanding of the Environmental Protection Agency and its aims, however, a great deal of the intimidation and surprise can be reduced. That does not mean that a phone message from the EPA appearing on an owner-manager's desk will become entirely anxiety-free, of course, but there is a way to cut down on the financial and emotional toll of an EPA encounter. It depends on knowing the agency and its rules and how those rules can be shaped by a politically active entrepreneurial community.

The role small business owners can play in changing environmental policy is underestimated by the owners themselves, and in interview after interview with officials the message has been the same: Entrepreneurs can make a difference, and those who write the policy are waiting to hear from them. After all, many of the EPA's most stringent requirements were created by another community of activists: the environmentalists. By adopting a similarly aggressive stance, and many of the same tactics, the small business community can advance its own regulatory agenda.

The whole chess game of environmental politics has started over with the shifts in power from Democrats to Republicans in Washington and from big to small business on the lobbying side. But, during the

EPA's heyday in the years just after the first Earth Day in 1970 through the 1980s, major corporations had the capital to meet the new technology standards. With Republicans in the White House and Democrats in Congress, the Democrats pushed their environmental agenda and tied the hands of the federal regulators when it came to figuring the costs of compensating the local governments.

In fact, the biggest worries for small business arise from the major legislative initiatives of the late 1970s and 1980s, as well as more recent restrictions on asbestos, protecting endangered species, and outlawing chemicals like CFCs and chlorine. These include:

- The Resource Conservation and Recovery Act (RCRA), which regulates hazardous and other solid waste and underground storage tanks (USTs)
- The Comprehensive Environmental Response, Compensation, and Liability Act, better known as Superfund, and its Title III component, the Superfund Amendments and Reauthorization Act (SARA), which established the emergency response mechanisms for incidents involving hazardous substances
- The Emergency Planning and Community Right to Know Act (EPCRA), which covers accidental releases of toxic substances
- The Toxic Substance Control Act (TSCA), which covers pesticides and other toxic substances
- The Clean Air and Safe Drinking Water Acts, both of which are due for reauthorization in the next two years

The cost of environmental compliance rose from $42 billion in 1977 to about $130 billion in 1994; by the year 2000 it will hit $178 billion. According to Resources for the Future, a Washington-based think tank that specializes in the economic analysis of environmental issues, the United States spends about 2.2 percent of the gross domestic product (GDP)—by 2000 that will go to 2.8 percent, according to the EPA—compared to 1.6 to 1.8 percent in Germany—which has long had the reputation of being "greener" than America—and about 1.0 to 1.5 percent in Japan. The figures vary from interest group to interest group. Environmental attorney Thomas M. Bradshaw says:

The number of substances and costs associated with environmental regulations are staggering. For example, there are approximately 70,000 chemicals on the EPA Toxic Substances Control Inventory. It is estimated that the cost to clean up the hazardous waste sites subject to the Superfund program could reach $1.25 trillion. Compliance with pollution control regulations could cost American businesses $1.6 trillion in the 1990s. And in order to comply with the Clean Air Act Amendments, as much as $25 to $40 billion could be added to that total annually.

PAYING A FAIR PRICE

The Small Business Administration's (SBA) Office of Advocacy commissioned several studies in 1994 to measure the extent to which environmental rules such as these and the other federal regulations that fill more than 11,000 pages of impenetrable text hurt small business more than large corporations. One study found that from the late 1970s to the present, environmental law greatly favored large corporations because it was found to present "a remarkably consistent deterrent effect on small establishment formation." (*Pollution Regulation as a Barrier to the Formation of Small Manufacturing Establishments: A Longitudinal Analysis*, by Thomas J. Dean, Knoxville, TN, 1994, 43 pp., available from the U.S. Department of Commerce.)

Another report on environmental financial responsibility examined the question of whether or not Congress had made any provision to ensure that small businesses had the funds or received the kind of tax treatment to ensure that they would accept the costs for complying with environmental rules. The study looked at private-sector mechanisms like trust funds, surety bonds, letters of credit, insurance for damages, and corrective action—as well as insurance against business failure. It also considered public-sector mechanisms like public bond pools and government insurance programs. It found that private mechanisms are unable to serve the small business community consistently. Many firms were driven out of business not just by the capital costs of buying more equipment but by the impossibility of covering the bonds or securing the insurance they needed. (*Environmental Financial Responsibility*, by Robert E. Burt, Silver Spring, MD, 1994, 78 pp., available from the U.S. Department of Commerce.)

The problem environmental regulations pose for owner-managers is not simply the cost in financial terms. When you run your own business with only three or four employees, you have to be the general manager, chief advertising and marketing decision-maker, bookkeeper, mechanic, even photocopier repairer. On top of all of these tasks, handling a stack of environmental compliance forms takes hours every month, and unlike the Fortune 500 companies that have whole departments to push this kind of paper, typical owner-managers have to set aside part of their workday to do it themselves.

The first signs of the severe financial strain that environmental regulations could cause for small business followed the enactment of The Resource Conservation and Recovery Act in 1978, when several companies went bankrupt because they could not obtain insurance letters of credit or surety bonds from the private sector to cover hazardous waste management. Because the rules governing waste management suddenly changed and the unforeseen costs of compliance were far above what small businesses could pay, many just threw in the towel. The SBA still finds that there are substantial gaps in the coverage of small businesses affected by new regulations. These gaps include a complete lack of financial relief mechanisms for covering corrective actions at hazardous waste treatment, storage, and disposal facilities, third-party liability after a facility is closed, or the care of a site after closure beyond 30 years.

In the meantime, unfair tax and bankruptcy laws hamper the effectiveness of firms that try to meet their environmental obligations through private means. Since tax laws treat funds set aside for environmental purposes, such as bonds, as if they were still under the control of the firm and so tax them as income or assets, these firms are in effect punished for compliance. It is not hard to see how the laws in this regard are heavily weighted in favor of large companies that can handle the financial aspect of compliance much more easily than firms that face chronic capital formation problems.

DEALING WITH THE EPA

If this litany of problems were all that entrepreneurs had to contend with, the burden would be heavy enough. What makes strategic planning vis-à-vis environmental policy all the more confusing is that the EPA itself is in a state of flux. Minor skirmishes and power struggles create the impression that one division of the agency is favorable to small business at the same time that another is going after entrepreneurs. Under pressure from the White House and Congress, the EPA is going through a re-organization that has angered some of the die-hard environmentalists who joined its ranks in the 1970s. The particular thrust of this reform is toward a more simple, less intimidating institution.

In July 1994, the agency launched its "Common Sense Initiative" to encourage flexibility and a more user-friendly atmosphere in its practices, particularly with regard to reporting, compliance, the permit process, and the promotion of pollution prevention as a standard business practice. With clarity and efficiency as the goal of the "Common Sense Initiative," the agency's new slogan is, "Cleaner, cheaper, smarter." The EPA is approaching "stakeholders" (as the companies that are targets of potential regulation are called) in six major areas—auto manufacturing, computers and electronics, iron and steel, metal plating and finishing, oil refining, and printing—to develop solutions to compliance problems. But the pace of change is slow, and few have noticed any great difference in the hit-or-miss enforcement tactics of the agency. Never a paragon of efficiency and organization, the EPA is likely to become even more chaotic until the "re-org" is through.

If the EPA really is going to redefine itself, then this is the perfect time for the small business lobby to give it a push in the right direction. The agency has already strengthened the powers of its small business ombudsman, who acts as an advocate for entrepreneurs in the regulatory process as well as a liaison officer.

Change is also evident in the way in which senior policy officials, with years of experience at the EPA, are thinking and talking about small business. One of these officials is Bob Hardacre, staff director for global environment and trade at EPA headquarters in Washington. The clear-thinking and plain-spoken Hardacre is head of a secretariat that advises the White House and foreign governments on environmental policy issues and how best to implement environmental standards in a way that does not strain the "human or economic capacity" of the countries involved. A key figure in the debate over NAFTA and its environmental implications, because of his expertise in international relations and contacts with the top management of large companies, Hardacre is clearly one of the "big picture" types. That is why it is interesting to hear how important small business has become to his work. As Hardacre explains:

> *The working groups in which I participate try to bring all the different views on humongous policy issues to bear and try to reach a consensus. There is a lot of concern right now about small and medium-sized companies and the implications and opportunities for them. They need to be represented at the table along with everybody else, and we struggle with the inability in a lot of cases to reach them, because there are so many of them and they don't have as much access to information in an organized way.*

Sending Business Your Way

One of the obstacles to outreach is the EPA's lack of staff to accomplish it, and the Republicans have vowed to cut back more. Being understaffed has its advantages for the small business community: It is one of the reasons that small businesses are not investigated more often. There is an attitude at EPA headquarters that there are simply too many enterprises out there to watch, and for the first time in its history, officers are admitting that there is no reason to start trying now. According to Hardacre:

> *It is fair to say that small business has not been the focus of regulation, and for good or ill they are not likely to be because I think that there are so many of them that it is going to be a physical impossibility for the government, more so after the staff cuts, to try to regulate these hundreds of thousands of small sources.*

What might look like a blessing at first—inattention—in fact has a decidedly detrimental effect. It may buy some time for a few individual businesses, but it does not guarantee the safety of all. More importantly, in addition to enforcement, the EPA and many of its officers also play a serious role as go-between for small business. They help entrepreneurs in the environmental clean-up and equipment business to get contracts at Superfund sites or on other projects. Each state, as well as the head office in Washington, has a special officer in charge of procurement who works full-time on getting contracts for American businesses in the environmental clean-up and equipment areas. In the regional offices of the EPA, I have often waited patiently during interviews as officials took a moment to handle calls from small business owners looking for projects to work on through a program that matches small businesses with projects that have set-asides for contracts.

The whole notion of the EPA being an aid to small business is revolutionary. Yet Hardacre and others are trying to reconfigure their jobs to becoming more service-oriented. For instance, he says:

> From an international perspective, there are lots of opportunities for small businesses as a result of NAFTA, where they don't have to travel 10,000 miles to do business with Asia. But still, a lot of these companies don't seem to be that interested and part of it is economics and part is their focus on a smaller radius. They feel they have potentially enough business within their region or the U.S., with its 260 million consumers as opposed to reaching across the border for another 80 million. These folks ought to be looking at those opportunities.

Outside of the EPA, one of the best sources of business opportunity information involving federal funds is a Washington-based organization called the Environmental Technology Network (ETN), which maintains a database of members that ETN staffers use for matchmaking between primary government and corporate sources. The ETN staff contacts the procurement officials to let them know that members fit the profile of the contractor they are looking for, and then turns around and helps the company decide if the agency's program is right for it. Since the laws regarding purchases between $2,500 and $100,000 have been changed to exempt long-standing paperwork requirements and bonds that had to be posted for construction contracts with federal and state governments, and these contracts have to go to small businesses by law, a major increase in procurement contracts for small business is expected in the next few years. The Office of Federal Procurement Policy has also reclassified purchases under $2,500 as "micropurchases" that are no longer subject to the competitive bidding process of the Buy American Act. This simplifies matters for small businesses seeking a way to begin working with the government on a minor scale.

Along with its advisory services, ETN also publishes a monthly bulletin filled with government procurement opportunities and regulatory news for small business. For example, in November 1994 ETN included the 1995 Procurement Forecast of the Department of Transportation, which includes brief descriptions and contact names and phone numbers for, to take a few examples, pollution prevention subcontracts ranging between $200,000 to $499,000 under the Coast Guard, a hazardous waste cleanup job estimated between $50 to $150 million, for the Federal Aviation Administration, and a dozen other opportunities, many of them minority 8(a) set-aside jobs.

The newsletter also maintains a calendar of trade shows and is especially good at tracking international developments such as the investment opportunities set up by the Overseas Private Investment Corporation, the United States–Asia Environmental Partnership, the United States–Mexico Chamber of Commerce, and the Environmental Enterprises Development Initiative of the U.S. Agency for International Development.

The development of a small business focus at the EPA, as well as in organizations like ETN and the U.S. Agency for International Development, is helping to give American enterprise a break. In Hardacre's view, the cutting edge of environmental services is dominated by smaller firms. "There is a lot of innovation in environmental technology occurring in small business, and we are trying to promote the transfer of pollution prevention technology and new machinery to build the human and economic capacity." The EPA offers grants, technical assistance, and what are called "cooperative research development agreements" provided for in the Technology Transfer Act of 1986, which favors small businesses that want to work with the government on pollution control.

Giving a hand to an entrepreneur does not always have to mean that the government has chosen small business over big business as a major policy decision. Hardacre views the relationship between large and small companies in a different light from most officials in Washington who tend to set them in opposition. He believes that a rapprochement between the two groups is possible, and that big businesses that have "reformed" their polluting ways can serve as models for smaller enterprises. "I think that the larger multinationals need to be working with small companies who represent their suppliers, to help broaden the base of the market."

Many of the large companies that were the focus of regulation have concluded that it doesn't pay to fight and that, in fact, there are economic rewards for pollution prevention: Pollution represents waste and waste represents inefficiency. Hardacre hopes that entrepreneurs will, in cooperation with larger firms, learn ways to minimize their exposure to regulation, and by eliminating pollution, take away the need for permits and regulatory oversight. As Hardacre recognizes, in a relative sense smaller firms need to be even more competitive because they stand to lose more and don't have as much flexibility—they can't spread out the costs of compliance over years or division budgets as a large multinational can.

MR. AND MS. SMITH GO TO WASHINGTON

The traditional picture of political battles over the environment is a fairly straightforward, epic scene of head-on conflict. Activists sound the charge against major industries, and politicians scurry back and forth between the two sides to gain votes where they can and to stay as far out of the line of fire as possible. The battlefield is national and occasionally global in scale.

But this picture can no longer be painted in such broad strokes of the brush. For one thing, it now has to include small business interests, which are not identical with those of big business and not always diametrically opposed to the environmentalists either. For another, the battle site has expanded. More and more, as lobbyists for the major corporations have found, the fight is also being waged on the local level. As the industrial lobbies redeploy their troops to cover regional action on the environment, they are encountering the small businesses that are the mainstays of those areas. Since knowledge of the home turf is an advantage, the immediate advantage lies with the entrepreneurs. The famous slogan of the environmentalists of the 1970s, "Think globally, act locally," is now the guiding principle of those who are trying to reform environmental law and make it more sensitive to the needs of small business.

Focusing locally works well because of a strategic flaw on the part of many environmental organizations, which are still the main proponents of stricter regulation. The organizers of Greenpeace, the Sierra Club, and other major groups have had to admit that they have lost touch with the grassroots constituencies that originally gave them life. Their top-down manner of managing, which can alienate regional members who have their own needs, is working against them.

In basic terms, the shift from federal to local has brought about a shift in environmental politics from broad-based policy concerns to the more detailed issues of implementation. Washington is the place for policy, but locally the emphasis has to be on implementation. Where landowners, developers, environmentalists, and the community must agree, the rules have to be flexible enough to allow for compromise. In this way, regulatory change is brought about by modifications and practical solutions to local problems rather than by national decree. It is easy to see how this shift favors the power of small business concerns, who are firmly rooted in the communities. The lobbyists for large firms that try to steer local issues inevitably appear in the role of outsiders telling the locals what to do.

The regulatory reform movement in Washington, which was started by the big business lobbies but is more and more in the hands of small business, is gaining a reputation for playing legislative hardball. So far, its tactics have been astonishingly effective by killing bills having to do with everything from health care to the environment. With the transition to a Republican-controlled House after the 1994 elections, the success rate is predicted to rise. By the beginning of 1995, a regulatory revolution was under way in the House. Under the rubric of the Job Creation and Wage Enhancement Act of 1995, House Republicans are hoping to radically change the regulatory process by introducing the most stringent requirements ever proposed—but these are requirements imposed on the regulators, not on the regulated. The bill would create a regulatory budget that limits the costs of complying with all federal regulations, which will bring down that ceiling year after year by 6.5 percent until the costs to the private sector are not more than 5 percent of GDP and the costs to the state and local governments are no more than 3 percent.

This would severely limit the agencies and Congress, while empowering the Office of Management and Budget not only to review the potential financial consequences of new rules but their grammar as well, to make sure that they contain "only sentences that are as short as practical" and no double negatives. Following in the footsteps of the recent review process, it pushes the early analysis of costs to both businesses and local governments and sets up outside review panels for assessing the costs of compliance in both fiscal and scientific terms, such as whether or not compliance itself would pose health risks.

Since the peer review process would involve financial and risk assessments by technical and industry experts, it would shift power to the regulated from the regulators, especially in the case of "major" rules involving 100 people or more and costing a person or corporation at least $1 million. The committee hoping to pass a bill would have to show that it would not exceed the budget, and even then it could not be brought to the floor without permission of three fifths of the entire House or Senate. Much of the maneuvering would occur even earlier than the standard comment process today, which is initiated when the proposed rule is first published. If enacted, the Republican bill will replace President Clinton's executive order on the White House's ability to shape regulation with former President Reagan's defunct order allowing the president to rein in the regulatory process.

The bill as a whole is expected, if passed, to severely curtail the regulatory powers of Congress, its committees, and the agencies and to return much of that authority to the White House. Since the budget would force a committee that wanted to write a new law to stay within an overall cost ceiling, the in-fighting over whose rules would pass and whose would be killed would be incessant. Every procedural change of this kind has winners and losers. The big winners in this case would appear to be the House and Senate Budget Committees and the White House, which regains the power to hold back new regulations. Since the White House is partial to small business, that's good news for small business.

SMALL BUSINESS AND THE PROPERTY RIGHTS MOVEMENT

One of the most striking demonstrations of Washington's shift of attention to the regionally based power of small business is the property rights movement. As landowners—including entrepreneurs who own the property where their business is located and particularly those who work out of their homes—take their protests about environmental restrictions to Washington, the "little guy" is getting an audience, because of populist sentiment.

In fact, the property rights movement has harmonized the interests of oil and gas companies, timber and agricultural businesses, and large-scale farms with those of individual landowners, who are frequently family farmers, small enterprises that have been on the property for generations. Rather than attempt to bring their Washington-style lobbying techniques directly to the grassroots level, the big-business associations have used coalitions with local small business to further their agenda on the local level. While the money and the strategic planning are drawn from Washington, the implementation is local.

The voices of the property rights movement are heard loud and clear in Washington. They include immediately sympathetic figures, like Bill Humphries, a cattle rancher from Colorado, who says, "I say property rights are like civil rights. You can't take anybody's away without hurting everybody." The private property owners' bill of rights was recently introduced in Congress. It would compensate landowners if government land regulations cut the value of their property by 50 percent. Even at a time when the federal government is under the gun to cut costs, it looks like it will be enacted.

The property rights movement marches under the banner of the Fifth Amendment to the Constitution, which says, "Private property shall not be taken for public use without just compensation." Its bible is a book by University of Chicago law professor Richard Epstein entitled *Takings: Private Property and the Power of Eminent Domain.* Numerous trade associations and policy wonks are getting in on the act, including Fred Smith, president of the Competitive Enterprise Institute and co-editor of *Environmental Politics: Public Costs, Private Rewards.* According to Smith,

> *This is a typical American spontaneous grassroots organization movement. It represents our society's unique outrage when it feels its rights are violated—that is when people get organized. They're small landowners, small business groups, and people who for various reasons—wetland law, endangered species law, whatever—have found*

that they can't do what they thought they could do with their land for development, for building a home, for selling for retirement purposes, cutting down trees that they'll save for the future. They don't feel that there's a conflict between their use of the land and national interests, and if there is, they feel they should be compensated for it. They're demanding that their rights be honored, and they're now in every state and there're hundreds of them, and they're doing an incredibly interesting job.

An indication of how closely identified property rights have become with the rights of small business is the fact that one of the strongest proponents of property rights is the National Federation of Independent Businesses (NFIB). Criticizing both the Endangered Species Act and local zoning restrictions, and pointing out that the federal government already owes $1 billion in outstanding compensation claims, the NFIB is urging Congress to amend the Act and re-examine the method and reasoning under which private property is taken for environmental protection. The NFIB is also looking for a classification system for wetlands according to their value and function and urging that better scientific data be considered when species are classified as endangered.

NO MONEY, NO MANDATE

The "no money, no mandate" measures are gaining respect on Capitol Hill. In January 1995 the Senate Budget and Governmental Affairs Committees initiated a landmark bill that will make it harder for Congress to impose regulatory burdens on states, local governments, or the private sector without making some provision for funding. Designed to cover not only environmental regulation but food stamps, welfare, foster care, and other areas, the bill is sponsored by Senator Dirk Kempthorne, a Republican from Iowa. Its main effect, if passed, will be to slow regulation for cost estimates, particularly for any new mandate that adds costs of $50 million or more a year on states and localities or $200 million a year for the private sector.

Even before the Republicans gained the majority in Congress the "unfunded mandate" issue was hot. Almost exactly one year ahead of Kempthorne's bill, the Senate passed a risk and cost-assessment amendment sponsored by J. Bennett Johnston, a Democrat from Louisiana, by a decisive 95-3 vote. And Vice President Al Gore's proposed Biological Survey, which would have allowed the federal government to take a census-like survey of the plants and animals across America, was stifled by the property rights movement.

Because "no money, no mandate" legislation has in the past had to take the form of an amendment attached to a new safety or environmental law, the green activists are placed in the defensive situation of having to defeat any new bill that involves the environment with the reform language attached to it. If the bills are passed with the amendments, then a precedent is set regarding who pays for compliance. In a more likely scenario, they will be shot down by the very powers that support them in principle just so that their antithetical amendments will not survive. There is talk in Washington of a constitutional amendment on unfunded mandates to institutionalize the kind of cost assessment that will change the way legislators view the regulatory process.

The gridlock caused by the use of unfunded mandate amendments to environmental bills has already slowed the pace of environmental legislation, and this type of gridlock is only going to be further exacerbated by the redeployment of Congressional power between the Republicans and Democrats. The traditionally Democratic orientation of the "greens" will clash all the more diametrically with the Republican Congressional committees over proposed legislation, especially in the coming two years when each of the major environmental acts of the 1980s, including Clean Air and RCRA, are up for reauthorization.

There is the potential for considerable change in Washington, but it will have to come from the top. A moratorium on new regulation, similar to the one that George Bush declared in the months leading up to his losing bid for re-election, is one possibility. A six-month moratorium on many types of new federal regulations was one of the first ideas to be floated by the incoming Republican Congress in January 1995. Tapping the antiregulatory feeling in the Congress, freshman representative David McIntosh, a Republican from Indiana, has secured a significant role in the House governmental affairs committee, which is promoting the idea of the moratorium.

What would be more valuable for small business is a coalition of environmentalists, regulatory professionals, scientists, economists, and business leaders—including entrepreneurs—which would study ways to make environmental regulation more cost-effective and rational and ensure that the environment and business are both served. With the shift in power away from the agencies themselves and constant talk of "zeroing out" wasteful government institutions, there is even a remote possibility that the Environmental Protection Agency itself could be eliminated one day.

That would not, however, eliminate the need for government regulation of environmental affairs or the concomitant need for small business to be on top of what the government is thinking and doing in this area. Whether the EPA survives or not, entrepreneurs need a direct channel of communication between themselves and those who make environmental policy, because there will never be a time when pollution control by some sort of government edict is "zeroed out."

A FRIEND ON THE INSIDE

The channel of communication between small business and the EPA is very much alive today. The office of the ombudsman for small business is an advocacy division within the agency that appears to be gaining power and credibility as small business itself makes strides in Washington. The main responsibility of the ombudsman is to update entrepreneurs on new rules in each area covered by the EPA and to serve a network of trade associations and umbrella groups. The ombudsman's office has experts on staff as well as contacts "inside" the agency in the policy and enforcement areas. By staying alert to the concerns of small business through close contact with trade associations and through the inquiries it receives, the ombudsman also serves as a mouthpiece for entrepreneurs inside the agency, in addition to providing such services as technical assistance, brochures, reports, audiovisual materials, seminars, workshops, conventions, and the fielding of an endless stream of questions and problems that it receives on a daily basis.

In a small office, staffed by a deputy and four veteran federal regulators as well as two secretaries, the ombudsman and her team keep vigil over an "800" line on which small businesses are invited to call from 8:30 in the morning until 4:30 with their questions and problems. Voice mail picks up after hours, and the office promises prompt answers to questions from small business within 24 hours in the case of phone calls and within 72 hours for letters. The volume of these calls has grown almost exponentially—a result of the proliferation of regulations but also because of an increasing awareness on the part of the small business community that the ombudsman's staff is available to answer their questions.

In the early 1980s, about 4,000 calls a year came into the office; now they get about 20,000 calls a year. Many of the calls come from Congressional constituency referrals as staffers have realized that the ombudsman's office is far better qualified to handle technical questions and issues than they are. Significantly, callers are promised complete confidentiality, and there is a solid Chinese wall of silence between the ombudsman and the investigative arms of the EPA, so that entrepreneurs who call requesting information or assistance do not have to worry about the ombudsman tipping off the agency to violations.

The ombudsman provides access to information of the most technical nature but also offers access to the agency, making the EPA more aware and responsive to the needs of small business. By working with the SBA on financing, the ombudsman's office can help companies get assistance for pollution control investments, mainly through commercial bank loans arranged through the SBA's Pollution Control Financing Guarantee Program.

Created in 1982, the office of ombudsman was designed to offer a liaison between small business and the EPA as a problem-solving mechanism and as an independent, objective source of reliable information. The key to the ombudsman's effectiveness is direct access to policy making. The ombudsman serves on the EPA's Working Group, where policy is written, and during the regulation development process the ombudsman has a voice in the deliberations over new rules and is able to convey to the Working Group the potential impact of proposed regulation on small business. When a new rule is proposed and published in the *Federal Register*, the ombudsman also acts as a conduit of information to trade associations and proprietary business organizations and is charged with the responsibility for carrying back to the working group the response of those institutions.

As Karen Brown, the current ombudsman, notes, "Our main objective is to promote an atmosphere between the agency and the regulated small business community that will enhance voluntary compliance with our regulations." By demonstrating that they do improve compliance, the ombudsman's office shows that it is worth the $200,000 annually that it costs the agency to keep it running.

Karen Brown is too energetic and enthusiastic to be considered a typical EPA employee, but she is a career government environmental officer. When she was in college at the University of the District of Columbia, she was a pre-med student; however, after a rocky interview at Georgetown University's medical school she changed course and joined the Environmental Health Administration of the District of Columbia. "I did everything you have to in the field, including climbing up to inspect smokestacks," she says. They put her through graduate work in environmental science at George Washington University. Brown worked her way up the ranks as a chemist and environmental health specialist for the municipal government and then moved into the EPA in 1981 as an administrator in the Solid Waste and Emergency Response division.

Brown was appointed to the position of Small Business Ombudsman by the Administrator, Lee M. Thomas, in June 1985, and in 1989 her title of Asbestos Ombudsman was added. Her deputy, Robert Rose, has been with the EPA over twenty years, working on both air and water enforcement. Before joining the Department of Defense as a production controller, he worked in the steel and electronics industry and in the Department of Defense.

When Ombudsman Brown is not answering questions or speaking at conferences, she baby-sits the legislative and regulatory process. Twice a year she and her staff review the Regulatory Agenda for new rules that will have a significant impact on small business. They make a list of the upcoming changes and get it out to hundreds of trade associations and small business groups for comments, then convey their input back to the EPA. In late 1994, Brown was actively tracking about 80 different regulations that she considered important for entrepreneurs to know about. For all the good her experts do on the phones as they answer the day-to-day worries of entrepreneurs, her most significant work on behalf of the small business community is probably done inside the committee meetings and hallways of the EPA.

When Brown took on the oversight role of ombudsman, it was initially a matter of reacting to legislation and helping small business cope. More and more, it is a proactive job that intervenes earlier in the regulatory process. Brown is a vigorous participant in the EPA's rulemaking. She speaks up about alternatives and options to the requirements that will hurt small business the most and promotes what she calls a "balanced approach" to legislation, on the basis of her promise to the agency that she can promote voluntary compliance. If a proposed rule strikes her as ominous, she expresses her reservations as a statement of "nonconcurrence" which in turn has to be answered point-by-point by the proposer of the new rule. While she cannot kill a rule on her own, she can slow its progress during the comment process.

The usefulness of an office such as that of the ombudsman is measured in part by the research material it can put together for the constituency it serves and the kind of information and data it can muster to go into Congressional committee meetings and state its case. In addition to the hotline services, the ombudsman's department is well-known for the material that it has put together not only for small business but for Congressional staffs as well. It has become a kind of "one-stop shop" for technical assistance and information. The ombudsman makes personal appearances throughout the country as a speaker or panelist and is a constant presence on the circuit of small business conferences and meetings, often working with the SBA. The network of small business trade associations that the ombudsman serves includes about fifty different trade associations representing several million small businesses from coast to coast.

Short of cloning herself, the only way that the ombudsman can serve the growing demand is to branch out, and that is precisely what the EPA is planning. With regional offices in North Dakota, Ohio, Oklahoma, Oregon, Pennsylvania, and New York, the office of ombudsman is on its way to establishing compliance advisory panels in every state. The new state assistance program will require states to have their own ombudsman, small business assistance program, and a compliance advisory panel. Acting as a local version of the federal ombudsman, the new officer will be the point person in the state for the EPA and will work with air quality experts, engineers, scientists, and leaders of the small business community.

Each state compliance advisory panel will have seven members who will closely monitor the overall relationship between small business and the EPA in the state. Four of the members will be small business owners or representatives selected by the state legislature. The governor of each state will select two other members to represent the general public. The seventh member will be chosen by the head of the state agency responsible for issuing operating permits. The panels will review and render opinions on the effectiveness of the ombudsman's office and send progress reports to the federal ombudsman about regional issues. One of the other functions they will serve—one not to be underestimated—is the relatively simple-sounding task of making sure that the information and rules are written in a style that is clear and understandable for owner-managers.

ENFORCEMENT: WHERE THE GOVERNMENT GETS TOUGH

Beyond their technical and legal complexity, the most confusing aspect of environmental issues for small business owners is the often contradictory nature of the signals sent out by the government. While Congressional leaders, the White House, and the Washington offices of the EPA, SBA, and Chamber of Commerce are united in a chorus of calls for regulatory relief, there is no apparent abatement in the day-to-day struggle to comply with the laws already on the books. Part of the problem is surely attributable to the old dichotomy between rhetoric and reality. As skeptics are apt to point out, very little of the regulatory relief has been signed into law as yet.

More importantly, the apparent contradiction between what Washington says and what local regulators do is attributable to another pair of opposites: policy and implementation. As fundamentally self-defeating as it sounds, the split between the views of policy makers and those of the officials charged with enforcement is often dramatic. Since implementation starts on the state and local level, this division can be all the more pronounced. For this reason, the increasing attention paid to small business by environmental policy makers has its good and bad side. On the one hand, entrepreneurs are getting an audience in Washington and in state capitols where legislators are finally becoming more conscious of their needs. On the other, since major polluters among the world's largest corporations have long since been identified by the environmental police, small business is viewed as a new target of enforcement. According to some experts, this could bring small business into the spotlight in a way that is historically different from before. Kenneth Vonderahe, CEO of Remediation Services Inc. and Chairman of the RCGA Energy & Environment Committee in St. Louis, says:

> *Corporate giants and small businesses alike are responding to the ever-changing environmental challenges. Years ago, small companies were not that involved in environmental affairs; however, today all sizes of operations must consider environmental issues in their day-to-day decisions.*

One of the best ways to take the pulse of the trend toward stricter enforcement is to visit the Federal Law Enforcement Training Center in Glynco, Georgia. The seven-week training course includes firing automatic weapons on the range, practicing high-speed car maneuvers on an obstacle course, and learning how to conduct a stake-out. Many of the recruits are headed for service in the Drug Enforcement Agency or the U.S. Marshals Service, but an increasing number are electing to work for the EPA. Since 1989, the size of the EPA enforcement team has almost tripled, rising from 47 agents to 123, and is expected to reach 200 by 1996.

This expansion, which may slow under the Republicans, has its price. The EPA's environmental-crimes division budget has risen by 400 percent since 1989 (much faster than the 29 percent growth in the EPA's total budget), to $15.6 million in 1994. The stepped-up enforcement effort was initiated by Congress to a greater degree than it was by the EPA itself. One of the key bills in recent history was the Pollution Prosecution Act of 1990, mandating the increase in budget and enforcement staff. Congress also created the distinction between the "knowing" violation and the lesser types of accident or negligence.

The environmental police already have more than enough codes to enforce. The past decade has been characterized by a pattern of legislation that has grown more stringent, as when the Resource

Conservation and Recovery Act of 1970 was amended in 1984 to double the daily $25,000 fine and one-year prison sentence. The 1990 amendment of the Clean Air Act of 1970 increased the fine from $25,000 a day to $250,000 for individuals and $500,000 for companies, and the one-year prison sentence went to five years. The reauthorization in 1987 of the Clean Water Act of 1972 boosted the fine from $25,000 per day and one year in prison for a first offense to three years in prison and a $50,000 a day fine for knowing offenses.

Enforcement depends in part on the follow-through efforts of prosecution and conviction. That is the province of the Justice Department, which not only handles the EPA's cases but also initiates some environmental cases of its own (just as it is becoming more involved in antitrust and securities investigations). Attorney General Janet Reno is planning to add 39 new attorneys and 39 support-staff positions in 1995 for environmental cases, pulling troops from criminal, tax, and civil divisions. Justice won convictions in 91 percent of the 630 cases closed over five years ending May 1993. The caseload is expected to double in the next two years. Most of these criminal cases—which can end in prison sentences—start with deliberate violations of environmental laws resulting from companies that do not have pollution control equipment, shut it off, or intentionally dump hazardous waste in the wrong places. The accidental violations, like a chemical spill, are prosecuted as civil cases and the fines are generally less severe.

Generally speaking, only about a third of investigations end up being pursued, and many of those are dropped as mere record-keeping problems. The vast majority of cases arise from alleged violations of the Resource Conservation and Recovery Act and the Clean Water Act. The EPA is now targeting violators of the Clean Air Act Amendments (CAAAs), which were last amended in 1990 and are due to be reauthorized, their penalties stiffened (despite the overall antiregulatory atmosphere of Congress), in 1995. Given the Congressional attention Clean Air will be getting and the fact that the EPA is willing to go on record saying it will be making a special effort to crack down on Clean Air violations, the business community affected by these laws can be sure that this will be one of the key issues of the coming three or four years.

The CAAAs are comprehensive and now applicable to industries never previously regulated. Once designed to reduce emissions from new, large industrial plants, they are now turning attention toward older and smaller plants, and, to the surprise of many policy makers who had understood that entrepreneurs were to get a break, even small businesses. The industries expected to be hurt the most will include utilities, oil, paint manufacturing, chemicals, auto, furniture, and dry cleaning. It will cost these industries an estimated $20 to $25 billion per year to comply, not including legal and consulting fees. The early warning signals of this crackdown have been evident for some time, and it is important for small business to heed them before the final stage of investigation and prosecution is reached.

The whole tenor of the relationship between government and small business shifts as we move from the level of policy to that of enforcement. The cordial, even collaborative, atmosphere of the offices of the ombudsman or Congressional representative eager to solicit the views of an owner-manager on upcoming policy changes gives way to the old adversarial relationship between small business and the EPA. An inspector calls at your manufacturing plant; questions are asked; a long-forgotten rule is invoked; the audit begins.

The Jekyll and Hyde dichotomy of enterprise-friendly administrators and intimidatory enforcement officers is beginning to worry not only business advocates in the private sector but federal officials as well who are anxious to develop the partnership between government and business so a genuine economic recovery can take hold. One of those worried is Charles Ingram, associate manager of environmental policy at the U.S. Chamber of Commerce. He believes that the get-tough policy on enforcement sends out the message that government mistrusts business—especially small business, which often struggles to decipher environmental regulation, and doubts its ability to police itself.

Entrepreneurs argue the logic of deterrence that drives this push toward the stricter interpretation of the existing laws is also a barrier to cooperation with the EPA. Rather than go to the agency for information or technical guidance, small manufacturers are worried that they may be drawing attention to themselves and prefer to stay in the shadows. According to Susan Cooke, a Boston-based environmental attorney with the firm of Goodwin, Procter and Hoar, "There is a government recognition that you can't have voluntary disclosure if at the same time you're going to whack them over the head with a board like the Punch and Judy show."

That is certainly the fear at Central Plastics Inc., a plastics recycler with 25 employees in Greenwich, Ohio. Their annual bill for publications to keep the president and managers ahead of new regulations is about $3,000. State regulators have been invited to visit the company to help advise on how best to keep emission levels low. But Robert Buskey, Central Plastics' president, notes that despite the help he gets from state officials, the Washington office of EPA is becoming "increasingly combative" in its approach to enforcement. As Buskey says, "It bothers me because it makes us and the government adversaries." This takes us a long way from the stated purpose of the ombudsman and the EPA's outreach goals.

If the small business community could work together on mending that adversarial gap between itself and the EPA, some of the anxiety surrounding environmental law could be allayed. Amnesty and confidentiality for small companies that come forward and request guidance on compliance could be one target of activists. Simpler and more clearly written guidelines should be another. Given the universal use of computers in small business, software should be designed that enables businesses to file reports electronically with local investigators.

The EPA's efficiency is undermined by the need to respond to media scares, like the periodic stories on asbestos or carcinogens that pull the agency's resources in one direction or another, away from where staffers themselves often consider the most important problems to be. According to Dale Jorgenson, a Harvard economist who studies environmental issues, "If we just regulated smarter, we could get the same environmental quality for half the cost." According to the EPA's administrator Carol Brown, "We need to create incentives for plant managers in companies all across the country to look for ways to get the most pollution control for the least amount of money. I need those guys working with me."

GETTING DOWN TO DETAILS

In 1994, the EPA was supposed to become a cabinet-level agency, and four of its seven major statutes were reauthorized. But the unpopularity of its "top-down" style of regulation caused all of these changes to be shot down. As always, the obscurity and complexity of its laws is an issue. On a certain level it is a joke, but nobody laughs when it suddenly becomes clear that the laws have a direct bearing on his or her own business.

One Size Doesn't Fit All

One of the main challenges for the small business lobby is changing the way in which the rules defining company size are drawn up. The "one size fits all" nature of most environmental laws is the most crippling aspect of all. Unlike many types of regulation, the size of the company usually has nothing to do with its potential liability for environmental crimes. Similarly, the costs of complying with environmental regulations for a small company are comparable to those incurred by larger firms, making the costs of compliance usually disproportionate. The EPA is working on developing regulation-specific definitions of small entities in consultation with the SBA's Office of Advocacy. Among the many points that entrepreneurs should push in their political agenda is a scale of rules that involves the size not only of the company involved but of the pollution it produces. Since the EPA is already leaning toward establishing a volume threshold to waive the annual emission reporting requirements for small sources, this kind of rider to environmental laws is possible if the right pressure is applied in the right places at the right time.

The definition of a "small business" for most environmental legislation is antiquated. It follows the rules laid down in the Small Business Act of 1953:

> That a business that is independently owned and operated and not dominant in its field, owned by a person who employes 100 or fewer individuals, and is not a major stationary source of either a primary urban pollutant or toxic air pollutant, and cannot emit 50 tons or more of a single pollutant a year, or more than 75 tons of all regulated pollutants.

State governments can modify some of these requirements provided that the particular source does not emit more than 100 tons a year of all regulated pollutants.

Taken to the Cleaners

Since the SBA figures that about 70 percent of the 3.5 million small businesses in the country are in sectors of the economy that produce little or no pollution (such as wholesale and retail trade, finance and services), it is a wonder that environmental rules leap to mind whenever the word regulation is used. But consider the example of dry cleaning establishments, many of which have underground storage tanks or come under scrutiny due to perchloroethylene emissions controls. In much-publicized cases that gain poignancy since virtually everyone visits his or her cleaners on a regular basis, the whole industry was hit by new rules on solvents that use perchloroethylene or perc. More than 84 percent of dry cleaners use them, and some use fluorocarbon or trichloromethane—the EPA figures only half of them have emission controls at all. The evaporation of percs from dryers or their presence in waste waters is considered hazardous.

Since the minimum investment for emissions control equipment is about $6,000 for perc and an additional $4,300 for RCRA controls, with additional compliance expenses of $2,800 as calculated by the EPA, it is not surprising that reports of cleaners going out of business appear in the press on a regular basis. These costs amount to about 35 percent of the median annual net profits, or 33 percent of median equity, for cleaners with one to nine employees. The smallest companies have to spend 60 percent of their annual profits, and over 150 percent of the equity, to comply.

Similar disastrous figures can be quoted for the impact of underground storage tank regulations on gas stations, trucking firms, supply stores, furniture makers, and the numerous other types of business that are still living in the shadow of the EPA's rules on toxic chemicals and wastes.

In certain ways, the laws are tougher and enforcement is stricter now than ever before. As on Wall Street, where regulatory inquiries are now aimed at both individuals and the parent organizations that are supposed to have some degree of control over their actions, so too the environmental police are picking up both the site managers and decision makers on lower levels, as well as the owner-managers of their firms, holding both corporation and individuals liable for violations. Generally, personal liability is found if an officer actively participated in a violation by, for example, directing the illegal dumping of hazardous waste. The trend shows up clearly in statistics. In 1992, 61 percent of defendants in EPA-initiated cases were corporations, and 39 percent were individuals. In 1993, only 25 percent of defendants were corporations, while 75 percent were individuals.

CIVIC ENVIRONMENTALISM

An understanding of the specifics involving enforcement will help the small business owner manage environmental compliance from day to day. A sense of what Washington is thinking allows one to look ahead a few years, but, for the longer term, new ideas are needed. Clearly there must be a different sort of relationship between small business and the regulatory institutions meant to protect the environment. The "command and control" or "top-down" style of federal regulation is antithetical to the kind of competitive, individualistic, and "bottom-up" nature of American business and life, particularly from the point of view of small business. To work this out, the government should encourage more informal cooperation between business and environmental groups instead of trying to impose detail-crazy nationwide standards.

One of the most promising new concepts is called civic environmentalism. The phrase originated in the 1980s when it became clear that federal programs were not sufficient—or well enough financed, since they were picking up only about 15 percent of the tab for environmental enforcement in many states—to solve most regional problems. Its chief proponent is Dewitt John, an economist who feels that federal authorities still play a role in the protection of the environment, but to restore credibility to the process, local communities have to have a far greater measure of authority. In a brilliant and forward-looking essay that appeared in the June 1994 issue of *Issues in Science and Technology*, John wrote:

> *Civic environmentalism requires of federal agencies an indirectness, openness, and self-restraint that do not come easy to any bureaucracy, especially one designed to regulate. But the times require new approaches and much can be done even without new federal legislation.*

John is the director of the Center for Competitive Sustainable Economics at the National Academy of Public Administration in Washington. His new model for governance bears watching by small business, because although he does not place particular emphasis upon the entrepreneurial community in his theory of who should step up to the plate and get involved in shaping policy, it is clear that they are the ones who can best represent the type of coalition that he favors.

As John points out, laws such as the Clean Air and Clean Water Acts are fragmented (addressing specific forms of pollution and satisfying different constituencies) and remain adversarial, including the split they cause between state and federal authorities. Similarly, a populist approach to environmentalism would be far too fragmented because it would reflect too many individual interests. The aim of civic environmentalism is to create a comprehensive, practical approach to environmentalism that retains the conscientiousness of populism but takes away its single-issue, often antigovernmental, quality. As he notes, when environmentalism had its start, the need for federal legislation came from the assumption that if state and local governments had to consider the economic consequences of pollution control and clean-up laws they would always choose jobs over environmentalism and never be able to enforce the rules. But in our time, that situation has changed.

John differentiates between "point" and "nonpoint" pollution. The major point sources were large corporations and industries that accounted for conspicuous amounts of pollution—and John says that most of these have been identified and controlled. By contrast, the biggest challenge for environmentalism comes from the "nonpoint" sources, including municipalities or farms that in the past have escaped scrutiny. In a landmark Federal court case decided in Los Angeles just before Christmas 1994, Judge Edward Rafeedie ruled that the California Department of Transportation (Caltrans) must stop releasing millions of gallons of contaminants that made their way to the ocean. Environmentalists from coast to coast hailed the decision as a momentous step forward in their efforts to stop untreated runoff from polluting rivers, streams, lakes, and shore areas. The stern order of the judge gave Caltrans only 120 days to deal with the problem.

While not all experts agree, including the EPA's Bob Hardacre, John identifies small businesses as nonpoint sources, too. According to

Hardacre, the official definition of "nonpoint" is pollution that doesn't come from a discrete source. He says that most nonpoint pollution comes from agricultural operations and the runoff from streets in urban areas or towns. As professionals recognize, it is difficult to regulate that kind of pollution in conventional ways.

Whether DeWitt John or Bob Hardacre is correct about what constitutes "nonpoint" pollution is almost immaterial when it comes to how closely entrepreneurs ought to be paying attention to this type of thinking. Small business should take heed of John's theory and its growing credibility among environmentalists. John notes, in a way similar to Hardacre's observation on the same topic, that small business remains relatively less affected by federal regulation and by its sheer number defies universal supervision. This opens the door to small business becoming more involved in the policy area.

As John points out, Washington's policy makers are likely to look for ways to recast nonpoint pollution as a point-source problem. He offers the example of rules that make car manufacturers install controls on new cars instead of trying to persuade millions of people to drive less. Since the nonpoint sources are more likely to include small business, this shift in priorities could be disastrous for small business. John recognizes that small business lacks the resources to comply with preventive measures and needs help from pollution-prevention and energy-conservation programs. He proposes to offer them technical assistance through university-based centers of applied research or economic development organizations.

Under the theory of civic environmentalism, the management of complex regional ecosystems has to be local instead of federal. The theory stresses cooperation among businesses, scientists, universities, and community activists. John advocates the creation of a "shadow community" of environmental professionals in agencies, business leaders, and environmental groups who can create a local collaborative forum of negotiation that solves problems for the good of the region instead of in a way that just satisfies the federal authorities. Given their stake in the outcome of many of the current debates over environmental policy, entrepreneurs should embrace the agenda of civic environmentalist—and make it their own. As a way of mediating disputes that could have a crippling effect on their businesses, the notion of a "shadow community" that includes local entrepreneurs could be invaluable.

The civic environmentalism model calls for the cooperation of state government in various forms beyond having environmental enforcement officers involved. Specifically, it brings in the state economic development agencies to help in the planning process. Given the eagerness with which most economic development agencies embrace the cause of small business, this means that enterprise will have an official advocate involved in the planning process if the theory continues to draw support.

Civic environmentalism makes sense considering what small business stands to gain both politically and economically from becoming involved on a local level in the management of the environment. As a viable way to secure a leadership role in the community and to make that position count by empowering the community to be able to decide for itself how its environmental policies will be implemented, civic environmentalism looks like the blueprint for a new generation of environmentally conscious entrepreneurs who do not want to be regulated out of existence.

Small business should have a great deal to say in the continuing debate over environmental policy for several reasons. The growing political strength of the small business lobby both in Washington and on the regional level offers the first justification for this hypothesis. At the same time, the declining authority—measurable in terms of membership, political clout, and fundraising capabilities—of what had been the chief environmental groups leaves a gap to be filled. With the exception of a revision of the Superfund law that will change the way toxic waste dumps are regulated, no major environmental legislation made its way through Congress during all of 1994. As *Fortune* magazine smugly observed, "For the first time since the green lobby swept through Washington more than two decades ago, environmental activists are on the run."

The third factor in this equation—the lobbies for big business—is similarly out of favor politically, at least in terms of environmental policy. The realization that this is the case has, in fact, led big business to pay court to (and even hide behind) small business on environmental issues.

THE SMALL BUSINESS AGENDA FOR ENVIRONMENTAL REGULATION

The need for a clear and pragmatic set of small business policy goals regarding the environment that will protect entrepreneurs before they become part of an endangered species is essential. Small business owners must work on a national and local level for:

- Greater access via the EPA to lower-cost pollution control technologies or standardized technologies.
- Ombudsmen for each state EPA office.
- Expanded educational, training, and service programs involving the SBA, EPA, Commerce Department, and other agencies.
- Greater tax incentives for capital expenditures to help comply with regulations.
- Far more rigorous and detailed screening analysis of the cost and impact of regulations, extending the scope of the Regulatory Flexibility Act.
- The amendment of the Resource Conservation and Recovery Act to exempt small businesses from mandatory waste disposal restrictions and burdensome reporting of hazardous wastes.
- Limited right-to-know standards that impose heavy chemical reporting requirements on owner-managers.
- A re-examination of property rights and the cost to landowners of local designations of protected areas and species.

A GOOD HEALTHY DEBATE
Small Business's Role
in Health-Care Policy

A quiet revolution is taking place in the circles of power that compose the Washington establishment. In the old David and Goliath struggle between the little guy and the powerful giant of bureaucracy, David has achieved a number of stunning upsets. What makes this all the more remarkable is that our David, representing small business and its interests, has taken on what amounts to two Goliaths: the government and the big business lobby. Judging from the results of the best-publicized and bloodiest bout—the repackaging of President Clinton's health-care reform plan—David is winning big.

The stakes are huge. Concomitant with the fear that health-care costs inspire in individuals (nearly 40 million of whom still do not have health insurance), entrepreneurs fear they will have to give up their businesses, unable to keep up with costs that are rising at a rate of 10 to 50 percent each year. The real-cost spending for health care per employee has jumped 200 percent since 1970. By 2000, some are predicting that health-care costs could eat up nearly 60 percent of pretax profits. In 1992, health care had already eaten up 13 percent of GDP, or nearly $800 billion.

Under the current system, health benefit costs make up 13.5 percent of payroll for businesses with fewer than 10 employees, and 40 percent of the current premium costs is just chucked down the rathole of administrative expenses. In addition to paying more to insurers, many small businesses—as much as 15 percent—are being "redlined" or denied coverage because of risk groups. These range from florists and beauty shops to logging and mining companies and even hospitals and dental offices.

Faced with a deepening crisis that threatened to go a long way past politics as usual and lay its grip on the pocketbook of millions of entrepreneurs, the small business community mobilized in 1992. After a two-year, precisely organized campaign against the original health-care reform package, by the summer of 1994 one powerful contingent in the small business lobby had the champagne on ice. Not only was the White House in retreat and one of the principal Senate committees responsible for the bill completely unable to come up with a draft

---

THE TOP HEALTH-CARE ISSUES
FOR THE FUTURE

- Insurance reform to reduce costs and allow workers to change jobs without losing insurance
- Subsidies or tax breaks for small businesses that offer full coverage
- New tax laws allowing deductions for insuring the self-employed
- Simplification of tax and labor rules governing health care
- Medical malpractice and antitrust legislation that will make coverage affordable for small businesses

---

version, but the entrenched old-boy network of the Business Roundtable, representing the nation's biggest industrial giants, had raised the white flag, recognizing that it had been outmaneuvered in a classic power play that suddenly put small business in the forefront of the nation's political-economic agenda.

But what comprises the small business lobby? While the David and Goliath analogy makes a neat Biblical distinction between the good little guy and the bad big one, the fight over health-care reform is not actually that clear-cut, especially when it comes to small business interests. As the summer of 1994 ground on, in fact, two very large small-business lobbying organizations clashed in what seemed more like a battle of sumo wrestlers. The National Federation of Independent Businesses (NFIB), which ended up winning decisively, opposed the President's plan, while an ad hoc organization called the Small Business Coalition for Health-Care Reform (SBCHCR), put up a stoic fight in favor of the President's plan.

Of course, without some kind of specialized representation in Washington, small businesses across the nation would have to rely on their Congressional representatives to remember their voting clout. That's not sufficient. There are three major lobbying organizations in the capital—and several smaller ones—that do not see eye-to-eye on all issues, mainly due to party politics. The biggest of them is the NFIB, a 50-year-old lobbying group with 607,000 members, including very small businesses: 11 percent with one employee, 14 percent with two, and 30 percent with between three and five. The National Small Business United (NSBU) represents 65,000 members, mostly businesses employing 15 or more workers. The Small Business Legislative Council (SBLC) is a coalition of 100 trade associations nationwide.

The National Association for the Self-Employed, the Small Business Survival Committee, and the U.S. Chamber of Commerce are also based in Washington, although they are not as aggressive or powerful as the larger organizations. Other, more focused groups that are getting the attention of the White House and Washington include the Minority Supplier Development Council, a New York–based association for the promotion of purchasing agreements between major corporations and minority-owned small business; and the National Association of Women Business Owners (NAWBO). While most of the general small business groups, particularly the NFIB and SBLC, are known for their conservative values and are basically identified with the Republican agenda, there are dissenters among them. The squabbling cannot help the cause, but it indicates that enough Washington insiders sense the kind of clout that is worth fighting over, and the turf wars over who *really* represents small business are a sign that the bragging rights are worth the effort.

The jostling for position was more than evident when Jan Meyers, the Kansas Republican who is head of the House Committee on Small Business, suggested that the major groups band together for a news conference in January 1995 to outline their legislative goals. Although the collaboration succeeded in gaining headlines, and they collectively made a number of points regarding tax legislation and the ability of small businesses to go to court to enforce the regulatory flexibility act, the divisions were also evident. The SBLC, for example, pushed a 10-point "Subcontract with America" that included a measure to raise the threshold for federal laws affecting personnel issues to 100 employees from the current 50, while the NFIB concentrated on tax and paperwork reduction proposals.

It was surprising to many that the NFIB showed up at all for the press event. Susan Hager, a former head of the NSBU, calls the NFIB the "just-say-no crowd" because they have maintained a nonnegotiable position on issues like health care and often refuse to participate in coalition meetings that are meant to be discussion sessions on legislation. Hager, a Democratic party fund-raiser, is also aware that the NFIB has opposed a number of Democratic Congressional candidates and has been openly critical of both President Clinton and his wife, Hillary Rodham Clinton. President Clinton has run into stiff NFIB opposition on everything from his "tax-and-spend" budget to the minimum wage raise and health-care reform. Hager is not above challenging the President, either. She pushed for two other nominees to head the SBA, including the former head of the NSBU, after Erskine Bowles, a North Carolina investment banker, was named by President Clinton.

For John Satagaj, president of the SBLC, the cool attitude of the NFIB is also destructive. "To say no is easy. It sells memberships. But it's hard to see how that's helping the constituency I serve," Satagaj comments. He is a frequent guest at the White House and testified before the health-care task force. Together with the NFIB and the NSBU, the SBLC opposes raising the minimum wage as well as health-care reform under the original plan, but these groups are willing to go much further than the NFIB in terms of sitting down with the White House or legislators to hammer out compromises.

TURNING THE TABLES

Long before the small business lobby concentrated its forces on health care as an issue, the lobbying organizations representing major industries and corporations were deeply involved in the problem. Big business and small business do not see eye-to-eye on health care. The opposite number to these small business lobbying organizations is in many ways the Business Roundtable, a group of chief executives from the nation's biggest corporations that has its own agenda. Tremendously powerful in the 1950s, when Alfred DuPont and others had the ear of President Eisenhower and Congress, the Roundtable suffered near-total defeat in the health-care reform debate of 1994.

There are other, more health-care oriented big business groups, such as the Corporate Health Care Coalition, a Washington-based organization representing 24 huge corporations, that support universal coverage through the employer mandate dreaded by the NFIB. Once a proponent of the Clinton Health-Care Reform Act as a way to contain soaring costs, big business woke up late to find that the small business lobby had shifted the burden of health-care costs to larger corporations and that all four of the reform packages spelled out dramatically different tax and employer-contributions for major corporations from the levels expected of smaller ones. All of this is the result of vocal opposition to health-care reform by the small business lobby. Washington decided: If small business does not pay, then the Fortune 500 has to.

Clearly, the health-care debate had some valuable side effects for small business in Washington. Tuned in to the small business concerns when it became clear that they were on the victorious side, politicians learned to appreciate the ripple effect of legislation in the small business community. For example, John Danforth, a Republican Senator from Missouri, told the Finance Committee that he feared the discrimination against large concerns would send the wrong message. "Businesses will be treated increasingly worse as the size of the business goes up. What it says to business is 'Don't grow.'" The White House and the Office of Management and Budget (OMB) also learned to treat small business better. Alice Rivlin, director of the OMB, says, "Small employers don't offer health insurance now because they can't afford to. Making it more affordable for these businesses is essential."

A CHALLENGER ENTERS THE ARENA

In a curious twist, the health-care debate spawned a rival small business lobbying organization in Washington: the Small Business Coalition for Health-Care Reform, which argued in *favor* of the employer mandate. The Coalition was created late in the game—in May 1994—to promote the interest of small businesses that are paying larger and larger insurance premiums to subsidize the cost of taking care of the uninsured, including those who work for small businesses.

The Coalition called into question the degree to which the employer mandate would harm small business, and the debate produced a barrage of new numbers about the cost of health-care reform. Mounting a publicity campaign that took direct aim at the NFIB between its founding in May 1994 and the peak of its drive to push through the Clinton plan two months later, the Coalition pulled together 29 national organizations with 626,000 small businesses employing over 5.6 million workers, to top the NFIB's stated membership. Although the NFIB at first said that the Coalition represented too many large concerns, the Coalition stated that the average size of their businesses was about eight employees. A few of the organizations include the American Booksellers Association, the American Institute of Architects, the Atlantic Apparel Association, the National Association of Black Accountants, the National Association of Chain Drug Stores (a major sponsor, which supplied staff and office space), the National Council of Non-Profit Associations, the National Family Farm Coalition, and the Women's Business Development Center.

In June 1994, the Coalition was a prominent guest at an event on the South Lawn of the White House that brought together over 400 owner-managers, members of Congress, and then-SBA administrator

Erskine Bowles. In a speech at the event, Brian McCarthy, a part-time activist and spokesperson and a full-time florist in Scranton, Pennsylvania, said:

We will never get overall costs under control without a system of universal coverage. Congress must hear the other side and know the silent majority of small businesses in America support health-care reform and support universal coverage with a shared responsibility for all.

Enlisting the support of several prominent Democrats, including former Senate Majority Leader George Mitchell of Maine and former House Majority Leader Richard Gephardt of Missouri, the Coalition pointed out that small business often pays 35 to 50 percent more than larger corporations to provide the same extent of coverage. Approving the employer mandate, and calling for subsidies for small business, the Coalition's main demand of Congress was a guarantee of equal purchasing power.

The Coalition asked for broad community rating in setting premium fees, the elimination of discriminatory practices such as redlining certain business categories, the prohibition of ways to deny coverage for pre-existing conditions of any employee, and provisions allowing health insurance to be transferred from workplace to workplace. The Coalition was also a firm supporter of the usual reform principles, including the simplification of paperwork, the implementation of cost-containment mechanisms, and the ability to cap payrolls to keep costs down. Touching on a pair of important issues for the self-employed, the Coalition asked for a full 100 percent tax deductibility for insurance costs, as well as assurances that participation in health insurance plans would not interfere with the current status of independent contractors.

By the time the Republicans scored their major victories in the November 1994 elections, the Coalition's staff had suffered enough defeats. As an ad hoc group, its future existence depends on health care continuing to be an issue. Howard Weiss, one of its staffers, notes, "We're evaluating the political landscape." But the experience of the

Coalition is an instructive one, because it shows how dynamic the political dimension of small business can be. As Weiss philosophically observes,

> Once they become informed on the issues there are a variety of ways in which entrepreneurs can express themselves civically. Small businesspeople are in demand right now. People want to know what they think, partly because the health-care reform debate has so polarized the political scene. I have to admit that the NFIB did a wonderful job of expressing small biz issues, and now everybody in this town wants to know what small biz thinks.

The issue-orientation of the Coalition is interesting in and of itself, since it points to a way that organizations can be formed and dissolved according to the needs of specific constituencies. According to Weiss:

> When we hear from people on a certain issue we raise our antennae. We place people on radio and plan events on Capitol Hill and in the White House. We do that by listening to small businesspeople and what they have to say, and realizing that they are tremendously articulate. We're the conduit between enterprise and the government. The changing political landscape provides a unique opportunity right now for the small businessperson.

The Coalition may not have won its first-round battle over health care, but its approach is right. To have the antennae raised and to pursue the issues that mean the most to a constituency of owner-managers ought to be the starting point for any political organization that claims to represent small business, even if that means going against the current of other small business lobbying organizations. The Coalition had the right attitude because it recognized the value of allowing entrepreneurs to speak for themselves on significant political issues.

THE "900-POUND GORILLA" OF SMALL BUSINESS LOBBIES

Enter the National Federation of Independent Business (NFIB). Called by some rival lobbyists representing small business the "900-pound gorilla that can sit where it wants," this Washington-based lobbying group played a decisive role in redirecting the health-care reform movement. Current President Jackson Faris is a veteran political campaigner who has been with the organization for three years—its three most successful years on Capitol Hill, measured in terms of legislative change and victories. Faris has one big trophy on his shelf now: altering the course of the Clinton health-care plan. The NFIB's well-oiled professional lobbying team, headed by Vice President John Motley along with directors Michael Roush in the Senate and Kim McKernan in the House, uses corporate tactics to represent its Main Street clientele.

The organization basically intimidated two Democratic members of the Senate Finance Committee, Max Baucus of Montana and Kent Conrad of North Dakota, into taking up their cause by organizing expensive phone and mail campaigns in their home states. As a result, the Finance Committee deleted the employer-mandate language from its version of the bill. The NFIB reached Democrats on the House Energy and Commerce Committee in the same way, including Representative Billy Tauzin of Louisiana and Jim Slattery of Kansas, and it completely tied up the Energy and Commerce Committee, which never even finished its work on the bill. Chairman John D. Dingell of Michigan had declared he was going to be a crucial player in the bill and had to watch his chance pass because the Democrats on the committee would not approve employer mandates.

The tactics used by the NFIB are anything but friendly. They painted the disastrous prospects of the employer mandate in the most vivid tones. As chief lobbyist John Motley said in a speech, "The plan would be like tying small businesses to a sled and pushing them down a mountain, hoping they'll remain upright."

When the NFIB swings into action, it uses a highly sophisticated computer database and communications system that can automatically pinpoint members in the district of a Congressional member who has a swing vote or is a committee member and can be used to identify members by zip code or sales figures as well. A barrage of faxes on legislative developments goes out to its members under the attention-grabbing headline "Action Alert." The telephone and mail campaigns, though expensive, use evening calls to guarantee they reach individuals across the nation, although the organization is strongest in the South and West.

The NFIB's battle plan on health care took aim at three significant committees in a deliberate order. It started with Energy and Commerce, which the NFIB basically immobilized with indecision. It moved on to the Finance committee and ended with Ways and Means, ignoring the various labor committees because they are "too liberal." The momentum generated by the NFIB during this campaign was phenomenal, making the organization the envy of other lobbying groups.

Arguably the most effective technique in the campaign was a series of regional meetings that the NFIB organized and sponsored to build a grassroots campaign against the bill beginning 14 months before the Clintons got on their bus in Independence, Missouri, to promote their agenda. These forums were targeted at towns such as Thibodaux, Louisiana, which is home to Energy and Commerce committee member Billy Tauzin. Tauzin, who attended the forum, returned to Washington proposing a separate vote on mandates. The most effective power tool at the meetings was the firsthand stories told by owner-managers about their fears regarding the bill. On July 4, 1994, the NFIB had over 40 of these meetings going in the districts of lawmakers who could be swing votes.

Democracy in Action

The NFIB is one of the strongest lobbying organizations on Capitol Hill, with annual revenues of $60 million, a staff of over 700, offices in all 50 capitals, and access to top lawmakers right up to the Oval Office. Its offices are on the seventh floor of a prestigious Washington office building right on the Mall, within walking distance of Capitol Hill and most of the agencies it wants to reach.

Behind its wood-panelled, elegantly appointed lobby, the NFIB is a lobbying machine (it spent about $785,000 on campaign contributions in 1994) like so many others in Washington, except that instead of one big check each coming from a few corporate headquarters it runs on hundreds of thousands of small contributions. To prevent undue influence by one member or group, annual dues start at $75 and are capped at $1,000. Nobody writes the big check, so nobody gets to dominate the discussion.

The organization has a simple way of finding out what is on the minds of small business in America. They ask them. The Federation has a sophisticated marketing and polling operation that uses a constant stream of polls (every two months) to keep in touch with the interests and concerns of its members. It uses direct balloting rather than steering committees or board members' decisions to determine policy. If the goal is to involve as many small businesses as possible in the determination of the crucial policy decisions that affect them, then the NFIB succeeds admirably. The polls serve as a means of alerting owner-managers to the hot issues and getting them to declare their position. The input received through the polling process gives the NFIB instant credibility as the mouthpiece for a geographically comprehensive sampling of American enterprise. Even if its professional staff tends to take over the whole advocacy process after amassing the poll results, rendering to a passive role the small businesses themselves, the NFIB manages to engage entrepreneurs in the political process through a participatory mechanism that is well-organized and effective. Five times a year the ballots are counted on federal issues and once a year on state issues for NFIB lobbyists to take to legislatures.

WHY HEALTH-CARE REFORM MAKES SMALL BUSINESS SHUDDER

The typical NFIB member has a staff of five and annual sales of around $250,000; total sales equal $747 billion. Counting the staff of the member organizations, the NFIB speaks for over 7 million voters. The

---

Long before the media focused attention on Hillary Rodham Clinton, its members were sending a strong signal to the NFIB that health care is their number one worry. In a decisive poll, 94 percent of NFIB members said they opposed a requirement to pay the bulk of the cost of workers' health coverage, and one third said they would lessen their opposition if they got an unspecified government subsidy.

---

range of industries is of course huge, but the general breakdown is dominated by retail (25 percent), services (27 percent), and financial services (6 percent). Over 13 percent are in the key category of manufacturing, which is particularly susceptible to health insurance and product liability concerns. About 19 percent of the member businesses bring in between $100,000 and $199,000 in annual gross receipts; a healthy 12 percent make between $500,000 and $1 million, while 17 percent top the million-dollar mark.

NFIB President Faris knows precisely what made the presidential plan such a nightmare for owner-managers. As he calculates it, only 40 to 45 percent of small business currently insure their workers, and 74 percent of those firms with four or fewer employees cannot afford coverage. Washington is rapidly learning that the total number of businesses affected is not small by any means. By requiring all of them to pay for universal coverage in some way—most businesses will have to pay about 80 percent of health-care costs for employees or about $6,000 on average per worker—it eats away at their bottom line. As Faris explains, "Cost. Cost. Cost. In three words, that's the reason many small businesses do not provide insurance. Sweeteners, subsidies, government promises aside, the number one problem is the cost of health insurance."

But the trouble does not end as the owner-managed businesses adopt coverage. Often, that is just the beginning of the problems. "Once insured, all it takes to ignite the cost rocket is for a firm to file a slightly higher-than-normal claim," Faris points out. It does not take a rocket scientist to envision the upward spiral in costs from there. Together with the modification of the Clinton health reform bill, the NFIB members are hoping to see insurance industry reform measures that would stabilize premiums, eliminate exclusions for pre-existing conditions, and guarantee renewability and portability. Another item on the NFIB wish list is a permanent 100 percent tax deduction for the health insurance premiums of the five million uninsured self-employed.

Making It Personal

Faris understands most of this from firsthand experience in the nitty-gritty world of owner-managed enterprises. He grew up in a small-business household. His father ran a gas station in Pensacola,

Florida, and his mother sold cosmetics door to door. After studying economics at David Lipscomb University, a small private college in Nashville, Faris worked as a senior loan officer and then moved on to executive posts in marketing and public relations at various Nashville banks.

He moved from banking to the construction industry as a marketing and planning executive for the Nashville-based Joe M. Rodgers and Associates firm, then got the political bug. He served as campaign finance director for Tennessee Governor Lamar Alexander in 1978 and was executive director of the Republican National Finance Committee from 1978 to 1981, when he joined the NFIB.

When it comes to hitting a nerve in Washington, Faris knows the word to use: tax. As he points out, "Through his employer-funded health plan, Clinton has proposed the largest payroll tax increase in history, larger than Social Security, Medicare, and Medicaid." When President Clinton declared in his State of the Union Address in January 1994 that small business would be getting a tax cut, the NFIB was quick to point out in their response that the President's break for small business would be severely undermined by the employer-funded health plan.

Above all, Faris is an eminently logical man, given to dispassionate, well-reasoned arguments that support his constituents' interests. Rather than argue on emotional or ideological grounds against the Clinton plan, he established a logical set of reasons for abandoning it. "To demand that all employers cough up the cash to pay for a national health care program makes no sense. That scheme pits business owners against their own employees and against other taxpayers and will inevitably result in pink slips for millions," he reasoned.

Faris says that he faces an uphill battle every day. Despite the Capitol Hill rhetoric that promises small business one break after another, the message that NFIB members still feel they get is mainly one of official indifference while they attempt to drum up support for their concerns. As Faris remarks, "The unceasing flow of antibusiness sentiment pouring out of Washington and the state capitals these days has set off a deafening clatter of alarm bells alerting the entrepreneurs of this nation to a serious threat."

Reflecting the general concern of NFIB members, Faris is not completely bullish about the prospects for owner-managed business under the remaining years of the Clinton regime. Just after Clinton's State of the Union Address he commented:

> *The state of the union from a small-business perspective is not an encouraging one. The government which provided security from cradle to grave can also dictate the details of your life. That is opposite and foreign to what small business is all about in America.*

That may be changing under the new Republican majority in both the House and Senate, particularly as more committee chairmen pay lip service to the needs of small business. With its strong recognition in the Republican camp, the NFIB should gain greater access on Capitol Hill in the years to come.

Like others with a personal belief system, it does not need to be articulated time and again, but Faris does refer to his faith in the free-enterprise foundations of the country in speeches, backing it up with references to his polls or other research. It is the fundamental credo of his organization. As Faris puts it:

> *No matter how the question is posed or the motivation assessed, research shows that these little Main Street firms are forms of economic and social self-expression. That is why small business owners see government-imposed health care, or any other mandate, as an infringement on their personal freedoms and as a type of economic censorship.*

THE SMALL BUSINESS AGENDA
FOR HEALTH CARE

Although the NFIB won the battle to defeat the Health Security Act in 1994, it is clear that something constructive has to be done about the health-care crisis. A combination of suggestions from the Small Business Coalition for Health Care Reform and the NFIB should ensure that small business pays its fair share, and no more:

■ A managed competition system that implements cost sharing and makes sure policies are affordable, renewable, and can be carried from workplace to workplace as needed.

■ Congress should implement insurance and medical malpractice reforms and regulations to bring down costs and stabilize the underwriting market.

■ Discriminatory pricing against small business has to be eliminated, so that all pay the same amount for the same plans.

■ Congress should limit variations in premium increases and prohibit increased rates or cancellations based on health status.

■ Small businesses and the self-employed should be allowed to fully deduct health-care expenses (as large corporations do), and owners ought to be allowed to self-insure.

■ The financial responsibility for any new plan should be shared by the employee, employer, and government.

■ Congress should push to get rid of "quill pen" laws that require providers and insurers to communicate on paper and establish federal guidelines for private electronic filing of claims.

■ Congress should oppose setting a cap on all health-care spending and encourage competition among providers and insurers.

3

THE TAX MAN COMETH
Getting a Hearing from
Congress and the IRS

The universal aspect of tax policy places it in a different category from other issues facing small business. Even before they own their own businesses, entrepreneurs have been in at least annual contact with the Internal Revenue Service (IRS) and state tax authorities every year of their working lives. From a personal standpoint they know the basic drill, including the fuzzy language of government forms and the instructions for filling them out, the cat-and-mouse game of trying to avoid detection as well as the intimidatory fines and exorbitant interest rates used to deter noncompliance. Dealing with the tax department is for many the initiation into the experience of government. The annual rite turns all of us into part-time strategists, and the pain is sufficient to leave us sensitive for the rest of the year to the issue of tax policy.

It's a pocketbook thing. When the word "tax" appears in the headlines, the story—even with a Washington or state capital byline that usually connotes boredom—is read thoroughly. Campaign literature that spotlights taxation is not immediately thrown away, and the television remote control is left alone when the news or a financial program turns to tax strategies.

For people in the business of policy making, the universal quality of tax issues is even more pronounced. As one small business activist and CPA points out, "Tax law is part of everything legislative—you can't separate it out." Indeed, up and down the list of issues that affect small business most, the role of taxes is insidious, from health care through labor and access to capital. Each item on the small business agenda comes back to the way Congress and the state legislatures prepare their annual tax bills and what consideration they give to the special case of small business.

There is a lot of finger-pointing in policy circles whenever tax problems come up. While most outsiders automatically assume that the villain is going to be the IRS, in fact Congress and the state legislatures often have as much to do with idiotic or unfair tax rules as the IRS, which is charged with enforcing them. The traditional model for regulation holds that a brief and vague legislative text conferring wide-ranging powers and jurisdiction would be entrusted to an agency—such as the Interstate Commerce Commission (ICC) or Federal Communications Commission (FCC)—for more detailed and interpretative work that produces a set of rules. This effectively gives the agency the power to write policy, after a legislative fashion.

However, in the case of the Environmental Protection Agency (EPA), the IRS, and the Labor Department, Congress since the 1970s has preferred to spell out in all its convoluted detail the specific requirements of business, from retirement plans to pollution-reduction acts. These comprehensive laws, which in draft form can run to two hundred or more pages, give less discretionary power to the agencies, which historically have been perceived as too closely tied to the industries they are supposed to police.

Similarly, the most onerous tax requirements on the books come out of the Congress and state legislatures and not from the IRS. This means that Congress and the states, not the IRS, should be the primary target of lobbying efforts. The first step for small business as a community is to alert federal and state government to the disproportionate tax burden that small business is bearing. By all accounts small business is in the excruciating grip of the tax bite. In a 1994 survey of 7,500 small firms by Arthur Andersen and National Small Business United, while a majority said business revenues and profits were up and expected to rise in 1995, one third also reported an increase in their corporate taxes, and 66 percent said they experienced a personal income tax increase. A similar survey in 1994 of small manufacturers was conducted by the National Association of Manufacturers. It found that more than half of the S corporations, which constitute 38.5 percent of small manufacturers, expected to decrease investment due to tax reasons—even though more than half of the respondents reported higher profits in 1993 and 1994 despite the higher taxes.

These are just a few of the many statistics that are the pawns in the chess game over the minutiae of tax legislation. Number crunchers on both sides of the issue—whether they are hoping to alleviate the tax burden on small business or raise tax revenue to reduce the deficit—are able to find similar figures to bolster their arguments, sacrificing one pawn for another. Since most of the lobbying groups for small business, led by the National Federation of Independent Businesses (NFIB), which has a solid tax team at work on a dozen different initiatives, are concentrating their efforts on tax incentives such as exemptions and deductions, the figures on the damaging effects of high rates tend to cancel each other out.

Among the promises that paved the way for the Republicans to roll into Congress and the governors' mansions across the country in November 1994, none was so potent as the vow to cut taxes on the middle-class family, which has been directly linked to helping family-run businesses. The Republican "Contract with America" explicitly signalled the party's commitment to small business, giving it a family-values spin. In a victory speech, Party Chairman Haley Barbour declared: "Ours is the party of small business, not big business; of Main Street, not Wall Street."

The most direct way to come through on that commitment will be through tax cuts. The key committee on taxes is Ways and Means, and

Bill Archer, a Republican from Texas, has already vowed to cut business taxes specifically related to capital investment and capital gains. New York's Alfonse D'Amato, who takes over the Senate Banking committee, and Oregonian Bob Packwood, who will head Finance, are also supporters of tax breaks for business. To stop the hemorrhaging of his popularity, President Clinton came up with his own plan to help the middle class that had a number of similar-sounding tax breaks. Small business should take his promise as an invitation to apply the pressure for the kind of measures government should be pursuing.

THE SMALL-BUSINESS WISH LIST

Most small business lobbyists have their roll call of hoped-for tax breaks ready. For the NFIB, the agenda is headed by capital formation and what Congress can do to stimulate economic growth through a tax relief package. As the organization's position paper states:

> Small business owners believe they would benefit most if the federal government just let them keep more of their own money. Instead of taking taxes from them and then refunding some of the money through an investment tax credit or a targeted jobs tax credit, small business owners would prefer to pay a smaller tax in the first place.

To do this, the NFIB favors increased and simplified expensing to encourage investing and to save time on paperwork since figuring out depreciation can be such a headache. Rather than the current $10,000 deduction for equipment allowed in the first year it is purchased, the NFIB would like to see the allowance go to $25,000. Together with an investment tax credit that will help in raising capital and reduced capital gains for small businesses, this package could assist entrepreneurs in raising capital.

For the first time in years, there is genuine expectation of a capital gains tax cut. Under current law, gains that are attributable to inflation are heavily taxed. Small business activists correctly point out that this is unfair because it takes years for a new enterprise to grow (most statistical profiles of a successful company stipulate five or more years), and so they are penalized. If taxes were indexed for inflation, small businesses and the investors who consider buying shares in them could afford to grow. The NFIB recommends that small businesses be allowed to deduct 50 percent of the profits they make on stock held for more than five years and 100 percent of stock held for 10 years or more. All of this is part of the tax bill, S.1932, that appeared before the 102nd Congress, although many of the breaks incorporated into that bill were more than offset by higher taxes in other areas, like estate and payroll taxes. No final action has been taken on the bill, and many of its provisions are finding their way into a similar bill introduced in 1995.

Not every small business advocate is convinced that a major campaign should be mounted on the capital gains issue. For example, Debra Lessin, who prepares the position papers for the National Association of Women Business Owners (NAWBO), asks, "Who's selling for capital gains? Small business has sold investments and whatever other assets it can to keep going. It takes years to make money. Five years from now they will know how little capital gains tax reductions really have to do with building capital." Lessin feels that the present proposals for capital gains tend to favor manufacturing and neglect the interests of service companies with four or fewer employees. By steering attention to more pressing matters, such as the home-office deduction, she feels small business lobbyists representing the "real world of small service firms" can get more bang for their buck.

Every entrepreneur can use a tax break, and one proposal on the table is to allow a zero corporate rate tax on the first $25,000 in earnings for businesses on the edge of profitability, along the lines of the zero tax rate that allows individuals to avoid taxes (partly because it would cost the IRS far too much to go after millions of them for such paltry revenue). According to tax experts, even those inside the IRS, the effort to track down small businesses that are just getting by is far more expensive than the tax revenues collected. The same negligible return on a substantial effort at enforcement has led small business advocates to question other taxes. The alternative minimum tax, for example, is a nightmare for both small business and the IRS to calculate, and it only brings in about 0.1 percent of all income taxes collected from individuals and small businesses. Eliminating it will have a negligible effect on Treasury revenues.

Parallel with the capital gains break, which would allow entrepreneurs to keep more of what they have built up over the years it takes to grow a business, activists are hoping to see reform in the area of estate taxes. When the owner of an enterprise dies, whether it is a small store or manufacturer or even a family farm, the value of the business is added to that of the owner's personal estate and can be taxed at a monstrous 50 percent rate. This drives many families to sell the business merely to be able to pay the taxes. While Congress enacted an exemption in 1981 for the first $600,000 in an estate, the 102nd Congress proposed that the exemption be reduced to $200,000. The small business lobby countered with a proposal that would have deferred the estate taxes owed on a small business until the business is sold outside the family.

No decisive action was taken in 1994, but the issue is expected to be taken up again in 1995. The key here is to allow the business to pass intact from one generation to the next and to avoid the elimination of jobs that would result from businesses closing down. Even if the business is liquidated, advocates of small business are hoping that Congress will find a way to structure taxes so that the rates will be no higher than those on ordinary income.

Home Is Where the Heart Is:
The Home-Office Deduction

The pressing small business taxation issues on a nitty-gritty level are the home-office deduction and independent contractor status. You would think, listening to the rhetoric coming out of the White House about keeping up with the trends toward working at home and being more entrepreneurial, that the home office deduction would be encouraged by government. After all, 9 million people work out of their homes, and futurists confidently predict that half of all American workers may well "electronically commute" before the end of the century. There are over 200 newsletters and 17 catalogs published exclusively for home-based entrepreneurs. As the National Association for the Self-Employed, a nonprofit lobbying group in Washington, argues:

> Home offices are popular because they make sense for businesses, families, and individuals. Narrowing the home-office deduction ignores or tries to roll back fundamental changes in the economy: More telecommuting, more two-income families with one parent working out of the home so as to supervise children, more elderly and disabled people

working at home, more people who have been laid off by larger businesses 'starting over' from their homes to minimize costs, and the 'flattening' of traditional business hierarchies as more functions are contracted out.

But the IRS does not seem to be paying much attention, and Congress is not applying much pressure to make the home-office deduction a comfortable proposition. In 1993, under pressure from a few of the small business lobbying groups (but not the NFIB), both the House and Senate considered bills to amend the Internal Revenue Code of 1986 in favor of a clarification of the rules regarding home-office deductions. Neither bill passed in its original form, but advocates are hoping that they will survive as an amendment to further tax legislation.

First, the basics. According to the current law, you should be able to take a home-office deduction if you pass the "regular and exclusive test," that is, if the office is used regularly and exclusively as the principal place of business and as a meeting place for patients, clients, or customers. The deduction is based on direct expenses of painting, repairing, and equipping the office and indirect expenses like mortgage interest, real estate taxes, rent, insurance, and utilities that relate to the entire home. The deduction cannot exceed the net income from the business after considering all other business expenses, so it cannot be used to create or bolster a loss from a trade or business.

As many of those who tried to take the home-office deduction quickly learned to their dismay, and thousands of others were told by wary accountants or the press, the deduction became a red flag for a personal income tax audit. The problem was started with the "focal point" question posed by the IRS, which wants to know if the goods and services are provided and the revenues are produced in the home. The customers of a home business must physically visit the office and the income must be generated within the home office itself. But local zoning ordinances can prohibit home-based businesses from having customers who visit, and many service industries work with customers at the customer's office, or work by fax and computer (saving gas and reducing pollution, according to the environmentally conscious telecommuters).

Rather than Congress changing the rules, the tax courts began to make the deduction harder and harder to take. The rollback of the deduction is particularly hard on parents trying to earn money while taking care of children, or women starting businesses who are concerned about security and prefer to meet their customers away from the home office, as well as the elderly and disabled who have difficulty commuting or working in traditional offices.

The landmark case in the history of the home-office deduction is the 1993 *Commissioner of the IRS v. Nader Soliman*. Soliman is an anesthesiologist in Maryland who worked 30 to 35 hours a week at four different hospitals, none of which gave him an office. He used one of his three bedrooms as an office and spent an average of three hours a day in the office doing administrative work, such as billing and records, but never treating patients there. The Tax Court decided, and the Fourth Court of Appeals agreed, that he could take the deduction, but the Supreme Court reversed the decision and the IRS announced it would strictly apply the Supreme Court decision to discourage others from using the deduction. The IRS is using new tests that advocates of small business are calling unfair and arbitrary. As Lessin asks, "If a business is generating enough income to claim an office deduction and has one office used exclusively for the business, why should the IRS concern itself with where the office is located?"

Giving Congress a Try

Considering the rocky road that entrepreneurs have found in the courts when they try to challenge the IRS on the home-office deduction, the most expedient way to re-claim this issue is by taking it to Congress. That is exactly what the National Association of the Self-Employed did. In a letter-writing and fax campaign, they won bipartisan support for House and Senate bills that eventually could make the home-office deduction viable again. Even though H.R. 3407, the Home Office Deduction Act, was introduced in the House in October 1993 by Peter Hoagland, Democrat from Nebraska, with a companion bill in the Senate introduced by Orrin Hatch, Republican from Utah, Joseph Lieberman, Democrat from Connecticut, and James Exon, Democrat from Nebraska, the home-office deduction was moribund under the Democrats.

Neither bill will probably pass on its own, particularly given the tight fiscal climate created by the 1993 Revenue Reconciliation Act. But the Republicans are vowing to find a way to attach language to a tax bill and allow more entrepreneurs to use the deduction, even though it could cost the Treasury Department about $400 million in lost revenues over the next four years. Representative Bill Archer favors allowing taxpayers to use the home-office deduction if the office is where the taxpayer's "essential administrative or management activities are conducted on a regular and systematic basis" and if the taxpayer has no other place to conduct them.

With the growth of virtual companies, it is harder and harder to tell where business is conducted today. As NAWBO's tax expert Lessin acerbically remarks:

> The guys who wrote the tax law on home-office deductions obviously never had a day job in their lives, because they totally discounted the administrative aspects of running a business and they have separated where you earn your money and run your business. It's being used as a scare tactic by the IRS against the fastest-growing business sector in the country.

In Lessin's view, the way the deduction is interpreted by the IRS, which permits a studio photographer to write off a home office but denies the same deduction to a location photographer who does everything but shoot at home, is illogical and shows the Treasury Department is out of touch with the way business is done in America today. As she says, "The IRS just doesn't get it. I spend half my days sometimes marketing, administrating, billing—and you're going to tell me that I'm not working?" To scare off potential users of the deduction, the IRS makes sure that a ruling that severely punishes someone for using it gets a lot of press just before April 15 every year. However, there are accountants who point out that home office claims do not have, statistically, that much to do with auditing figures.

There is bipartisan support for making the home-office deduction more fair without inviting abuse. Even Newt Gingrich has said that the home office rules are outdated on the basis of the new technology. That prompted a powerful response among even die-hard Democrats, like

Lessin, in the small business advocacy community. As Lessin admits, "My jaw drops and I'm going, "Wow! Cool! Newt's got it.""

This time around, the small business lobby might actually get it in writing. The key will be to track the progress of the House and Senate bills and apply pressure, through fax and mail campaigns as well as the use of mass media, such as call-in radio shows or the editorial pages of local newspapers, on elected officials to make sure they pass.

Declaring Independence

The other nuts-and-bolts issue for small business involves sorting out the difference between an employee and an independent contractor. For a seemingly minor detail, it impinges on many legislative areas, including labor and tax laws. Even the health-care reform bill took a stab at more strictly defining independent contractor status. The guidelines suggested that anyone who derived 80 percent of his or her income from one payor was an employee, not an independent contractor. That measure was not passed, but the IRS is looking for authority to write its own rules to reclassify any worker, including direct sellers or real estate agents. They probably could use some *de minimis* rules for the number of hours a week and percentage of income, just so that the contractors themselves have a quantitative way of knowing how to file.

In order to implement those proposed rules the IRS is asking for $405 million to hire 5,000 more examiners. While they hire more investigators, tax professionals note that the IRS has never issued promised guidance interpreting the applicability of the safe havens for businesses treating workers as independent contractors, even though several times the Treasury has announced that they would be published "imminently."

Congress came up with the "service industry noncompliance" (SINC) plan in its 1993 deficit reduction package, which would have required businesses to report payments to corporations, partly to capture information on individuals who say they are incorporated. The Senate killed SINC after strong business lobbying—mostly on behalf of large corporations—but there are rumors that the IRS will refloat the idea in the form of one of its own rules.

From the point of view of businesses large and small, there are several legal and tax reasons for preferring to use independent contractors. The major savings from a tax perspective is that the employer does not have to pay Social Security tax or federal or state unemployment taxes, since the independent contractor is responsible for them. The employer also does not have to file payroll tax returns, even though a Form 1099-MISC for each independent contractor making $600 or more during the year has to be filed, or, in the case of a direct seller of consumer products, anyone to whom the company sells $5,000 worth of goods during a year has to be reported. Since the crackdown on independent contractors began, these 1099-MISC forms have become the main way for the IRS to identify businesses that represent employees as contractors.

In the eyes of some small business advocates, a basic change in Schedule C of Form 1099-MISC could solve many of the problems for the IRS. Instead of reporting income on line 1 as "Gross receipts or sales" without breaking it out from sources, there could be separate lines for each 1099-MISC statement that would help the IRS match the forms submitted by the firms that hire the contractors, just as they do for interest payments. It sounds like a relatively minor matter, but as a way of clarifying a highly problematic area for many small businesses it could save millions of dollars not only in taxes but in legal costs as well.

The Hidden Devourer of Profits: Payroll Taxes

One of the least-publicized ways that small business gets stung by taxes involves the most basic of routines: the payroll. Each of us who has at one time worked for a company doubtless remembers the horrible shock of looking at our first pay stub and realizing how much of our salary is eaten up by taxes and deductions we never remember authorizing. The same misery befalls an owner-manager on pay day. Through a series of payroll taxes covering unemployment, social security, and a whole slew of employee benefits, as well as bonds and insurance costs that have to be covered, the simple act of meeting the payroll becomes a nightmare.

For example, take the question of unemployment tax liability. Small businesses with high turnover rates, especially seasonally affected businesses, pay a much higher unemployment tax than larger firms that have lower turnover. Unemployment taxes—essentially wage taxes paid by the employer—amount to 6.2 percent of the first $7,000 of annual wages for an employee, although a credit for up to 5.4 percent is given for state unemployment taxes. The credit fluctuates depending upon the amount of claims by former employees upon the company. The more benefits claimed, the higher the unemployment tax rate becomes.

Since 1935, when unemployment insurance was created by Congress (by the Federal Unemployment Tax Act), the relative burden on small business of unemployment taxes has been disproportionately large by comparison with larger firms. The general consensus in Washington and among the states is that unemployment benefits are sufficiently funded for now and probably will be cut back, but periodically bills arise to increase payroll taxes in order to expand the unemployment insurance program.

Similarly, the apocalyptic fears for the future of Social Security became a source of panic about five years ago, when Congress voted a tax rate increase in 1990 on top of a similar amendment passed in 1983 that established a schedule of increasing payroll tax rates to ensure the solvency of the Social Security system. Since those increases were based on projections that the recession would be deeper and steeper than it has been, a surplus of $255 billion built up in the system by 1991, with projections that it would increase to $1.16 trillion by the year 2001. Pro-business groups, including the small business lobby headed by the NFIB, want to see a pay-as-you-go program for Social Security that will free up funds to start up and expand businesses.

The NFIB and other groups are hoping that the payroll tax increase of 1990 will be rolled back, despite Congressional action in 1993 that makes it more difficult to reduce FICA tax rates. As the NFIB points out, "Because small businesses are primarily labor-intensive, FICA taxes are a significant burden on them. Small business owners generally pay more in FICA taxes than income taxes." Small business trade organizations of all stripes have to keep their ears to the ground to detect the first stirrings of these bills, just as they have to be vigilant regarding the rumors of a national sales tax or value-added tax similar to the consumption taxes in force in Europe.

Some legislative ideas seem to be going the entrepreneurs' way, however. According to a plan authored by Representative Ron Wyden, a Democrat from Oregon, the tax codes would be rewritten to provide for "partnership pay," by which the amount of a worker's wages depends on the performance of the company. Wyden notes that the tax code encourages investment in equipment but does nothing to encourage firms to hire workers: "In effect the government, through our tax policy, is encouraging companies to replace workers with machines." His bill would encourage partnership pay and ensure tax fairness to small business owners who sell one company and use the proceeds to buy another firm.

No Good Deed Goes Unpunished

On top of the issue of pay, the small business owner faces the nightmare of complex and costly rules on benefits. By state law, businesses have to obtain workers' compensation insurance covering job-related injuries or illnesses. Insurers can be reluctant to work with very small businesses unless the compensation policy is tied to other types of policies. Businesses that provide fringe benefits, like group insurance other than workers' compensation, pension, or profit-sharing retirement plans, have to deal with one of the most onerous sets of regulations ever devised by Washington: The Employee Retirement Income Security Act (ERISA) of 1974. The ERISA rules are so convoluted that many businesses break them without even knowing they have, and a whole management consulting industry has grown up around interpreting them for businesses. Congress set criminal as well as civil penalties for unintentional noncompliance with ERISA, and many individuals make their living as benefits consultants helping small companies to avoid those penalties.

The confusion only deepens when more than one federal agency becomes involved in supervising the payroll deductions. Tax-qualified retirement plans, such as Keogh plans as well as profit-sharing plans, are monitored by both the Department of Labor and the IRS. Between the two agencies, there are a multitude of reporting requirements. They include a mandatory Summary Plan Description and half a dozen annually filed forms. The demands of Labor and the IRS can overwhelm a small business that is trying to minimize its administrative activity to concentrate on becoming more productive in its real line of business. What may be even more frustrating is the way in which entrepreneurs who want to do the right thing in terms of benefits have to pay a higher price. The cost of these plans has multiplied several times since ERISA was enacted, and a fidelity bond has to be posted for assets of a pension or welfare plan. When withholding became mandatory on distributions of pension and profit-sharing benefits, the burden of paying the taxes in advance passed to the businesses themselves. The business that wants to set up pension plans beyond the minimum stipulated by the government is severely punished for doing so.

A CALL FOR CLARITY

There are two ways for small business to attack these problems—and have its wish list recognized. One involves holding the government to its promise of greater interagency coordination and the elimination of redundant regulation. Since the Small Business Administration (SBA) has sponsored a series of meetings on this very topic that have included representatives of the IRS and Labor, they should push to have the process of supervision simplified so that one or the other is in charge of monitoring benefits for small businesses. The second way that small business can bring about a modicum of relief is by seeing to it that another government promise is kept: clarification of the rules. If the language in which the rules governing benefits were simple and clear, then most of the unwitting violations of those rules could be eliminated.

As in most other areas of regulation, even the government is realizing that some of the fog—and what bureaucrats call FOG or fear of government—coming out of Foggy Bottom has to be dispelled. Beyond the monetary breaks brought by changes in rates and exemptions, entrepreneurs need a break on the costly preparation time—amounting to an estimated 1.2 billion hours or $24 billion worth of aggravation—that the IRS imposes on them annually. However, every bill proposing a simplified tax code for small business was vetoed in 1994. They went down in flames despite the strong support of the NFIB, the SBA, and even conservative organizations such as the Heritage Foundation. The crippling factor was the need to keep the tax bill revenue neutral—and the inability of the lobbying organizations to find a way to do so hurt their efforts.

In 1994, state by state White House conferences on small business ran straight into the same assault on the unclear and prolix wording of regulatory documents, including tax instructions. A dramatic effort at changing the current reporting process was acknowledged, and Congress was exhorted to get back to principles, such as those that guided legislators to create the individual 1040EZ form.

There are many other ways to clear up the mess. Legislators are only finally noticing that small businesses are forced to handle long and misleading forms and that the introduction of more simple paperwork requirements, as pioneered by the Small Business Administration in its Low-Doc loan application program, results in greater voluntary participation and compliance.

The very method of accounting used by small business could be changed by an act of Congress. According to the NFIB, instead of the present system, which uses accrual and completed contract methods of accounting as well as uniform capitalization rules for all sizes of businesses, a cash accounting system would be simpler and probably far more accurate. Much of the complexity is attributable to the sheer impenetrability of the rules of incorporation. The original notion of the S corporation was simplification. Because the protection of incorporation is valued but the requirements for C corporation status were so stringent and complicated, the lighter burden of S status was created. But now the rules are so contradictory and the forms so lengthy that many accountants are urging their small business clients to rethink their decision to file as S corporations and to consider becoming C corporations.

HOW THE IRS GETS AROUND CONGRESS

As with environmental regulation, where policy and enforcement often part ways ideologically, there are discrepancies between what the IRS promises and what is actually delivered. One of the real dangers of IRS rule changes is that they can be interpretive rather than legislative in nature, and so they escape some of the scrutiny and analytic requirements regarding their cost to business that most legislation has to undergo, as stipulated by the Regulatory Flexibility Act. The Act ensures that any new regulation "will not, as promulgated, have a significant economic impact on a substantial number of small entities."

Some agencies, such as the EPA, have taken that a step further and made it policy that "*any* impact is a significant impact," as a recent in-house memo from the deputy administrator of the EPA reads. The impact analysis requires not only a strong argument on the part of Congress for taking action and the legal basis for that action, but an estimate of how many small businesses would be affected, how they would have to report and what kind of records they would need to keep, a check to make sure that other federal rules do not overlap or conflict with the proposal, and a thorough consideration of alternative rules that would have less economic effect. Small business advocates argue that this litmus test should apply to IRS rule changes as a vital source of protection for small business, but it takes a vigilant entrepreneurial community, including the SBA's Office of Advocacy, to ensure that the IRS does not skirt these safeguards.

In the eyes of the small business community, the Treasury Department is out of sync with the otherwise supportive attitudes of most federal agencies. In particular, many perceive that a new effort on the part of the IRS to propose partnership antiabuse rules, which would be the virtual opposite of the idea of partnership pay as proposed by Representative Wyden, is really an attempt "to create new law" that will be detrimental to the interests of entrepreneurs. Since regulatory flexibility or cost analyses are required of any new law, lobbyists argue that the IRS should undertake some sort of analysis of its proposed rule changes as well.

The SBA addressed this issue in a letter to the IRS in November 1994. Jere Glover, the chief advocate at the SBA, wrote that he was "troubled, although not surprised," by the IRS's determination that the proposed regulation is an interpretative rather than a legislative rule. Under the proposed rule change, the IRS can *recast* transactions involving partnerships to reveal the underlying partnership arrangement and in this way prevent the use of partnerships in circumventing taxes.

As Glover observes, "While it is by no means clear what constitutes an interpretative or legislative rule, it is beyond the realm of reason that the proposed antiabuse rule can be considered an interpretative rule." The proposed regulations will, with certain limited exceptions, apply to virtually all 1.5 million partnerships, regardless of size, in the United States, and it will cost money not just in terms of taxes but in litigation and other compliance expenses. Glover is urging that small partnerships be made exempt from the rule, which should be fine-tuned to target abusers rather than sweep up more than a million small businesses in its net.

Another proposed IRS rule change—again, a measure that did not come through Congress—is meeting with stern disapproval from the banking community and should be on the SBA's list as well as that of other tax watchers. It concerns the allocation of the profit derived from sales in which two or more members of a partnership are involved, and hinges on the amount of taxes that have to be calculated and paid in advance of the distribution of those profits. Although it is a mere footnote to the tax rules that cover partnerships, and in particular international partnerships, it is a good demonstration of how the IRS can slip one through the comment process.

One group that was watching was the American Bankers Association, which stated in its position paper on the subject:

It is unlikely that small business, or smaller businesses, could afford to undertake that search or that analysis, if challenged on audit, let alone undertake it in advance for determining its prices or filing its tax return. . . . Clearly, if it is in the public interest to encourage small business to export and expand their respective markets overseas, and the latter does so through foreign subsidiaries, rather than through branches, to reduce the exposure of the small business to the risks of doing business in a foreign jurisdiction, it hardly is in the best interests of the country to impose upon small business taxpayers the financial burden that will be imposed upon it by the application of the proposed regulations. In sum, such taxpayers will simply have the choice of capitulating to any demands by the IRS, unless the demands are so extreme that the small business taxpayer would feel compelled to challenge notwithstanding any substantial financial burden of doing so.

The drafters of the proposed regulations seem to have lost sight of the fact that not all taxpayers in the country are multinationals with large staffs, better able financially, in varying degrees, to absorb the burden of compliance or resisting IRS challenges in the application of the rules that would be imposed by the proposed regulations.

While the ABA does not always come to the aid of small business, in this case by catching a quiet rule change, they did entrepreneurs a service.

AN INSIDER'S VIEW OF THE IRS

Recently, the IRS itself decided to create a watchdog unit inside its own halls to do this job. In a move that parallels the EPA, the IRS appointed an ombudsman in March 1994. She is Barbara Jenkins, who became the director of Small Business Affairs for the IRS on the basis of thirty years of loyal service to the IRS. Not everyone is convinced that the creation of the office of ombudsman is enough, of course. When I told one activist whose specialty is taxes that I had an interview coming up with the small business ombudsman from the IRS in Washington, she just laughed. The image of the IRS among entrepreneurs is no different from the way it is perceived by individual taxpayers. The assumption that the IRS does not care about the rights of the little guy is universal.

As with the EPA, the ombudsman at the IRS is supposed to be there to handle complaints and boost compliance. Unlike the EPA position, unfortunately, the IRS does not welcome continual input on new policy or rule changes from Jenkins, although she does meet with the chief officers, the deputy commissioner, and the commissioner on enforcement procedures as they affect small business. As with most IRS officials, she is quick to point out that it is essentially Congress that sets tax policy, and their job is merely to carry it out.

Jenkins, a native of Philadelphia, had her start on the lowest rung of the IRS ladder at the Philadelphia Service Center in 1964, where she eventually became a supervisor and then went out to Fresno, California, to open a new center in 1971. She has been a top-level supervisor in Memphis, Brookhaven, San Francisco, and Detroit and was named executive assistant to the assistant regional commissioner in charge of data processing in Philadelphia. She came to Washington in 1992 as assistant director for operations management and then moved into telecommunications.

Jenkins is, in short, the ultimate IRS insider. It even shows in the way she talks. When she refers to the IRS, she calls it "the Service," as a CIA veteran would refer to "the Company." No outsider, no matter how intimately his or her job was involved with the IRS, would call it "the Service." Just as with Karen Brown at the EPA, Jenkins has had no small business experience from a personal standpoint, except across the desk as an IRS official in contact with small business. For some, this perspective could raise eyebrows. Jenkins feels she understands the spirit of enterprise, however. She says, "I dream about one day becoming an entrepreneur myself, after my work here is done."

Jenkins loves her job, because it suits the way she has learned to approach her work:

> I've always had that customer-oriented focus since starting with the Service and this really affords me the opportunity to be a bigger player. It's the first office of its kind to focus on the small business client base, and it's fascinating to be able to interact with the executives and to be a spokesperson for the small business community. Entrepreneurs don't know that side of the IRS. When you talk to people about the IRS their immediate reaction is the tax side of it, which only reaches a small percentage of the public.

Jenkins meets periodically with senior executives at the IRS and her six-member staff, but the emphasis is less on policy, which she considers a Congressional matter, than on implementation. The main job of ombudsman is to be an educator within the IRS:

> We need to educate and influence those with program responsibility to be more sensitive about how what they do affects more small business. We are a matrix organization that will be effective when others understand and recognize that one size does not fit all.

A big part of the ombudsman's responsibility is also to serve as a communications link to the trade associations that serve small business as well as the SBA and state and county agencies. In addition to Jenkins, the Problem Resolution Program of the IRS is also available for what the IRS calls "chronic tax situations."

Since assuming her responsibilities, Jenkins has been:

. . . trying to assimilate all the information I've heard from small business because the IRS cuts across all industries and has the same perspective as the SBA. I learn every day from small business executives—now my focus is much broader than in my single functions in other jobs. I can look across functional lines and spend more time considering our business situation. In today's economy, keeping in mind the agenda for a reduced deficit, it's difficult to talk about tax cuts without having an idea of how to pay for them. We're in the middle, looking for ways to help small business and still be revenue neutral. That's the dilemma.

TAXES AND THE ECONOMIC OUTLOOK

Jenkins's view is broader than most. Scaling the mountain of paper created by the tax code and all the proposed changes to it and the responses to the proposals is such an arduous task that experts and amateurs alike can be forgiven for not turning to have a look, from those lofty heights, at the view around them. But at the summit, taking in this view is essential. The ultimate perspective on taxes emerges from neither the personal nor the IRS point of view. It is bipartisan, and it is global in nature. It involves asking the basic questions regarding the "common wealth" of the nation and whether higher taxes and the services they create are good or bad for economic growth.

By 1995, most Americans realized even intuitively that the economy was still in the grips of a troubling, paralytic recessionary force. While historical patterns generally show an average growth rate in GDP of more than five percent during the three years following a recession, the growth rate of the American economy is half that, and further corporate layoffs continue to be a weekly staple of the business news, while job creation is about one third what one might statistically expect at this "postrecessionary stage." While taxes have climbed, the deficit remains about the same at more than $200 billion (back in 1990 the nation was promised a budget surplus if the tax bill was enacted), and interest rates have begun to rise. Despite its strong performance during this troubling period, small business continues to feel the chilly grip of the recession.

Anecdotal evidence as well as statistics also point to the heavy cost on small business and investment brought about by the current level of taxation. Particular regions of the country are also the victims of new tax hikes passed in 1993. For example, according to the Heritage Foundation the economy of the state of California will see a decrease in its GDP of more than $37 billion over the next five years, and on a per-capita basis, Connecticut, which will lose $5.8 billion in all, feels the impact to the tune of $1,711 for every man, woman, and child. All four U.S. Senators representing these two states voted for the tax bill, by the way. The same Heritage Foundation report claims:

> *No state or district will benefit from the higher taxes. These figures notwithstanding, the White House still maintains that taxpayers come out ahead because higher taxes will stimulate economic growth, lower interest rates, encourage job creation, and reduce the budget deficit.*

A tragic contradiction in public policy is that as the states are striving to attract new business and promote small business through expensive promotional programs and capital expenditures on industrial parks or other facilities, they are effectively undermining these efforts by allowing tax rates and rules to keep business away. The strongest magnet for enterprise is a favorable tax environment, and enterprise is the key to economic growth nationwide.

THE SMALL BUSINESS AGENDA FOR TAX POLICY CHANGES

Whatever arguments are made on behalf of this, that, or the other new modification in the tax code, their validity should be tested against the big picture. In preparing the agenda for tax policy changes, small business advocates should keep a long-range, macroeconomic outlook in mind. They need to press their state and federal representatives to:

- Pursue a policy of tax relief that stimulates the general economy and particularly the growth and prospects for capital formation for small business.
- Provide tax incentives such as investment tax credits for capital expenditures that help carry out federal policies regarding health care, the environment, and exports.

- Raise the deduction on equipment purchases or improvement and allow small business to expense the upgrades.
- Cut capital gains taxes and index them for inflation.
- Defer estate taxes until a business is sold outside the family.
- Make the home-office deduction a reality, not a red flag.
- Clarify the rules regarding independent contractors.
- Rewrite the rules for creating S corporations.
- Change small business tax computation to a cash accounting system.
- Give the small business ombudsman at the IRS policy-making responsibilities and create a similar office for each state tax body.

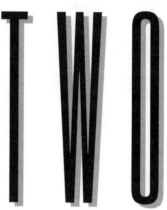

GOING GLOBAL: THE SMALL BUSINESS PERSPECTIVE ON INTERNATIONAL TRADE

4

LET'S TALK
Trade Negotiations and
Their Importance for
Small Business

World trade has never been unimportant for the small business sector. With entrepreneurs in all industries now looking overseas to expand markets and to work with new suppliers, following negotiations among heads of state and their specialized deputies—and understanding the rhetoric of those trade talks—is more important than ever. As a result of trade shows, or through the services offered by federal and even state and local export initiatives, small business owners are finding more buyers and suppliers at their doorstep. While local and federal governments are often involved in staging those trade fairs and are in general eager to see "global fever" take hold in small businesses, there is remarkably little recognition as yet that small business ought to be included and informed about its stake in ongoing trade negotiations that will necessarily affect any business with global aspirations.

Here is just one subtle indicator of how government has forgotten entrepreneurs and their needs in this area. The Commerce Department has a 24-hour fax hotline on the General Agreement on Tariffs and Trade (GATT) that invites anyone dialing a toll-free line to choose among hundreds of different reports about the impact of GATT on industries, regions, and laws. Not one of the reports is devoted to the impact of GATT on small business, nor is small business even mentioned in Commerce's basic rundown on the impact GATT is likely to have on American business.

If government ignores the interests of small business in this issue, it may be partly attributable to the way in which the key lobbying organizations representing small business themselves have stayed away from the issue of foreign trade. Most of these lobbying organizations never took a position on GATT and, in fact, have left the subject of trade off their agendas in favor of more domestic pursuits.

Clearly we have not only a vacuum of interest and information but a logical contradiction. On the one hand, entrepreneurs are told by the government that they are the standard-bearers in a march to globalization that the federal and local governments are counting on to help heal the trade deficit and bolster the national economy. On the other, they are left out of the loop when it comes to trade talks. And they are not making a big enough effort to get into that loop. Someone in government is assuming that what small business does not need to know about a complex set of issues will not hurt them, and those who are entrusted to look after the political interests of small business are not bothering to speak up and say that entrepreneurs can be hurt by ignoring what goes on in international trade negotiations.

Major industries and multinational corporations have the luxury of assigning experts full-time to monitoring these developments, and their adroitly packaged promotional materials attract the interest of the federal officials in charge of the negotiations. When a delegation visits Beijing or Tokyo or Brussels to carry on preliminary trade conversations, individual corporate heads from telecommunications, aerospace, computers, and particularly the automotive trade are inevitably brought along. This inside track is meant to carry its weight politically. A major McDonnell Douglas contract from Saudi Arabia spells jobs and votes. So the government hands the ball to McDonnell Douglas, or Boeing, or IBM, and very often they fumble—losing the contract and continuing to lay off workers. Time and again it has been proven that job creation and a rise in American exports will stem from the small business community while the big corporations stumble along; yet small business is never part of the agenda for trade delegations.

This gap is waiting to be closed. For entrepreneurs, it is going to be a matter of education in the meaning of trade for them. For the officials who represent national interests, it is going to involve an education in the importance of putting small business on the table along with the familiar interests of giant corporations.

Of course, world trade has never presented a more complicated and confusing picture than the one we are facing in the mid-1990s. This has required a fundamental shift in Washington's view of foreign policy. The strategic thinking that used to be focused on military aggression, foreign aid, and other concerns of the State Department is now linking State and Treasury and Commerce in one business-oriented consolidated effort that has to be brought to bear on trade issues. As former Treasury Secretary Lloyd Bentsen comments about Washington, "Everyone's been saying for a long time that foreign policy is becoming economic, but like everything else, it's taken a while for the message to sink in around here." The State Department has handed off responsibility to Commerce and the trade negotiators in the cases of Japan, China, and Latin America, the new "Free Trade Area of the Americas."

The need for new strategic thinking on trade is dire. As in Europe, where the chorus of praise for unification rapidly dissolved in a chaos of conflicting voices, so too have trade accords that looked promising from an American point of view run into trouble. Just as the North American Free Trade Agreement (NAFTA) ran straight into the fury of H. Ross Perot and his supporters, so too the General Agreement on Tariffs and Trade had its vocal political opposition.

Sorting out the good guys from the bad in these disputes is far from easy. The hidden effects of the major trade agreements have a way of emerging only after the ink on the signatures has dried. Because the language of the accords is so specialized and abstruse and the

Congressional bills that make their ratification possible have a way of accumulating prolix twists and turns of their own, there is a built-in level of obscurity that makes straight talk so rare. While Perot and others who are not in office make a political issue out of it—that is to say, a partisan means of attacking the position or career of a rival under the pretext of a debate on trade—the officials in office view the debate on trade bills as an opportunity to advance their own agenda on business and trade, tacking on pork barrel clauses requiring major construction projects in their constituencies or blocking the entry of Japanese or other foreign entities that could knock local businesses out of the area competitively. In this way, what looked like a relatively straightforward progression toward the opening of borders and the relaxation of tariffs rapidly became an exercise in backtracking and hidden agendas that is typical of Washington.

One of the sad consequences of the confusion is that small business in Washington, as well as on the local level, is losing out on trade to a great extent. The attitude on Capitol Hill regarding the interests of American enterprise in the trade bill is an arrogant posture, based on the assumption that entrepreneurs cannot handle the issue intellectually. That is dead wrong. Provided with the information and time to sort it out, like all good businesspeople, small business owners can understand international trade policy and help shape it in ways that will benefit their companies and the country.

Given their superior understanding of the culture and politics of their native lands, many foreign-born entrepreneurs would be better equipped to sort out the misunderstandings that plague trade negotiations than the American-born representatives who only get them into more of a muddle through ignorance. If the negotiators consulted with professionals from communities including the Korean-Americans, Caribbean-Americans, Mexican-Americans, Chinese-Americans, and others before proceeding with trade pacts or making significant decisions regarding policy toward those regions, the federal government could save money and the businesses that operate under those pacts could be much better off. Among those who would be in a position to advise the federal government are small business owners involved from day to day in trading with those countries who know the politics, culture, business practices, law, strategic subtleties, and taboos of countries that are very different from the United States.

THE FUSS OVER NAFTA

Just like any government policy that undergoes changes and is rewritten to suit the interests of a few privileged insiders, some small businesses stand to gain while others can be hurt by the outcome of these negotiations. While a few trade organizations representing small businesses lobbied in favor of NAFTA, most were wary about offending part of their membership that stood to lose business across the borders. One of the exceptions to the cautious approach of small business lobbying groups was the National Association of Women Business Owners (NAWBO), which fought wholeheartedly for the accord after receiving a strong message from its members in California, Texas, and Florida that it would be very good for their business.

Betting the right way on NAFTA has already put millions of dollars into the pockets of informed and forward-looking entrepreneurs. A year after NAFTA went into effect, many entrepreneurs and relieved politicians were calling it an unqualified success. President Clinton declared that it had created 100,000 new jobs and that within six months after the pact was adopted exports had increased by 20 percent, or three times the rate of overall export growth. The prize was tarnished to a degree when the Mexican stock, bond, and currency markets went into a tailspin in January 1995. When the U.S. government agreed to guarantee $20 billion in loans to restore confidence in the peso and the Mexican economy, the old opponents of NAFTA cried "bailout" and reiterated the old arguments against NAFTA. For small businesses involved in trade with Mexico, the aid package was particularly significant.

These high-level decisions regarding economic aid to developing nations, designed to encourage them to maintain market economies by guaranteeing short-term government securities and credit markets, are not simply of interest to major investment banks like Merrill Lynch or Goldman, Sachs, with their vast exposure to developing nations' debt. They are also significant for entrepreneurs of many different kinds that are looking for a stable situation in which their considerable investments will have a chance to pay off. In the case of Mexico, the threat to economic stability in the border states, the possibility of an influx of illegal immigrants, and the need to keep the peso from sinking further would have been dire enough. But other political issues joined the dangers to joint ventures or day-to-day trade in forcing the U.S. government into the role of helping to manage the crisis. Similar aid packages for South Africa, Eastern Europe, Israel, and Latin America deserve the attention—and support—of small business owners.

The happiest group in the small business community benefitting from NAFTA had to be the farmers. The amount of corn exported to Mexico tripled in the year after the pact went into effect. Companies that import Mexican goods are also doing well, and experts were surprised at the reversal of the predicted trend toward exporting high-skill, high-wage products to Mexico and importing simple products and raw materials, since the Mexican imports have been products that are very like the high-tech, high-wage California products that are now being manufactured in Mexico. The "giant sucking sound" of jobs being lost to Mexico has been all but inaudible during that first year. Calling the shots on GATT is more difficult but no less important for those who are looking abroad for small business.

SORTING OUT THE GATT MESS

The extraordinarily slow pace of the Uruguay Round of the negotiations of the General Agreements on Tariffs and Trade is just one dramatic example of how the professional politicians can tie knots in a process at the expense of the business community. The Uruguay Round of the GATT is the most comprehensive trade agreement in the world's history. Taking the place of a set of rules subscribed to by 117 countries—rules that were almost universally considered unreliable, incomplete, and unfair—the talks began at a meeting of trade ministers originally held in 1986 in Punta del Este, Uruguay. The ministers wanted to update a set of rules that had been basically the same since the end of World War II and scarcely touched upon areas such as services and intellectual property that have taken on new importance in recent decades.

The new GATT—which now includes 124 countries with several more (including the People's Republic of China) knocking on the door—creates a supervisory body called the World Trade Organization (WTO) that will be located in Geneva and will be responsible for resolving disputes among member nations. These multilateral trade talks formally came to an end on December 15, 1993, after which the baton was passed on to members to ratify the accords. In the United States, this meant a trade bill in Congress that, like the bill supporting NAFTA two years before, looked like it would pass easily. But GATT became a tactical battle rather than one involving the people of the United States or the representatives of its small business interests. It was taken out of the hands of the people it would affect and turned into a political football. By seizing the initiative on GATT, Senator Bob Dole and Representative Newt Gingrich engaged in a power struggle with the Republican right as well as Congressional Democrats and President Clinton. They were not thinking about the interests of small business at all.

The tangled web of the GATT debate is certainly proof of the old saying that politics makes strange bedfellows. The anti-GATT contingent was an unusual amalgam of varying interest groups, including the pugnacious H. Ross Perot, conservative senators led by Bob Dole (until he sorted out a truce over the Thanksgiving holiday weekend in 1994), the archconservatives Pat Buchanan and Democrats like Ernest Hollings, a senator from South Carolina, and Ralph Nader. Even though GATT was a Republican initiative from the start, a pet project of Presidents Reagan and Bush, conservative senators like Jesse Helms of North Carolina and Strom Thurmond of South Carolina held it up as a way to cross President Clinton and tie up Congress. Even though they did not expect to defeat the pact, by voicing their concerns about its impact on the American economy they made a number of Congressional moderates uneasy, particularly those who were up for re-election in November 1994. The GATT debate was far from the most burning issue of the Congressional and gubernatorial campaigns of November 1994 because leaders of both parties put it on a back burner until after the campaign. But it was a significant issue behind the scenes where Congress and the White House make their deals.

Trying to determine if GATT is going to be a good deal for the American entrepreneur is a matter of putting together the evidence from among the fractured arguments advanced by consumer and political groups. The regulatory impact of the accord is sure to change business, particularly with regard to tariffs (both foreign and those imposed by the United States), copyrights and patents, open markets in services, export and import status of agricultural products, quality and safety standards, labor laws, and environmental regulations.

Since even conservative estimates put the figure of jobs owed to merchandise exports at over 7 million, with an additional 3.5 million workers owing their jobs to American service exports, and with those in export-related jobs earning about 17 percent more than the U.S. average wage, the impact of trade on GDP has gone from 13 percent two decades ago to 25 percent today. The Clinton administration has taken the position that GATT will pave the way to an additional $100 billion to $200 billion for GDP annually and a net employment gain of 1.4 million jobs within the decade.

Many are not impressed by these numbers and are more worried about the bureaucratic superstructure that the new GATT accords will create. According to Ralph Nader, the creation of the World Trade Organization (WTO) represents a giant step backward on many of the consumer protection measures he championed, because as a court-like governing body it would override existing regulations. As Nader views it, the "trade uber alles" regime that the WTO represents would signal a regression on environmental and safety standards throughout the world. Nader has warned that the legislative, executive, and judicial power given to the WTO through unaccountable tribunals based in Geneva could declare the laws of the United States (or any other member organization) invalid if they are in conflict with the pro-trade principles of the organization.

For example, American fuel efficiency and product labeling laws that have already been challenged by members of the European Union could be declared invalid by a three-member, closed-door tribunal of trade experts. Nader is concerned that their deliberations are too secretive and questions the provisions allowing council members to pursue their own business careers without worrying about conflict of interest problems. Nader stated in an op/ed piece that ran in *The Wall Street Journal* in September 1994:

> *The WTO's mandate is based on the supremacy of trade matters over consumer, worker, and environmental safeguards, even including*

existing environmental treaties. The agreement's controlling provision is that any domestic law that affects trade in any way must be the 'least trade restrictive' possible.

His call for a delay in the Congressional vote ended up being a prophecy—shortly after the piece appeared the bill was postponed. The debate became so heated that it surprised many in Washington, and the vote on GATT was rescheduled for a date past the November elections in order to spare the incumbents holding on to their seats by the narrowest of margins the difficulty of another controversy. In this way, the suspension of discussion in the House and Senate about GATT became yet another victim of the "do-nothing" Congressional session that has been blamed on Bob Dole and on the skittish Democrats. Senator Dole and President Clinton's agreement allows the United States to withdraw from the WTO if an American commission, consisting of five Federal appellate judges, reviews the WTO's rulings against the United States and determines that three of them are unreasonable. This "three strikes and we're out" rule means that Congress is empowered to order the United States to withdraw from the pact, an idea of Senator Dole's that was considered a major concession on the part of President Clinton. This was the provision that clinched the deal in Congress—both the House and Senate voted resoundingly in favor of the trade bill before the close of the 1994 session.

WHERE WAS SMALL BUSINESS?

The role of small business advocacy groups in this process was nominal. One reason for their silence was the huge diversity of individual opinions among their members regarding the potential harm or benefits of GATT. The consequences of the trade bill are far more varied than those brought about by health-care mandates, for example. The trade bill has diagonally opposite effects upon small businesses that need trade protection and those that thrive on the use of foreign labor. For an organization as vast as the NFIB, it would have been next to impossible to accommodate all the various contingents in one unified position. So it is not surprising to find that in the NFIB's handbook of legislative priorities for the 103rd Congress there is no mention of

GATT or the trade bill at all, and the organization did not take a stand. While individual trade associations representing small manufacturers of electronics, textiles, and other specialized products all had a very specific stand on GATT, the general small business advocacy groups stayed clear of the debate. The only exception to this was, once again, the National Association of Women Business Owners (NAWBO), which under the leadership of strong free-trade proponents supported the ratification of GATT and conducted a letter-writing campaign on its behalf.

Under the old GATT agreement, American companies can refuse to comply with the rulings of the tribunals (and often do). But the stricter enforcement under the new GATT, and the complete lack of opportunity the tribunals offer for companies or state governments to participate—federal governments have to sit back and watch what happens after submitting their written homework, and no transcripts or appeals are allowed—angered so many that 42 state attorneys general, 30 state treasurers, and other trade associations protested the creation of the WTO. Their top demand was that Congress had to authorize any federally mandated, WTO-required preemption of state and local laws. But that demand was not even carried to the talks by U.S. Trade Representative Mickey Kantor, who rejected their plea for him to add it to the agenda. The exclusion of local government from the enforcement process is a bad sign for small business. While major multinationals can afford to lobby the WTO in Geneva and generally enlist federal assistance in carrying their message to officials, small business wields more power on a local level, in its own back yard, where it has an audience with officials. That desire to control one's destiny is why Bob Dole and others wanted an "escape clause" for the trade bill.

According to Ralph Nader, this extra layer of international governance, which only involves officials at the federal level, means that the only access big businesses, especially foreign competitors hoping to get around United States regulations, will have to the process will be through trying to "rent a government" to represent them in Geneva. While Nader is known as the champion of the individual consumer or environmental groups, the cautionary note he sounds here should alert small business to a major discrepancy between their access to power in matters of international trade negotiations and the access enjoyed by major corporations.

The whole "rent-a-government" scenario dramatizes this distinction. The United States has just one vote in the 123-nation GATT, putting it on the same level as any other member, for instance, St. Kitts. Critics of the WTO point out that the United States insisted on weighted voting as a condition of its membership in the World Bank, International Monetary Fund, and United Nations Security Council. Sanctions can be passed against a country with a two-thirds majority vote. Under the old rules, the vote had to be unanimous. If a company knows who has the swing votes on a particular issue, they can target their lobbying efforts toward them. In one famous example of how the structure can be manipulated that actually ended up benefiting the United States, GATT failed to override U.S. laws against importing tuna in huge nets that were shown to kill dolphins because the vote was not unanimous.

The consequences of the WTO for certain small businesses are potentially grave. Many in the American textile industry, for example, are worried about the prospect of a completely free market without import quotas, and a similar fear of Far Eastern cheap labor grips the car parts manufacturers. Entrepreneurs who are located far from the borders and think they have only a remote chance of engaging in foreign trade are perhaps understandably indifferent to the progress of these trade measures. Yet that changes remarkably fast in many lines of business, which suddenly benefit from free trade in unexpected ways.

One of the vehicles of change is the computer network, which can transform local operations into international ones at low cost. Take the example of Martin Rood, who runs a Nissan/Volvo car dealership that has been in his family for three generations in Lynnwood, Washington. Unwilling to dump a lot of capital into traditional advertising, Rood attended a seminar on information technology and decided to work with a local computer consulting firm to create a custom software code and start the Dealer Internet Services Corporation (DISC). Using the Internet, and Compaq personal computers in conjunction with Windows NT, Rood blew away the boundaries of his local market with an online electronic catalog of new car information and auto parts. His "virtual showroom" attracts 3,000 inquiries a week from customers in countries all around the world. The success of the venture led Rood to spin off DISC as a service business of its own. The new reach of the business also means that Rood has become a "stakeholder" in the advance of free trade. Heavy tariffs or restrictions could curtail part of his operation, so he is paying attention to trade negotiations in a way that he never had before.

Specific examples of the benefits or problems caused by free trade abound. There is another level on which this argument is fought, however. It involves the macroeconomic and legal forces that affect businesses both large and small. The main arguments against free trade are that it will increase the federal budget deficit by taking out $11 billion in tariffs (nearly a third of all tariff revenue) over the next five years, that it will weaken America's influence abroad, and as Ralph Nader pointed out, it will take the teeth out of laws designed to protect workers, consumers, and the environment. Even Newt Gingrich argued that the WTO sets up world government instead of world trade.

On the other hand, the economists who view GATT and other trade accords as a significant force in expanding the nation's overall economy and promoting growth in GDP feel that the benefits in terms of job creation and export promotion far outweigh the dangers to consumer and environmental laws. They also point out that the growth in GDP will raise tax revenues and offset the loss of tariffs for the budget. From the perspective of small business, which is in a position to fuel (and profit from) an export-driven growth rate for GDP of 3.5 percent or more, but also recognizes how perilously close to an economic correction the country is sailing, any government moves that improve global capacity and real demand for their products or services should be welcome. To paraphrase the argument for free trade as a global stimulus, a rising tide lifts all boats.

However, the official advocates of small business are suspicious of joining forces with big business in the area of international trade. While every major industrial lobby was pounding away at promoting GATT (and before that, NAFTA) for more than two years, the position on trade of the small business lobby was ambivalent, and therefore weak. The general worry is that the treaty favors wide-ranging big concerns that have their fingers in many different types of business at once. At the NFIB, where practically every other legislative issue draws a distinct pro or con response, the leadership decided to take a "wait and see" attitude, polling their membership to look for direction. "Our best guess is that

GATT is not a real burning issue among small businesses right now," said Jim Weidman, an NFIB spokesperson, in late fall of 1994. In the last poll conducted by the NFIB, import and export concerns were ranked 75th out of 75 possible problems faced by small businesses.

Clearly, international trade is a blind spot for the NFIB, and the group will have to make progress on preparing for future debates on this issue. Other and smaller groups, such as the National Farmers Union and the United States Business and Industrial Council, based in Washington but representing about 1,500 family-owned businesses mainly in the Midwest, were fervently anti-GATT out of fear of the competitive edge it will give to large foreign multinationals.

In addition to NAWBO, one of the few groups to turn its attention to the specific needs of small business in trade talks is the Small Business Exporters Association (SBEA), which in July 1994 declared its formal support of ratification. In a significant development, and the only idea of its kind so far, the group also said it would put pressure on the new World Trade Organization in Geneva to establish a small business advocacy office, under the proposed title of "Small Business Directorate." According to Don Cassil, the SBEA's president, "Small and midsized exporters comprise the largest group of America's traders and they must have a continuing voice in the ongoing processes of the WTO." This is an idea that deserves the support of President Clinton and Mickey Kantor and that should be hammered home by other small business advocates as the formalities involved in GATT are addressed.

THE ARGUMENT FOR FREE TRADE

Economists who are in favor of free trade estimate that GATT will raise world merchandise trade by some 12 percent, or $745 billion, by 2005, and set the growth in world income at about $230 billion a decade after 1995. More aggressive figures, including those coming from the President's Council of Economic Advisers, estimate that in the next decade U.S. output will be boosted by $1.1 trillion as a result of the accord. By providing a level playing field, for the first time, in services, it would allow for growth in a sector that already is estimated to account for $3 trillion of world revenues per year.

Economists also look toward lower consumer prices for imported products thanks to lower tariffs, and an increase in wealth thanks to those savings as well as bolstered production. The pro-competition forces view GATT as a way to make producers more efficient and enable them to lower prices, which will benefit consumers. For those who want to see more invested in technological innovation and research and development, the argument is that increased competition and revenues will spur growth in these areas.

Individually, entrepreneurs are beginning to wake up to the potential benefits of free trade despite the rough ride it promises for certain specialized industries. According to Peter Kirsch, executive director of the Wisconsin World Trade Center in Milwaukee and a frequent counselor for small business:

> *We have a lot of people coming in who want to find out more about GATT. Overall, the feeling from the standpoint of business in the state is that it is going to be a big plus, especially for agriculture and telecommunications. People were a lot more involved with NAFTA, but you do have 117 trading partners involved in GATT.*

That tentative sense of something in the air characterizes the feeling shared by most consultants to small business. But in cases where tariffs add to the cost at several stages for a product made or assembled by a small business, the elimination or lowering of these costs will make a huge difference. For one Milwaukee company with extensive business in South America, the abolition of tariffs will have an immediate effect on profits. Peter Albrecht is the name of a specialty construction firm that produces entertainment spaces, stage and studio systems, and lighting equipment for entertainment. With annual sales around $3 million and 25 employees, the firm fits the profile of a typical American small business. According to Albrecht's president and chairman Paul Birkle, "We sell equipment in $100,000 clips to Mexico and South America. Almost 40 percent of our total sales comes from export." On everything sold to Mexico and South America, the company has to pay import duties of up to 15 percent, passing the cost on to the consumer. For Albrecht, the effect of GATT will mean more competitive pricing and a hefty addition to the bottom line.

The Fear of Dumping

One of the main areas of contention in the GATT negotiations has been dumping—the export of goods at prices below their production cost or for less than they sell for in their home market. In Europe, Asian-based companies were selling televisions for 8 to 34 percent lower than the normal price; prices for televisions rose 30 percent after antidumping duties of 5 to 30 percent were set in October 1994. The question has dogged the bilateral negotiations between the United States and Japan for years. Most of the controversial amendments to the Congressional bill representing GATT involved dumping, which angers free trade purists because antidumping laws are essentially protectionist by nature. According to Mickey Kantor, who is ardent about bringing antidumping measures to the negotiating table, the point of these laws is to "keep industries properly competitive."

From the small business perspective, protection against dumping is likely to be a good idea, because dumping not only favors foreign concerns but gives the advantage most of the time to large foreign concerns and their large subsidiaries or large American companies who use the parts or products they sell. The leading example of this has always been the automotive industry, not just with respect to finished cars themselves but parts and replacement parts, which account for two thirds of Japan's exports to the United States. It is an area that involves small business on every level, from supply to manufacturing, and it is a major bone of contention in bilateral trade talks, even outside the GATT, between the United States and Japan.

If GATT delivers as promised, the auto parts industry will be rid of unfair dumping practices despite strong pressure from the Japanese. Specifically, the new GATT rules should help American firms, including small businesses, to seek disciplinary action against circumvention, enhance the "transparency" of supply agreements, and allow for "cumulation" of imports to determine whether American small business is injured over a period of time.

The Controversy Over Patent Laws

One of the sore spots for entrepreneurs in the new GATT agreement is the way it will affect the American patent system. The involvement of small business and government in the patent debate is a new twist on the issues of both trade talks and the relationship between American enterprise and big business. The main focus of debate is called "patent harmonization," under which the United States would change its patent rules to make them more closely resemble those of the other nations involved in both NAFTA and GATT as well as other global and regional trade agreements. This is sacred ground for entrepreneurs and inventors who rely on the American patent system as an individual-friendly mechanism for protecting their livelihood.

According to Jerome Lemelson, who holds the unofficial title of America's most prolific inventor with 500 mostly mechanical and electrical patents to his name, the danger of harmonization is that it makes concessions that will allow large foreign companies, equipped with many lawyers and those able to do the paperwork, to beat the small guy to the filing date. "The United States patent system is the envy of the world, literally. No other nation offers so strong a patent system, so strong an incentive to inventors and new business ventures, and no other nation has produced the wealth of invention and innovation that has made the United States the greatest producer nation in the world," says Lemelson.

Lemelson recently created the Lemelson National Program for Invention, Innovation, and Creativity to help the nation's economic recovery by assisting a new generation of innovators. For Lemelson, the role of small business interests in patent law is an essential part of the tradition of success: "The hallmark of American success is a history of independent inventors whose bright ideas created small businesses that grew into gigantic industries."

Edward L. MacCordy agrees. Retired associate vice chancellor for research at Washington University in St. Louis and past president of the Association of University Technology Managers, MacCordy suggests that only multinational corporations would benefit from switching to a first-to-file system. "Very few independent or university-based inventors can afford foreign patents or even seek them. Only multinationals stand to benefit from abandoning first-to-invent."

In January 1994, when Commerce Secretary Ron Brown announced that he was not convinced that changing to a new, "first-to-file" patent system would benefit individual inventors and entrepreneurs, the news was greeted enthusiastically by inventors and entrepreneurs. Adding their names to the list of opponents, fifty prominent American inventors, whose inventions range from the cardiac pacemaker and the integrated circuit to Kitty Litter and the water bed, addressed a letter to President Clinton expressing their opposition to the pact. The letter, which was put together by the Intellectual Property Creators, a coalition that includes the United Inventors Association of the U.S.A., the American College of Physician Inventors, the Inventors Voice, the National Congress of Inventors Organizations, and Donald Banner, who was Patent Commissioner under President Jimmy Carter, stated:

Most of us are not only inventors but technology entrepreneurs. . . . It is the people of the United States who benefit from the high-growth, high-paying industries that are created by inventors and technology entrepreneurs. If Congress is to change the patent laws, it must understand how the patent system works from the perspective of not just big companies and patent lawyers but from inventors such as us.

Here is another voice raised in the wilderness on the part of entrepreneurs. As a key issue in the GATT process, the patent controversy should be one area in which small business continues to be heard.

According to a 1994 study by BDO Seidman, a Manhattan-based accounting firm, nearly half of American companies with annual sales under $100 million exported their products in 1993, a long way up from only 36 percent in 1990. These figures reflect the anticipation of GATT on the part of entrepreneurs but were posted without the assurance of free trade. The main impetus behind the rise in global trade is just the need to grow, to expand revenues, and reach new markets at a time when the domestic market is stagnant.

Economic forces, rather than political ones, set the ball rolling. Much of the growth has come at the expense of months or years of learning about the cultural and business idiosyncrasies of foreign countries; that homework was augmented by an understanding of other nations' trade regulations as well as a comfortable grasp of the U.S. regulatory attitude toward trade with a foreign nation. All of the small businesses that have already made the move to go global prior to the establishment of a global order, such as the one GATT hopes to create, have found out how tricky the current situation can be. The trade winds shift quickly!

UNDERSTANDING EUROPE

The great shocker in this area has been the inability of European nations to effectively organize a true common market. Just to illustrate how long it takes for free trade to become a reality, consider the recent history of the European Community. Back in the 1970s, I remember how my aunt, Margaret Harvey Anderson, who was then the deputy speaker of the House of Commons and a member of the 1922 Committee, the British equivalent of the Cabinet, worked hard at the upcoming entry of the United Kingdom into what was then called the Common Market. The heady conversation in her office and the corridors of power in the House of Commons was all about a single currency, parliament, and set of trading rules for a genuinely unified Europe. That vision looked prophetic in 1991, particularly after the dismantling of the Berlin Wall. But in the months following the "official" launch of the new European Community in 1992, it became obvious that very little had indeed changed. My aunt would have been terribly disappointed in the lack of progress made toward unity by the end of 1994. Two decades is a long time for politicians to wait for their dreams to come true. For small businesses that work against the clock for their survival, it is simply impossible to count on an investment that depends on developments that are two decades away.

But why should small business sit back and wait for certainty before opening trade routes to Europe? At least until the World Trade Organization (WTO) sets up shop in Geneva, the key to dealing with Europe in any broad way lies in understanding and operating in Brussels. The home of the European Union and the main regulatory organizations that oversee Europe, Brussels is at the moment more of a European capital than Berlin, London, Paris, or Rome. It is the heart of the lobbying trade in Europe. As Ronald Facchinetti, a New York–based trade consultant who specializes in assisting major corporations in Europe, notes: "If American companies want to succeed in the global economy, they will have to learn something about lobbying: it's not just for Washington anymore." In Brussels alone, according to a recent study, there are about 10,000 lobbyists, employed by 3,000 groups, who schmooze the headquarters of the European Commission. Since the Commission has regulatory powers over the 12 European nations, it is no wonder there is about one lobbyist for every 1.3 commission officials—twice the per capita rate of 1990.

The reason for the intensified activity is a very active schedule of business issues before the commission including antitrust and mergers, corporate structures and alliances, labeling and packaging requirements, environmental controls, waste disposal, procurement guidelines, and of course the usual routine of import duties. Moreover, as Facchinetti observes, "Perhaps the best reason for American companies to start lobbying in Europe is that right now the basic rules for doing business in Europe are being set for years to come. For all companies, it is an unrivaled opportunity."

This is terra incognita for many Americans, so experts like Facchinetti have an operating niche that is valuable. Most of the lobbyists hire political insiders, usually for exorbitant retainers and fees. As in Washington where former regulatory officials fill the offices of lobbying organizations, where they are better paid then when they worked for the government, the Eurolobbyists are often former members of the European Parliament or ex-officials who were on the staffs of regulatory bodies specializing in telecommunications, waste management, industrial fields, or agriculture. In his advice to large and small American companies who want to navigate the political waters of Brussels successfully, Facchinetti stresses the stylistic and philosophical differences between Eurolobbying and its American counterpart.

The Europeans are far more open, even honest, about their agendas, and it is not unusual for Eurolobbyists to provide help and information to the regulatory officials to help them see the big picture. An American lobbying organization will typically present a more narrow wavelength in the hope of protecting the specific interests of the firm represented.

In a similar vein, European officials are more likely to help the lobbyists, supplying statistical information and technical advice. A course on the essentials of lobbying in French and English is offered in Brussels by the European Institute for Public Affairs. Several key sources of information, including the 180 Euro-Infocenters throughout Europe, have statistics and definitions covering most markets for both large and small companies. Another key player in the information area is the American Chamber of Commerce in Brussels, which is renowned for its detailed and readable reports on particular issues.

The invitation to lobby in Brussels is not just open to major corporations. Through the American Chamber of Commerce and other institutions, American entrepreneurs should also be involved in the historic policy decisions that are in the making in Brussels and Geneva. The best way to make their views known, as in Washington, is through trade associations and professional lobbying groups, perhaps in conjunction with major European small business advocacy groups. Trade associations that have an export/import slant should be a presence in the lobbying communities of Europe. Moreover, American trade negotiators under Mickey Kantor's direction should be raising the question of small business interests during discussions of treaties and agreements. For all the same reasons that lobbying in Washington is important, so too the European front has to be covered.

For American businesses, which have always been famous for their parochial attention only to what is happening within the borders of the country, the ability to stay on top of developments in Europe can spell the difference between recurring profits and one-time, heavy losses from the wrong capital investment in the wrong place.

COUNTING ON TELECOM AND THE ELECTRONIC TRADE ROUTES

These are precisely the kinds of fast and responsive shifts that will make or break American enterprise in the coming decade. If inroads into global trade are made during that time, the U.S. government is expecting them to follow the spread of fiber-optic capability. Even before President Clinton met with the Group of Seven leaders in Naples in the summer of 1994, he had a plan for a future telecommunications parley that would give American telecommunications firms the chance to state their case for a broader global presence. In the same way that GATT and NAFTA were supposed to relax trade barriers, so too the global superhighway of information would bring together disparate trading partners. The key factor is access. To make this network available to small business, as the Clinton administration promises it will, the hardware, software, and data passed along will benefit American firms, large and small. Since telecommunications companies have the fastest growth rate in the U.S. economy currently, Clinton's advisers confidently predict they can create 1.4 million new jobs in the United States during the next decade. All along that new route, like the storefronts on Main Street, small business should be able to set up shop.

The regulatory side of this global superhighway is still in the process of being worked out. The bulk of the trade negotiations revolving around the idea will be devoted to nit-picking over copyright protection and definition, privacy issues, uniform standards, usage and compensation, and managing the frequency spectrum so that one medium, such as cable or satellite, will not have an advantage because of the way the standards for the spectrum are established. The goal of regulation is nearly always the establishment of a level playing field. Since access is already an important issue in the information technology field—politically, legally, sociologically, and commercially—the trick is to find a way to make sure that the technology, which will inevitably benefit the G-7 nations who are its main exporters, can also help underdeveloped nations along to the point where they can be more equal partners.

The telecommunications parley among the G-7 members represents a groundbreaking departure into a specialized field, but it raises certain questions that are familiar in the area of trade negotiations. For example, it is always a problem when the major industrial companies from the G-7, or the governments themselves, through "checkbook diplomacy" take on a major role in establishing the infrastructure of a developing nation and then find that the revenues that foreign companies can take out of those countries are capped. This has been a major problem not only for companies dealing with the People's Republic of China, where in 1994 under pressure the government finally moved to more favorable currency and tax guidelines for foreign investors, but with the former Soviet Union as well.

It could be that small businesses—which probably operate well within the limits set by foreign governments—have an advantage over their larger counterparts who stand to forfeit huge sums to laws that are rewritten after they have made their commitment to joint ventures abroad. However, the marginal costs of doing business in China, for instance, include innumerable bribes that are more burdensome for entrepreneurs on a tight budget than they are for larger concerns. Because small business owners do not have the legal clout or large administrative staff to fight for their rights in cases of this kind, they end up being stung particularly hard by the need to grease the palms of local authorities. This is an area where the American Chamber of Commerce and trade liaisons ought to go to work on behalf of American small business interests: to work with foreign governments and international authorities on safeguarding the welfare of entrepreneurs who attempt to do business abroad.

Another major element of United States foreign policy that is of interest to entrepreneurs is the promotion of American-style competition among companies as well as among industries (such as satellite, cable, and telephone) as a means of keeping prices down and as an incentive for further research into new and better products. In pushing its plan for telecommunications, the White House cites not only the example of the industry in the United States but also the progress made in Sweden, the United Kingdom, Chile, and Argentina, all due to a more competitive environment. Despite overtures between cable and telecommunications giants to set up shop together, the kind of competition the White House prefers pits cable against the phone companies or satellite.

This also has important ramifications for small businesses that are both suppliers and niche competitors. During the summer of 1994, Bell Atlantic won clearance from the Federal Communications Commission (FCC), after a two-year effort to get its application through, to create a cable television arm called FutureVision of America, based in West Conshohocken, Pennsylvania. Bell Atlantic will take on the local cable operator in an area near Philadelphia that includes 38,000 homes and businesses. To do so, the phone company has had to devise an innovative new system that will begin offering 60 cable television channels and interactive-multimedia services this year. The new service is called video dialtone, and it will let FutureVision reach consumers as easily as telephone marketers. The big worry is that phone customers will end up paying the bill for the new video-dialtone technologies, and of course the National Cable Television Association is using that argument to block future applications from phone companies seeking to operate cable networks.

As irritating as this is for the cable companies, who enjoyed a virtual monopoly in most regions until 1992, it dovetails beautifully with Washington's hopes not only for domestic competitiveness but for the models it wants to set up in Latin America and Asia. Despite the worry about phone customers footing the bill for the building of the network, most consumer groups were delighted to learn that FutureVision would be priced 20 percent lower than the existing cable operator, Adelphia Cable Communications, which does not have the two-way connections for home-shopping and information delivery. Small business advocates ought to be happy as well.

This kind of deal is not just the province of major entities like the telephone companies. Consider BroadBand Technologies, a family start-up based in Research Triangle Park, North Carolina. In their modest workshop-style factory, BroadBand created the technology that drives the new video-dialtone system for Bell Atlantic. Without it, the phone company could not have made the basic units affordable. BroadBand devised a way to allow households to hook up to the interactive information highways to enjoy a virtually "limitless" range of services and programs. The old estimate of how expensive this would be per household was about $1,500; BroadBand found a way to deliver the same power for less than $500.

More importantly, BroadBand found a way to read the political writing on the wall and time their product accordingly. By staying tuned in to the lobbying efforts of the telecommunications industry and the day-to-day progress of the debate inside the chambers of the FCC, BroadBand's leadership was able to play the game perfectly. Like a nimble little running back following a massive front line, BroadBand let Bell Atlantic and the telecommunications giants do the lobbying job in front of it.

Bell Atlantic has a further application with the FCC to offer the video-dialtone service to 3.5 million homes in a six-state region, and other phone companies have applications pending as well. Look for them to become major players in the domestic cable market. More importantly, with the help of the White House, watch the way the telephone companies take the lead in exporting not only their own traditional services but cable television and interactive shopping in developing nations where they have been in the forefront of public relations and political efforts over the past decade. By coattailing those trade expeditions, and paying attention to where they have succeeded and failed, small business can benefit as well.

UNDERSTANDING CHINA

A lot has been made of the image of China, which looms like the mythic mountain of gold that, paradoxically, used to lure Chinese to the United States' shores. Too much of this is based on the fleeting impressions left upon coddled business visitors and politicians who have briefly toured, under strict supervision, the coastal cities of Shanghai, Shenzhen, Tianjin, and Guangzhou where special economic zones have created a facade of burgeoning capitalism and rising standards of living.

The real China is another matter, and far more dangerous for business. For entrepreneurs who do not have longstanding business or, more importantly, family ties in China, the risks of doing business there are tremendous. For one thing, it involves understanding not just Washington, but Beijing as well. If you think that the political winds shift precariously in Washington, you are in for a surprise in China. Perhaps only Latin America brings as many political surprises, one on top of another in the brief time span of months or a year, as Beijing.

In the next few years, China will be the major arena for trade negotiations. Because it is not a member of GATT but has been the subject of tremendous lobbying efforts for and against its inclusion, the membership issue will be one significant battle. Another will be the annual debate over China's Most Favored Nation (MFN) status. The bilateral nature of trade negotiations during the 1980s that pitted the United States against Japan time and again will shift to a similar bilateral series of heavyweight bouts between Washington and Beijing over the next decade. When China's MFN status was under review in May 1994, many experts were uncertain until the last moment whether President Clinton and the Congress would buy Beijing's promises to ease up on its political dissidents. Major corporations, sensing weakness in Washington's position, bet on MFN being extended year after year—they can afford to. For smaller firms the annual question of whether MFN will be renewed is a time of nail-biting. In February 1995, U. S. negotiators narrowly averted a trade war with China over copyright and patent infringement.

This is yet another area where small business advocates have a difficult time deciding what position to support because while there are a number of industries that directly benefit from China's MFN status (including toy and food importers), others would, for financial reasons alone, like to see Washington put the squeeze on Beijing for a year or more. They would buy time under the protection of specific restrictions that keep less expensive Chinese goods out of the United States. But there are even more important issues involved than a year or two of protectionism. These involve the role of the United States and of the WTO in creating a lawful, fair playing ground for trade.

Ever since the Tiananmen Square massacre in June 1989, there have been signs of unrest and downright lawlessness in China in rural areas, giving many people the feeling that when Deng Xiao Ping dies—the preeminent ruler in his 90s is suffering from prostate cancer—the country could lose central control. Among the many lines of division perceptible in Chinese society, the split between the rural poor and urban middle class has dramatically widened in recent years, leading to open rebellion on the part of the peasants. Judging by its swift reaction, Beijing is taking the incidents seriously enough to make significant policy changes—think of them as Deng writing his own insurance policy for the transfer of power. Small businesses considering an investment in China ought to take them seriously, too. Foreign businesses in China should be prepared for a sharp downturn in volume and a steep rise in tariff-related costs in the coming years as central control is strengthened.

Power is the issue both in Washington, where President Clinton had to show he was in control of export policy, and in China, and as a priority it seems to outweigh the $20 billion trade surplus with the United States that has helped fuel economic growth. As Beijing's leaders demonstrated when the International Olympic Committee was considering China for the 2000 games, they know how to make a show of human rights reform when the price is right. But, the reason they rounded up the dissidents and gave the cold shoulder to Warren

Christopher during his 1994 trip was not to impress the Americans but to send a message to their own increasingly more restless people.

In the meantime, the anti-China lobby at home is growing. Some industrialists are disenchanted with the fact that the China market never materialized. In an NBC *Dateline* report, accusations were made that Chinese state-owned industries are using offices in the United States as a front for intelligence gathering—they cited China's acquisition of secret night-vision technology that could end up in Iraqi hands—as well as the sale of a million automatic weapons every year. At the end of 1994 a new round of patent and copyright infringements was angering the American pharmaceutical and entertainment companies that had played the waiting game in China without bringing back the contracts they expected. And the Chinese stock markets were racked by wave after wave of fraud and price fixing. None of these developments helped to justify the special status China had been granted as a trading partner. In fact, the confidence in China was badly shaken, to the extent that not only business but also political leaders were losing confidence. Most of the House and more than two thirds of the Senate have already indicated their opposition to extending MFN again, and the global environmentalists are just beginning to weigh in.

There will be many losers whenever MFN status is denied to China—and there is no guarantee that it will always be renewed. American industrialists, led by Boeing, which fears that China will turn to Airbus for its next contracts, have projected that tens of thousands of jobs could be lost. For Hong Kong the price would be particularly high—experts predict that revocation means that up to 3.1 percentage points could be shaved off the colony's projected 5.5 percent economic growth for 1995 if MFN is revoked, costing more than 75,000 jobs and $24 billion in trade.

These signs of trouble have taken the bloom off the rose for China investors. The market for dragon bonds (Asian debt excluding Japan) reflects these jitters, as a shaky $1 billion Chinese government issue in the U.S. market in 1994 showed. Moody's has given Chinese debt a Single-A3 rating, and S&P grades them Triple-B, both citing concern over "internal political conflict" that has hampered earlier $500 million and $150 million issues in American and European markets. Ford has indicated that they may reconsider a new manufacturing venture in

China, and Nintendo has pulled out altogether, blasting the Chinese for patent infringement. "This attitude of contempt is not only offensive; it makes China a dangerous place to do business as well," says Howard C. Lincoln, chairman of Nintendo of America. Playmates, which has made Ninja Turtles in China since the mid-1980s, just moved their operation to Macao because they expect MFN to be denied eventually. The Ninja Turtles gave themselves a head start. Can others be far behind?

Small Business in the Land of the Dragon

If these secure companies with deep pockets are feeling nervous about China, what is an entrepreneur supposed to think? The answer to this question is more important to world trade with China than many government officials in either Washington or Beijing have realized. While the major corporations perform this slowly wheeling dance with the central government in Beijing or top trade officials in Shanghai, a massive number of small, family-run concerns have already whirled through the preliminaries and are deep into what is for them the major investment of a lifetime in small factories in provincial cities far from Beijing's watchful eye. Most of them are owned by overseas Chinese investors whose clan-like, tightly held leadership belies their international scope. Praised by the media and by management guru Peter Drucker for their lean and mean style, they are far from being what one would ordinarily call politically active. In fact, if there is one thing Drucker criticizes in these organizations it is their tendency to be too closely knit and too eager to keep a low profile. Much depends on their becoming more conscious of their public role and more willing to participate in the efforts of business to regularize trade with China.

On Washington's part, it will be up to President Clinton's advisors to take stock of the growing economic and political power of entrepreneurs who will build a capillary network of manufacturing. More importantly, the service industry's ties with China deserve government support and fair, consistent regulation.

The professional political forces involved will inevitably have new faces in their midst, as well. As the overseas population of Chinese finds its political voice around the world, scoring election victories in not only California and New York but elsewhere in the United States,

Australia, and Europe, it will have the right and responsibility to direct some of the crucial policy decisions on trade with mainland China and Hong Kong after 1997.

The continuing debate over MFN status for China, for instance, will have a new entrant with not just an agenda but a stronger knowledge of how to deal with China, because within the decade it will be, at least in part, Chinese. For many generations now the Chinatown communities of San Francisco, New York, Boston, and Chicago—to name the most conspicuous enclaves—have stuck to their personal and financial priorities and turned their backs on political involvement. However, starting on the local level with city councils and gradually moving upward through the state assemblies and federal structure, more Chinese-Americans are becoming involved in the political process, and their motives for doing so are still consonant with the original goals of prosperity and the upward mobility of their children.

Targeting issues such as taxation, education, the municipal infrastructure, and the regulation of business, the newly political Chinese community is working to ensure that the wealth it has already created (in many instances, very considerable wealth) will be preserved and increased rather than excavated by unfair government interference. In an October 1994 feature on the emerging economic power of the Chinese diaspora, *Fortune* magazine estimated their number at 55 million, with unrivaled reserves of capital and political power in the Asian marketplace. In the United States, national groups such as the Organization of Chinese Americans, the Asian Pacific American Bar Association, and the Independent Federation of Chinese Students and Scholars are gaining recognition in the media. They are even able, on occasion, to influence the media, as when their protests over a CBS television report, originally appearing in May 1994, on Chinese spies in the United States brought an on-the-air apology and "clarification" from CBS anchorwoman Connie Chung. As Ginny Gong, president of the Organization of Chinese Americans, commented, "We'll no longer be the silent minority when negative stereotypes continue to perpetuate the image of Asian Americas as forever foreign." The old cliché that this community is apolitical does not hold any longer.

Although it ranks below taxes and education in the list of top priorities for most Chinese political leaders, Washington's position on trade with the mainland is bound to be one of the crucial areas of political interest to the overseas Chinese community, which has more than $700 billion in trade that could be affected by a sudden change in the rules or a breakdown in the relationship between Washington and Beijing. Since much of that trade is on the level of small enterprise, the input of the entrepreneurial lobby should be heard.

The signs of political change in China can be as subtle as the choice of ties for the news announcers in Beijing, but the level of awareness is very high. As a lesson for those in a society where political change, although never easy to predict, is relatively open compared to the volatility of a regime like Beijing, the example of small business owners in China is valuable.

The Small Business Perspective in Asia

Viewing trade with China through the lens of small ventures is not just a matter of turning up anecdotal evidence of two entrepreneurial cultures. When Peter Drucker looks at the massive Chinese market, he does not think in terms of a billion mouths opening to Coca Cola or two billion feet slipping into Nike sneakers. Instead, he sees pockets of entrepreneurial activity that need advice, information, and guidance. The growth area lies in service opportunities for small and medium-sized operations that rely on brains rather than corporate brawn. "China may be the first country to be integrated into the world economy through services rather than through goods," predicts Drucker in *The Postcapitalist Society*. Among the most promising areas he identifies are higher education and training, health care, financial and legal services, telecommunications, and information and transportation.

Drucker's take on the enigma of China is tremendously valuable for entrepreneurs. The notion of going global can seem a daunting prospect for a small business owner whose picture of international business is the familiar image of the multinational corporate officer being whisked by limo from the Concorde to a boardroom in a gleaming office tower in Paris where a multibillion-dollar contract for heavy machinery is waiting to be signed. But globalization can be as easy as picking up a phone or sending a fax.

This accent on services and small business is driving one of the most active areas of trade negotiation outside of the GATT machine. It involves Japan and China. Tomohiko Kobayashi, ambassador and special adviser to the minister of foreign affairs of Japan, observes, "Service industries have become more internationally tradeable than before, because of technological advances in the telecommunications and transportation industries. The need for them will continue to grow as people's standards of living rise." Kobayashi points out that the share of services in the GDP of developing countries increased about 10 percent since 1980, while it remained almost unchanged in developed countries.

In fall 1994, a major conference of Asian trade ministers was held that focused exclusively on issues involving small business. As an example of what governments can do on behalf of their small business communities when they set their minds to it, even in the face of severe ideological and political differences, it is a development that bears watching. The first Asia-Pacific Economic Cooperation (APEC) conference about small and medium-sized companies brought together trade and industry ministers from APEC's 17 members for two days of talks, hosted by Ryutaro Hashimoto, Japanese Minister of International Trade and Industry (MITI). Despite harsh warnings from Beijing that Hashimoto's earlier meeting with Taiwanese authorities could jeopardize trade agreements, the consensus in the meeting was that enterprise would become an integrating force in the development of an Asian trading community. As Hashimoto said in his opening remarks, "It is an important time for us to gather because in the 21st century, small and medium-sized enterprises will play an important role in sustaining economic growth and creating new jobs in APEC." The conference was held in Osaka, which has long been regarded as Japan's most entrepreneurial city.

One of the crucial items on the agenda of the conference was the endorsement of the candidacy of Kim Chulsu, Korean Minister of Trade, Industry and Energy, as the head of the new World Trade Organization. This campaign, hardly known in the United States, is another movement that bears watching, since it would be a coup not just for Korea but for the Asian community—and the small business forces that were the first to endorse Kim—if he were to become

WTO's head. The conference also focused on familiar small business issues, such as new technology, education and the labor force, finding new sources of finance, and empowering business through information.

In the 1970s, when similar conferences sponsored by MITI quietly laid the foundation for the rise of Japan's electronics and car industries, the planning and cooperative efforts between government and industry were all but ignored by the West. Later, that close degree of cooperation was severely criticized as an incubator for unfair industrial assistance that made competing with Japan nearly impossible. Here we see a new wave of government policy directed toward business in Asia. Significantly, it is not focused on major industries but on small business and its ability to bring together nations with marked political, cultural, and ideological differences, as well as dramatically different levels of prosperity and industrialization. Be assured that Asian entrepreneurs are hearing and reading a lot about trade talks on a daily basis, and trying—as we all are—to sort out what is in it for them.

THE SMALL BUSINESS AGENDA FOR FOREIGN TRADE

This is an area that has not involved the advocates of small business to any great degree as yet, so the work to be done must begin with fundamentals. Among the tasks:

- Small business must become more involved in shaping U.S. trade policy through direct interaction with the federal officials in charge of it.
- Free trade accords involving regions and countries not covered by GATT ought to be supported.
- Congress should enact stringent antidumping measures to ensure that GATT does not unleash a flood of cheap imports into world markets.
- Congress and trade representatives must safeguard patents and copyrights beyond the levels specified by GATT.
- Trade negotiators should push for an American-style patent system in the WTO.

- The federal government should support the research and creation of electronic trade routes accessible to small businesses.
- Trade agreements and laws should foster competition.
- Congress and the White House should keep the pressure on the People's Republic of China to raise its standards for copyright and patent protection as well as labor, environmental, and safety laws.

BORDER BLUES
Understanding and
Influencing Export
and Import Issues

Christopher Chapin, the president of Global Business Access, a Washington-based consulting firm, is angry. Even though he makes his money explaining tariffs and trade barriers to small business clients, he thinks the U.S. government should and could do more to help entrepreneurs. He is right. Compared to the information and assistance provided by most European and Asian governments, the American system is outdated and inefficient. The principal target of Chapin's frustration is the Commerce Department's United States and Foreign Commercial Service, the federal government's primary export-promotion agency. It operates the commercial sections of 70 large American embassies abroad and 47 district offices around the United States and has a budget of $100 million. Its main function is to let American businesses know about export opportunities and sales representatives abroad, as well as foreign competition through the for-fee Agent/Distributor Service.

Although the services are available in 170 countries, Chapin thinks Commerce is not doing its job. In a 1994 op/ed piece for *The New York Times* he noted that the Agent/Distributor Service charges companies $250 to locate three or four potential distributors in a particular country, a very low price that renders poorly researched information, including the names of unqualified distributors. The service is understaffed, with 1.8 export-promotion staff members for every $1 billion in exports; this is compared with 2.5 people in Germany, 6 in France, and 8 in Britain.

Chapin suggests that Commerce should privatize the agency, raising fees and running it like a law firm with incentives for those who bring in and link up the most business. For the small business community that stands in need of this kind of service, the idea is on target and the sense of urgency behind it—of the sort that spurs a private-sector expert who is in the business of guiding others through trade problems—is palpable. Small businesses both in the United States looking outward and outside looking toward American markets need more in the way of government assistance and information than they are getting. Given the computer and telecommunications resources that are now at their fingertips, the only obstacles that remain for them to get this information involves staffing and the facilities to load it up and make it available. It is another item to add to the small business wish-list of political priorities.

There are those in Washington who are listening. In 1994, on a cold February night in Washington, Jeffrey E. Garten, the undersecretary of commerce for international trade, rose after dinner to speak to a hotel ballroom full of members of the National Association of Manufacturers. His topic, "Competing in the Global Economy," was familiar enough to sound boring, but there were surprises in the speech. In light of more recent developments in world trade we can recognize the subtle hints of a White House link between foreign policy and trade that will be played out over the next two years, unless world events take a bizarre turn for the worse.

The new note sounded in Garten's speech was the special attention it paid to small business. Within the first minute, he was talking about "reaching out not only to the Fortune 500 but also to small and medium-sized firms and developing a broad international commercial policy to open foreign markets." Later in his speech, he outlined the government's goals to allow small business to gain the knowledge, experience, and power to "go global." He announced that as part of the new administration policy, the international commercial plan would place the federal government in a new role: "We tell ourselves that the answer is for the federal government to be the 'wholesaler' of export promotion services." The rest of the speech lacked specifics in this regard, except that he promised that Commerce would be pledging manpower to the "wholesaler" effort, but the message should cheer small business.

Clearly, the most important part of Garten's message was not intended for the ears of the Fortune 500 executives at the meeting. It was an invitation, and a promise, to entrepreneurs. Everyone in the room knew how hard Washington had worked over the past five years, starting with President Bush, to open up foreign markets to American exports, but the overwhelming majority of the benefits from this policy push accrued to huge corporations. Bush took the leading automakers with him on an ill-fated trip to Japan—all anybody remembers about that is his violent illness and the barrage of criticism aimed at the "fat cat" auto executives whose massive and growing salaries failed to reflect the heavy losses their companies were suffering.

After that, the White House went to bat for the computer industry, easing restrictions on the type of hardware that can be shipped abroad in light of the relaxation of cold war tensions and the paranoia over national security, and then President Clinton and Ron Brown helped McDonnell Douglas land a $6 billion deal with the Saudis—which later fell apart at the seams. But some computer companies ended up in Clinton's doghouse when they ran afoul of the Justice Department for antitrust violations or went ahead with massive layoffs, and the defense and aerospace industries, through a series of mergers, ended up contracting and losing jobs as well as foreign customers, so the political return on these investments was nearly disappointing enough to be called a liability. Garten's speech reflected a new realization regarding who should benefit from trade strategy in the future: the spotlight swings to small business.

YOUR TAX DOLLARS AT WORK

It would be unfair to say that the U.S. government does absolutely nothing to help small business go global. In fact, there is so much going on that a small business owner-manager might have trouble deciding where to start in looking for assistance. But much of the government's activity is wheel-spinning of the worst bureaucratic kind, because it is not coordinated and remains only partly accessible to the entrepreneurs who need it most. The responsibility for pulling together these varied forces into an integrated, effective system rests with the top players in the political arena, including Jan Meyers, the head of the Small Business Committee in the House, Philip Lader, the administrator of the Small Business Administration, and the members of the Congressional small business caucus. They should be urged to take on the job by the small business lobby, which has not shown any great skill or energy in the area of foreign trade so far.

Most government intervention starts with a study of the reasons for intervention. But the importance of small business to the nation's export strategy does not need to be studied further. It is time to get on with the active process of facilitating trade.

Recent history offers convincing proof that helping small business with a national export strategy will be a good investment. With growth in most sectors of the economy stalled by 1992, exports started to loom larger in significance for politicians who wanted to keep their jobs. Economists who for years had warned about the trade deficit realized that the prospects for a spurt in exports needed an extra federal effort to keep the tide going in the right direction. Between 1986 and 1992, exports as a percentage of GDP moved from 7.5 percent to 11.6 percent, and increased in value in real terms by nearly 95 percent. That's about 60 percent of GDP growth during the same period and covers one in six manufacturing jobs or about 7 million people. With the addition of services, the numbers grow larger, and the pay is better. The White House estimates that workers engaged in exporting earn 17 percent more than the average wage. Since small business is delivering more of this kind of good news than large corporations, it makes sense for the White House and Congress to put some hustle and muscle into meeting the needs of entrepreneurs regarding free trade, high-technology transfer, and other export and import issues.

Before government can really do the job of helping small businesses across the nation, it has to clean up its own act. The current export assistance programs come under so many agencies that they take on the complexity of a tangled skein of yarn. Business owners have to deal with the Departments of Commerce (where a new Advocacy Center has been opened that offers information and resources for nearly 100 major government procurement projects abroad), State, and Treasury. It is also important to stay apprised of the day-to-day battles waged by the United States Trade Representative, Mickey Kantor. For financial assistance, deals typically involve the Export-Import (Ex-Im) Bank, the U.S. Trade Development Agency, and the Overseas Private Investment Corporation. Technical assistance is available from the Departments of Transportation and Energy and the Environmental Protection Agency. As an interagency liaison and, more and more, legal advocate, the SBA is often involved in all phases of dealing with the government on foreign trade. Just to give one example of the type of confusion that could hamper a small company's export effort, it used to be necessary to file separate and quite different loan application forms to the SBA and the Ex-Im Bank; the two now have a single application that is used by both. Clearly it's time for the federal agencies to tighten up.

In an admirable attempt to rectify some of these problems, the federal government deserves some points for the establishment of export assistance centers, which started in Miami early in 1994 and now have offices around the country. The White House likes to call them "one-stop shops" for finance and legal counseling, involving Commerce, the SBA, the Ex-Im bank, and local officials. The Miami center, which is right near the airport, has experts in the subtleties of trade with Mexico, Brazil, Argentina, and other nations. But the centers have not been sufficiently publicized and remain underused, perhaps because it is difficult for many small business owners to reach them or take the time to visit in person.

In fall 1994, the SBA and Ex-Im Bank launched a new collaborative program to help small business succeed in the burgeoning export market. In an unprecedented move, the two federal agencies joined forces to offer easier access to financing and to train their staffs in the problems that confront entrepreneurs who have never been involved in export and import. Since small business makes up 96 percent of all U.S. exporters but accounts for only 30 percent of total exports, the need to help out was obvious. As former SBA administrator Erskine Bowles commented:

> The biggest problem is that small businesses can't match the capital resources that big businesses can draw on to finance their export transactions. Now we're doing something about that. We've taken our export loan program apart and put it back together again, blending our strengths with those of our partner, the Ex-Im Bank, to establish a single U.S. government export loan program that retains the best features of each agency's programs. There is enormous demand out there and there's enormous potential in this new program. I think we can double our volume for export loans as a result.

Under the harmonized system, the two organizations guarantee commercial bank loans providing small businesses with the capital they need to build inventory, buy raw materials, and market their products overseas. The application is available at the agencies and at "one-stop shops" around the country. The guarantees cover 90 percent of the loan amounts, and the cutoff point between the agencies' areas of responsibility is clear: The SBA handles loans up to $833,333, while the Ex-Im Bank handles loans of $833,334 and over. The Ex-Im bank raised the limit banks may commit from $750,000 per borrower to $1 million in some cases and $2 million in others. SBA for the first time will allow qualified lenders to approve export working capital loans under its Preferred Lender Program.

All of this is part of the Ex-Im's Business Development Group, which aims at eliminating red tape and hopes to make the Bank more accessible and attractive both to borrowers and to commercial banks. This includes a number of changes in its insurance programs. To give brokers new incentives, the Ex-Im Bank increased commissions from 30 to 40 percent in some cases involving small businesses and eliminated caps on commissions. It also expanded eligibility for small business insurance policies to include companies with annual export credit sales of up to $3 million, up from $2 million. The Bank also increased its medium-term insurance coverage of both commercial and political risks from 90 percent to 100 percent, which should allay some fears where political instability is a concern.

Already noted as a key agency that is in need of new management is the United States and Foreign Commercial Service, a network of about 1,200 federal employees who are assigned from their jobs in the Commerce Department, Ex-Im Bank, the Trade Development Agency, and the Overseas Private Investment Corporation, and are specifically targeted to work with American firms abroad and foreign firms hoping to invest in the United States. Here is a prime target for Vice President Al Gore's "reorganization" initiative. At a time when interagency coordination is being promoted as a way to make government more efficient and avoid redundancies, the need for the careful division of responsibilities in an institution like the Foreign Commercial Service is pressing.

As one subtle indication of the work that is yet to be done in integrating the Service, consider the curious fact that the foreign and U.S. components of the organization have separate career tracks. There is already a plan to pull these together and to make sure that the two-way traffic, and cross assignments, are handled by the same personnel. The problems inside the Service can all be related to divisions of this kind, and the noble aims of the Service will be better served once the organizational bugs are worked out.

Scouting New Markets

One of the most important tasks faced by international government organizations in the import and export field is picking the spots where small businesses can safely and profitably do business. This is an area in which the World Bank, the InterAmerican Development Bank, and other multilateral lending institutions are already involved, albeit on a level that benefits large corporations more than small businesses. These international trade organizations are focusing their attention on the Big Emerging Markets, where nearly 75 percent of world trade growth is expected to occur over the next two decades. The top 10 list includes Mexico, Brazil, Argentina, India, Indonesia, Turkey, Poland, South Korea, South Africa, and a combined Chinese area that comprises the mainland, Taiwan, and Hong Kong. Together these countries are supposed to produce about 44 percent of the total "new trade opportunities" globally, and their projected share of global GDP in two decades is expected to double. By that time they will surpass Europe and Japan combined, purchasing 25.6 percent of total world imports.

The World Bank is probably not the first organization that comes to mind when the question arises of finding resources for small businesses interested in global trade. However, the information it provides, and its strategic role in providing a stable economic base for trade, are vital forces behind the scenes for small business. An awareness of the work done by these international organizations can help the individual owner–manager strategically. To put that information to use, though, more specialized organizations are necessary, like the Small Business Exporters Association, headquartered in Annandale, Virginia, as well as the Small Business Administration.

It should not be surprising to find the SBA on the front line as American small businesses struggle to get a toehold in foreign markets. Herb Austin, assistant district director for business development in Manhattan, sees doors opening all over the world, including Eastern Europe, Latin America, and, thanks to NAFTA, Mexico. Up until a few years ago, Latin America was too risky because of soft currency and the trouble with collecting bills. Now the situation has improved. Austin observes, "Immigrants who have an understanding of the culture and language have a great advantage, and my only recommendation is to start small. Don't go to Europe and get lost." Every three months, due to heavy demands, Austin and the SBA run a special seminar in Manhattan on exporting.

Austin's colleague, Sidney Zierler, who is an international trade specialist with the Service Core of Retired Executives, is even more bullish on small business moving abroad. "There's a whole revolution going on out there, with small business picking up where the big corporations have left off, especially when entrepreneurs provide not only a product but a service." Echoing Peter Drucker, Zierler explains that the success stories involve businesses that bring expertise together with a product that finds its niche. "It's necessary for an entrepreneur to search for a way to sell a product, but with the product to sell a service that puts it all into motion," notes Zierler. He helped two African businessmen to export discarded and reconditioned computers to African companies where they would conduct the training themselves. He loves the story of the American who bought up used X-ray equipment and peddled it around the world to developing countries based on his ability to teach the locals how to use and get the most out of it. In a similar story, he helped a medical engineer who invented hospital equipment to get a start in a tough market by accompanying his machines with service and training. The market? Switzerland.

The training offered by the SBA is of particular value because it gets down to the level of detail that allows entrepreneurs to create budgets and plan financially for a foreign foray. Beyond advice on marketing and the logistics of setting up a business abroad, the SBA can tell a small business owner-manager what to expect in terms of tariffs and customs requirements for destinations around the world, and how those rules have been changing. In the case of the medical engineer who took hospital equipment to Switzerland, for example, there was a wide range of customs regulations as well as Switzerland's version of the Food and Drug Administration to negotiate his way through. Before these rules can present nasty surprises for a first-time exporter, the SBA sees to it that they are understood in advance.

From region to region the degree of government assistance varies, and its quality is based on the expertise of the officials who are lined up to help small business. Up around Puget Sound in Washington, for example, it is no surprise to learn that federal offices and local business consultants are gearing up for action along the Pacific Rim. The savvy entrepreneur who is looking for the best combination of assistance must seek out the help of various agencies, and even, perhaps to the surprise of some, the assistance of a foreign government.

The SBA's international trade officer for the district is Connie Alvarado, a resident of Seattle, whose previous experience included marketing and sales for Pollution Control Systems Corporation for five years, as well as finance for Honeywell Inc. for three years and a stint as a banking officer for Security Pacific. Her role today? "To ensure the U.S. Small Business Administration plays a pivotal role in positioning the Puget Sound region as an international gateway for small business," she notes. By concentrating on local banks and established organizations, she is hoping to use trade expositions and joint ventures to bridge the gap between American small businesses in her region and the Japanese and Chinese in particular.

At the World Trade Center in Tacoma, Washington, Constance Bacon, the Center's executive director, has similar goals. A transplanted Easterner, Bacon is a former public relations expert and aid to Governor Booth Gardner who was appointed to her position in 1992. The Center is a state project that must coordinate with federal initiatives. This involves tact and diplomacy in dealing with a problem that is endemic to the government effort to help entrepreneurs: the lack of cooperation. While she views Washington's geographic location as a major asset, Bacon is also worried about "turf considerations which take priority over developing the best possible integrated agenda" for helping small business.

The third major player in the Seattle area has nothing whatsoever to do with the U.S. government. He is Hsi-Tsan Chen, the director general of the local office for the Coordination Council for North American Affairs for Taiwan. A veteran diplomat who started out in 1967 as a desk officer for Taiwan's Ministry of Foreign Affairs, he served as a member of Taiwan's United Nations delegation and held diplomatic posts with the nation's embassy in Swaziland and consulate in Mozambique. Chen joined the Coordination Council's Los Angeles office in 1986 as deputy director general and was appointed director general of the Seattle office in 1990. Chen sees the sea and airport facilities as the key to Seattle's ability to help small business trade with Taiwan.

For owner-managers who are interested in doing business in Asia, the information and assistance offered by professionals who are focused on small business is the most crucial type of aid to be found. Who cares if it comes from the federal or state government, or from the U.S. government at all? If the Taiwanese consulate has the information and contacts that are needed, entrepreneurs will find it there. The issue of how difficult it is for small business to find out what it needs, and how much easier it would be if the U.S. government were better coordinated, remains a significant one, however.

IN SEARCH OF HIGH-LEVEL FEDERAL ADVOCATES

One measure of assistance for small business, limited as yet but with great potential, is offered by the Commerce Departments's International

Trade Administration (ITA). The goal of the ITA is to push American technology, made by both large and small businesses, in the global marketplace, especially their use in computers and software, microelectronics, telecommunications, medical devices, pharmaceutical, biotechnology, motor vehicles and parts, aerospace, oil and gas equipment, and environmental systems and technologies. In addition to opening up markets, the ITA hopes to expand and improve the information on trade for small business. Much of what the ITA does simply involves collecting data and putting together descriptive reports, both about American companies that ought to be better known abroad and foreign opportunities that might otherwise escape notice in the States.

The ITA aims to increase what it calls "commercial advocacy," or pushing American goods and services to foreign buyers. Since American companies have had trouble in the past when foreign governments lobby hard and offer concessional financing for their own firms in high-tech bidding wars, the Clinton administration is stepping up its advocacy efforts on behalf of American businesses and actively countering foreign government efforts. One sign that the power in Washington's foreign policy circles has shifted dramatically from the State Department to more economically oriented arms of the government such as Treasury and Commerce: The new high-tech situation room is not the war room in the State Department but the "Advocacy Center" in the Commerce Department.

This hub of a developing advocacy network for landing procurement contracts is located in the ITA offices. The general in charge is Commerce Secretary Ron Brown, and his staff uses state-of-the-art computers and databases to monitor construction and service projects around the world for which U.S. businesses are eligible to compete. By collecting the data and using it in conjunction with trade delegations that go to India, China, Latin America, the Middle East, and other regions, the ITA is hoping to give American firms the same sort of high-tech advantage enjoyed by the Japanese, French, German, and other foreign businesses. As Brown told the press in December 1994, "The idea is to bring the whole force of the Government together to press the case for American business— ambassadors, commercial officers, the Ex-Im Bank, or OPIC."

In 1993 the Department of Commerce announced its National Export Strategy, which calls for the establishment of an interagency Advocacy Coordinating Network to improve the teamwork of the federal government's advocacy efforts. The principal industries involved in these projects are energy, transportation infrastructure, telecommunications, aerospace, and environmental technology. In addition to the Advocacy Center and the Advocacy Coordinating Network, the industry and country specialists of ITA have stepped up their efforts to apply selling pressure to the "advocates in country" at the United States and Foreign Commercial Service posts and the American embassies around the world. The ITA is also reviewing procurements funded by the multilateral development banks to ensure that U.S. companies receive their fair share of new contracts.

Not surprisingly, so far the main beneficiaries of the ITA's situation room have been large corporations going after contracts amounting in the hundreds of millions of dollars for infrastructure projects in developing nations. As the game plan develops, there will be a change in favor of small business. Being included in the databases and strategy of the ITA should be high on the list of priorities for small business advocates in Washington. As the databases are expanded, they should include both procurement opportunities and the names of small businesses capable of handling jobs that become available, much in the way that other agencies, such as the Environmental Protection Agency, are taking the trouble to find procurement contracts for small businesses. The ITA ought to be working on behalf of small businesses that help to fund it through their tax dollars and that can deliver on the promise of expanding international exports.

It is ironic that the old situation room in the State Department was devoted to watching the former Soviet Union, and the new one at Commerce is also focused in part on Moscow. To promote trade and investment in Russia, ITA's Jan Kalicki was appointed as the administrator for energy and commercial cooperation with the Russian Federation. His job is not just to win contracts project by project but to help shape the Russian environment for trade and investment as a whole. As with the Cold War, the task of agents in the trade wars is to infiltrate and gain the confidence of the former Russian authorities. More directly, the creation of aid packages and loans as a way of maintaining the market economy not just in Eastern Europe but other regions as well is part of the tactics that are decided on the highest level in Washington.

A great deal is made of the idea of opening up markets. The rhetoric of this process is familiar by now, but the real job of making it possible for American products to gain a toehold in China or Latin America is a very complicated one that requires official negotiating and bargaining long before any business can be done. One of the key bargaining chips, particularly as the United States deals with developing nations, is the promise to provide technical assistance to foreign governments that are only now drafting regulations for high-tech industries. As a quid pro quo for assisting these governments in drafting legislation governing high tech, American authorities, many of them with the Commerce Department, are gaining in turn favorable regulatory terms, including stricter environmental and quality control regulations that are in line with our domestic guidelines. In the eyes of Commerce, by recommending U.S. standards and regulations they will undoubtedly foster a preference for U.S. technologies that meet them.

The biggest concern of small manufacturers remains market barriers, such as high tariffs, import quotas, incompatible standards, and unexpected testing and certification requirements. Even the federal and state governments can set up barriers, including special licenses and restrictions especially on high-tech products that might have military applications. While the most conspicuous examples of this kind of interference involve major corporations, like IBM or Martin Marietta, they can be more of a problem for their smaller suppliers who lack the indirect means of access to or alternatives to markets that are forbidden.

Given the end of Cold War tensions and its attendant paranoia regarding how much Moscow knew about computers and other trade secrets, you would think that many of these restrictions could be lifted. Unfortunately, the great worry now is that terrorists will be able to buy what we previously feared the Soviets would acquire, and nobody wants to be the country of origin for weaponry, or even the seemingly innocent plumbing supplies and hardware so often made by small businesses, that terrorists can put to their own evil uses.

The accent is still on large firms when it comes to tariff reduction. When the ITA met with the chairmen of 14 major firms in May 1994 to discuss regulatory issues, the agenda was a big business one. As American negotiators work on bilateral accords with their Russian and Chinese counterparts, the hot issues are industries such as health, energy, aerospace, and telecommunications. The development of infrastructures for Eastern Europe and China is a prime issue, while semiconductors, computers, cars, and other retail issues are the focal point of bilateral negotiations with Japan. The ITA is involved in U.S.–Japan medical/pharmaceutical market-oriented sector-specific (MOSS) talks, the U.S.–European Union Bilateral Agreement on Trade in Large Civil Aircraft, U.S.–Korea Motor Vehicle Market Access Negotiations, Brazilian informatics policies, and other important negotiations. The ITA has also worked jointly with the Commerce Department's Technology Administration on the U.S.–Israel Science and Technology Commission, which aims to promote deals between the United States and Israel that can benefit the civilian high-technology commercial sectors of the two countries.

For entrepreneurs who may be novices in the export game, it is of greater interest to know that the ITA also assists new-to-market and new-to-export businesses. The services include help in identifying markets and finding financial assistance, through seminars, conferences, a host of trade shows and one-on-one consulting at four U.S. Export Assistance Centers (USEACs), which provide local export communities with a single point of contact for all federal finance programs, covering credit insurance, pre-export loans, and guarantees to overseas buyers, or through direct contact with U.S. district offices and industry and country experts at the Commerce Department.

SEEKING EXPERT ADVICE

The strategic challenges of going global often require expertise that is not immediately available from the routine channels. For that reason, small business owners are turning for assistance to their local public universities as well as nonprofit organizations, which are finding that their charitable contributions are making a difference when they are channeled through enterprise.

The prospects for franchising in developing nations are a special interest of S. Prakash Sethi, a professor at the City University of New York and a renowned authority on international business and society.

An adviser to former New York Governor Mario Cuomo as well as South Africa's President Nelson Mandela, Sethi has followed the recessionary pattern of franchises going abroad because domestic markets have dried up. He sees the global move as an ongoing deal. "Unlike in the past, where small companies used foreign markets only during slow periods, now these markets are a permanent part of their total reach," Sethi remarks. The most efficient way of achieving this is with a franchise:

> *Franchising has a phenomenal future in a country like Africa because it provides a package of equipment, service, and skills that is uniform and does not cost a great deal, and it creates a tremendous number of jobs and social benefits. Think of how much it would cost to set up an operation like MacDonald's, but the package can be delivered quite cheaply now that it has been developed.*

The key to making globalization happen for American small businesses may be a support system of some kind that channels the brains and opportunities to the right connections. As Sethi points out, the international reach of German, Japanese, South Korean, and Taiwanese middle-sized and small businesses is partly attributable to government-sponsored networks that operate through or parallel to the embassy structures to help promote those nations' small business interests abroad. Sethi complains, "Our small businesses don't get nearly as much help abroad from embassies as the Germans or Japanese because our embassies are not as well staffed when it comes to providing these resources." Sethi points to the Japanese trade houses which, acting like freight collectors in a transport system, marshall the needs of local businesses and work on both the huge and small scale to see to it that business is done. "The South Koreans and Japanese need the American and European markets to survive, so they do everything they can to support small business—it's a matter of life and death."

For the small business lobby, getting in touch with experts like Sethi, and having the chance to meet with other owner-managers in a similar position, is important. Since the public universities are now finding it sexy to have "entrepreneurial studies" as part of their business programs, the small business lobby is in a position to ask for more from state governments in terms of access to academic facilities and training at no cost or for nominal fees. The state university systems in California, Texas, New York, Florida, and Ohio have already attempted pioneer programs, and the expansion of these privileges to small businesses in every state will in part be a matter of entrepreneurs as a political constituency putting pressure on local government to make the nominal investment, in conjunction with the SBA, to set up the programs.

Not all of the help comes from Washington or state capitals. One of the major nonprofit organizations that has spent two decades helping out what it calls "micro" enterprises is the Ford Foundation. Because the Foundation is always on the lookout to fight poverty—not just to develop business success stories—it concentrates its donations and loans on urban and underdeveloped regions that need capital. Among the organizations it has supported are favorites of President Clinton, like the Arkansas Enterprise Group, which received grants totalling $450,000, the Southern Development Bancorporation, which got $2 million in loans, and loan guarantees and equity investments to help the Good Faith Fund in Arkansas. These development banking projects support small-scale enterprises that work locally as well as internationally. It is all part of the style of "social purpose investing" that has in the past worked through major banks and corporations but is being targeted more and more toward smaller enterprises.

Because the Ford Foundation is committed to global thinking, it is in a good position to support projects that have an international flavor. One recent grant to Accion International provides microenterprise assistance for Hispanic businesses in border counties of the American Southwest. Accion International has been around since 1961, providing loans and technical assistance to tens of thousands of small businesses in Latin America and the Caribbean. The border project so far has created or stabilized more than 350 jobs, with an investment of only about $1 million. The initiative is just one of hundreds funded by the Ford Foundation each year that adds to the international climate for small businesses.

TAPPING INTERNATIONAL SOURCES OF ASSISTANCE

Beyond the U.S. sources of information and assistance, several international groups are invaluable. The upside potential of trade liberalization for entrepreneurs is keyed to the use of computer and telecommunications networks as well as organizations that provide information, like the United Nations and in particular its Trade Point Program, which sponsors a network of centers dedicated to providing cost-efficient ways for small and mid-sized businesses to enter the global marketplace. The UN figures that its programs could save as much as $100 billion in capital expenditures and regulatory compliance costs through education and networking. It has pilot centers set up in Bangkok; Tunis; Cartagena, Colombia; and Columbus, Ohio, where a recent conference brought together American mayors, representatives from nearly 200 international governments, including Commerce Secretary Ron Brown, Customs Commissioner George Weise, UN Secretary General Boutros Boutros Ghali, and entrepreneurs eager to understand how they can function in the new GATT.

About 60 countries—primarily in the developing world—are in the process of establishing permanent Trade Points. Columbus won its selection as the site for the conference and as a trade point back in 1992 because of the availability of databases, software companies, and telecommunications facilities. In particular, it is their use of Electronic Data Interchange (EDI) that made Columbus the choice since it allows the computers of domestic and international trading partners to communicate using a standard document format. EDI automates and simplifies the complex paperwork process currently required to conduct international trade. The cost savings for small business, particularly in Trade Point facilities that are essentially free of charge, is tremendous.

THE STABILITY QUESTION

Business travelers are always urged to learn the customs of the country they are visiting; it's probably more important to get to know that country's Customs. In addition to learning when to take your shoes off and how to present your business card, it is important to know the political and regulatory events that are shaping that country's business environment. What happens when, in addition to American regulatory agencies, you have Russian or Chinese regulations, language barriers, interpretations, and rule changes?

For small business owners itching to go global, one of the main points of hesitancy involves political stability. Much depends on the political changes that can alter the environment for trade overnight. If political surprises are common at home for small businesses, imagine how much likelier they are overseas on unfamiliar soil. Without a day-to-day reading of the shifts in power among factions in and out of the government, the chances of an unpleasant surprise increase. Businesses—no matter their size—love political stability. If a government changes its ministers of trade, taxation, and finance every year, that exacerbates the difficulty of getting the job done for a solo entrepreneur. Political instability is a trade barrier of its own. That is one of the reasons why much of Latin America, Africa, and the Middle East are still considered minefields for most small business, which cannot afford to gain a toehold inside a country, as IBM or Chrysler can, and then wait out the emergence of a stable regime.

Ireland is one of the best examples of this paradox. While American cities in particular are full of Irish entrepreneurs who would welcome the chance to set up a joint venture in their old homeland, the recent history of small business and trade with Ireland has been filled with brief spurts of activity followed by long periods of almost complete inactivity. During the 1970s, a steady torrent of "the Troubles" gutted the towns and city centers of Northern Ireland and drove away foreign investment. Over a decade ago, a special push to create an Irish "Silicon Valley" just outside of Dublin looked like it might have legs, but it was overtaken by new waves of violence that kept investors away. In early September 1994, it looked like peace might be coming to Northern Ireland after the Irish Republican Army signed a nonaggression pact with John Major's government, ending 25 years of terrorism—they hoped.

With British companies and foreign investors long gone, the country's economy has been in ruins for most of that time. Essentially, it is a wartime economy. Nearly 40 percent of all jobs are on the government payroll, compared to 25 percent in all of Britain, creating an excess of spending around $6 billion over tax revenues received and making Northern Ireland one of Europe's poorest countries.

Unemployment in parts of Belfast is as high as 60 percent, and for males throughout Northern Ireland it is 17.5 percent. As peace arrives, it could mean further job loss—as many as 10,000 to 25,000 from a reduction in the police force alone. The black market is vast and includes IRA and Protestant paramilitaries that run money laundering and drug operations.

Economic unification with Ireland is still a long way off, and so the aid packages and foreign investors will be courted. The Clinton administration is considering a massive increase in its $20 million a year contribution to the International Fund for Ireland, and New York City proposed a bond issue that would draw money for job-creating projects. However, according to Graham Gudgin, the director of the Northern Ireland Economic Research Council, a nonpartisan research institute, "Economically, unification is completely out of the question. If people have even confronted the economics of it, they are not treating it seriously. People in the South are going through the motions of rhetoric, not reality."

If you were an entrepreneur, with Irish roots and a desire to see the country pull out of this abyss, would you go back? That question haunts a whole generation of South Africans, Chinese, Haitians, Cubans, and others who know that small business is, in addition to being the salvation of the American economy, the best hope for their various homelands. But doubts about stability can hold them back.

The Community Approach

In September 1994, a delegation of entrepreneurs returned to their native Vietnam from California to drum up joint ventures. The trip stirred up considerable controversy back home in Westminster, California, often called "Little Saigon." About 60,000 Vietnamese live in this town just 30 miles south of Los Angeles, and 1,500 Vietnamese small businesses went through a boom that lasted until 1992, and then started to feel the pinch of declining retail activity and real estate values. The fuel that drove the growth of Little Saigon was a burgeoning underground economy involved in trade with home through third-party countries like Thailand and Taiwan. Now that the United States has lifted its embargo on sales to Vietnam directly, many of the stores and offices in the shopping malls and office centers are empty, and turnover is high as shops open and close within months. To bolster the sagging economy of the region, the Vietnamese Chamber of Commerce dispatched its delegation to home. Among them was a gynecologist, Dr. Co Pham, who comments, "We want Little Saigon to be the Hong Kong of Vietnam in the future."

The controversy in the community involves going back to the same Communist leadership that the expatriates fled a decade before. While the delegates are hoping to make Westminster the funnel for exports, travel, banking, and overseas investment by Vietnamese officials as well as Vietnamese living in the States who want a part of the action, many are less than sanguine about the prospect of helping out the Communist government.

In fact, the Vietnamese community is deeply divided over contact with home. Often, families are reluctant to tell their neighbors about a visit to the homeland. A travel agency arranging such visits was fire bombed, and a newspaper editor was killed for advocating negotiations with the Hanoi government. Some right-wing political activists in the community have picketed Dr. Pham's offices to protest the 10-day visit of his delegation, and Pham's life has been threatened, while his patients are harassed. The protesters hope that the Communist government will collapse and fear that American investment dollars will only prop it up longer. They contend that without foreign capital, the government will collapse sooner.

The main force behind this flurry of activity, and even behind some of the carping, is small business. In the eyes of Philip Nguyen, who is a partner in Environmental Group Products International, which manufactures water-filtration systems and has sales of $200 million a year, the opportunity to work through government officials to conclude deals is a model for how government and small business should interact. He already has a contract with one Vietnamese business but views these visits as a chance to network in both Ho Chi Minh City and Hanoi, where the group will meet with four high-ranking members of the Vietnamese government. Since water quality and plumbing are well behind the times in Vietnam, Nguyen is optimistic about setting up systems that will pass international regulations for hotels, restaurants, and other institutions that will be attracting foreign visitors when Vietnam opens up.

THE REWARDS OF INTERNATIONALISM

One of the most stunning success stories in the management of a global operation from modest beginnings is exemplified by a petite, soft-spoken businesswoman named Josefina Cruz Natori. When a phone call breaks the early-morning quiet in the charcoal-gray executive suite of Natori Ltd., one of the fashion world's fastest-growing companies, it is as likely to come from Japan or Paris as it is from the company's design loft around the corner on Madison Avenue. For Natori, the founder and president, thinking globally is part of the daily routine. With a manufacturing plant in her native Philippines, a Paris boutique, showroom, and warehouse, and a burgeoning market and licensing operation in Japan, the world is a small place even when you only have about 125 staffers—80 percent of them women—to cover it. "This business has always been thought of in a global manner, from day one, because we have always had to look at an international market," Natori explains.

Natori is politically savvy and dedicates part of her schedule to keeping up with legislative and legal changes in all the countries where she does business. She was invited to take part in President Clinton's preinaugural economic summit in Little Rock, Arkansas, in 1992. Before the summit, Natori addressed a long letter to Clinton in which she urged him to loosen credit through the Federal Reserve, implement an investment tax credit that would help small business, and address the health-care crisis. With one employee who is HIV positive—not an uncommon situation in the fashion industry—she has had firsthand experience with the problem of finding a reasonable insurance package. Natori also wrote to Clinton about helping the homeless and continuing the progress toward GATT and NAFTA trade agreements.

At the summit, she just listened. "I didn't have the guts to speak—I was starstruck," she recalls. In private, she has strong feelings about the challenges facing the Clinton administration regarding job creation and fostering small business. Philosophically, she feels the country has moved from corporate culture to a more entrepreneurial zeitgeist:

In this country we are inclined to have our own thing, control our own destiny. Before, people wanted to join and climb the corporate ladder, but now it is a choice that involves quality of life and being master of your own destiny. Allowing small businesses to get started and expand is a big job for this administration.

As she wrote to President Clinton:

I believe a speedy stimulus to the economy would be to create better liquidity as soon as possible for small businesses whether it be through the SBA or other appropriate government agencies. This means broadening guidelines or providing assurances to banks in order to induce them to make loans.

But Natori is not waiting for Washington. For her, progress starts at home. Natori's trim and highly profitable operation is living proof that small business can have a global reach and that entrepreneurs have something to say about the way the country's policy on foreign trade should be shaped. The people who know both the American way of doing business (she has a Wall Street background) and the Asian way ought to be the first to be heard when it comes to forging tariff and customs rules for trade with Asia. That is where the 47-year-old Natori had her origins. "Strangely enough, we started in Asia and we're going back. We wanted to make sure we were perfect for the Asian market before we went back," Natori says.

Natori does not change even a buttonhole of her designs for the Asian market. The big push is a marketing effort. "The Far Eastern market is the last frontier that we have focused on, and the market is picking up," she notes. Natori just hammered out a licensing agreement with Japan's Pola Cosmetics, a $2-billion-a-year company.

Fashion and textiles are the most hotly contested, controversial areas in the realm of export and import negotiations. Between problems with the French and Chinese governments over textiles, American negotiators have had more headaches when it comes to the question of quotas, rules of origin, copyrights, and licensing than in most other industries combined, and the textile conundrum has jeopardized trade relations with China for more than two decades. But in the midst of all that, Josie Natori keeps her eye on the ball politically. It is a matter of knowing not only the law as it stands but the mindset of the White House and the policy makers who are likely to change that law. It is a matter of survival.

THE SMALL BUSINESS AGENDA
FOR IMPORT AND EXPORT POLICY

In another area that calls out for a more active small business advocacy community, the most pressing issues involve finding a way to enable small business to become a larger part of the nation's export strategy. This is how it can be done:

- Small business advocates have to participate more in the interagency planning process for increasing exports.
- There is a need for more "one-stop shopping" export-import centers in gateway cities throughout the nation.
- A federal-state task force for paperwork reduction should address lingering problems with customs and tariffs.
- Small business needs a solid trade bridge with Japan to permit growth in exports.
- The federal government needs to create a network of technical assistance involving not just the Commerce Department but Justice, Energy, Transport, the EPA, and other agencies as well.
- Export financing for small business has to be more readily available through the Export-Import Bank or some other federally guaranteed institution.
- The advocacy program of the ITA must be strengthened to create a "wholesaler" in foreign countries for American enterprise.
- Federal negotiators should push for international quality standards of testing, safety, and other trade requirements.

**GETTING
ORGANIZED:
HOW SMALL
BUSINESS
AND
GOVERN-
MENT CAN
WORK
TOGETHER**

6

BIG BROTHER
Political Teamwork
Between Small
Business and the SBA

Friend or foe, the key to working with the federal government is getting more out of them than they get out of you. If your tax dollars are being pumped into a massive political effort to create jobs and jump-start the economy in time for an election year, then you want to know where those dollars are going and how they can end up invested in your industry—and back into your business. Given the labyrinthine nature of the government budget process, and the string of broken promises that confounds any attempt to track down the waste and diversion of resources, this aggressive attempt at making government accountable can be frustrating. But the newly empowered, more savvy entrepreneurial community that is flexing its voice in Washington and capitals around the world is getting results from its efforts toward getting government's attention.

There is no doubt that small business is gaining not simply respect but an irreversible momentum in the top circles of federal government. The challenge for American enterprise is to apply pressure in the right places to ensure that this continues to be the trend. Just after the 1994 elections, when it was clear that the Republicans were on their way to Washington with a mandate to eradicate whole nests of bureaucrats, the Small Business Committee of the Congress was one of three committees that looked like it would be eliminated completely. However, Newt Gingrich and his advisers decided it would be politically incorrect to phase out the committee, particularly as Jan Meyers was next in line to become its head and it would look particularly mean-spirited to take something away from a woman and from small business at the same time. Even though the committee is relatively insignificant in the legislative process, the decision to hold on to it reflects the "untouchable" status small business has in Washington these days.

The reason for this turnaround is obvious to those who have followed the interaction of business and government over the past five years. The major industries and Fortune 500 have struck out mightily each time they have come to the plate, and that is leaving both political parties angry and ready for a change. In terms of jobs, wealth creation, and ethics, the high-profile failures of corporate America have been an embarrassment to every Congressional leader who supported big business. Meanwhile, the only consistent performer has been small business. It is no wonder, then, that federal programs that directly benefit the entrepreneurial community are now being embraced by the executive and legislative branches. In the future, it will be up to small business to continue to hold the government's feet to the fire and retain this set of priorities.

The starting point for any entrepreneur who wants to work with the government is the Small Business Administration (SBA), a massive bureaucratic network of over 4,000 employees in one hundred regional offices that is headquartered in Washington and funded by Congress to the tune of $800 million a year. For well over two decades beginning in the early 1970s, it was a dead spot in Washington—when it wasn't in the news for lining official pockets through kickbacks and fraud. For career politicians, the SBA was marked as a bureaucratic backwater and even a political dumping ground (its last three heads before Erskine Bowles were losers in senatorial races).

For veterans of the SBA, the stigma has been particularly difficult to bear. One highly placed official with ten years' experience, whose job involves presenting a better public image for the SBA, admits:

> *The agency has for too long been known as an agency that did not serve or even understand the business community it was supposed to help. We were perceived as out of touch, often a hindrance and not a help, and that poor image problem was in part caused because the headquarters in Washington was like an ivory tower where people just sat around in their little offices waiting for businesses to come to us.*

In the eyes of business, the image of the SBA for at least twenty years has been associated with anything but success. Since the SBA was involved in bailing out disaster-struck areas and had a lousy track record on loans, it seemed jinxed. Presidents and prominent Congressional leaders preferred to distance themselves from the SBA. As Oren Teicher, the head of public affairs for the American Booksellers Association, notes, "Our members looked at the SBA as an entity that had very little to do with who we are. It was a whole orientation toward small businesses that employed 200 people and more. There may have been useful things they were doing for those firms, but for our members it seemed just plain irrelevant."

For its part, the Small Business Administration has deserved its image as one of the trouble spots of federal bureaucracy. As welfare agencies are now learning, it is not easy to distribute the taxpayer's money equitably without either making mistakes or incurring the wrath of those who consider their own constituents to be more needy than the customary recipients of aid. Moreover, it is tough to keep the ranks free of corrupt or opportunistic agents who channel the funds in the direction of those who have paid them handsome kickbacks. The SBA was even implicated in the Whitewater affair. What hurt the SBA the most, however, was a consistent lack of judgment. The rate of failure for SBA loans was atrocious by most banks' standards.

But all of that is changing, and will continue to as it evolves. There seem to be three schools of thought. Many think the SBA should continue as small business' fallback loan and guarantee institution;

they perceive the SBA as a much more efficient lending organization under new management that can fulfill its old role much better. Others are prepared to ditch the idea of the SBA as a financial institution and reinvent it as a political and legal strategy group for small business. It could become a central power in the advocacy movement that is reforming regulation to reflect the needs of small business. The third and far more skeptical view suggests that the SBA be abolished as redundant and outdated (almost as soon as the Republicans gained control of the House there was talk of abolishing the agency). If that idea prevails, small business may have a battle on its hands to keep its official "Big Brother" in Washington.

Instead of accepting its role as a political football, the SBA has fought to improve its status in Washington. In the first two years under President Clinton there were signs that the SBA was making strides. By 1994, when President Clinton elevated the director of the SBA to a Cabinet role, it had attained far more direct access, both officially and unofficially, to the President than ever before. As President Clinton noted in making the announcement, "This appointment and the elevation of the SBA administrator to cabinet status reflect my equally firm commitment to address the interests and concerns of our nation's small-business community." This penetration of the inner circle of power is a measure of the rapid progress made by entrepreneurial interests in Washington. During a flurry of dramatic changes that took place in October 1994, the insiders could see that the SBA had won a major power struggle and had made its way into the limelight. The shake-ups in its leadership have given it new life, new power, and a few stability problems.

Whether it stays hot or not, the SBA will become the focus of political attention in a way that will be markedly different from its shadowy role over the past twenty years. That means it is in danger of becoming part of the tussle for power as the Republican majority reshapes Congress and the next presidential election draws near.

The specific role of the SBA as an advocate will be in enforcing the Regulatory Flexibility Act of 1980, meaning it could conceivably go to court against federal agencies to make sure they go through the proper cost and impact analyses before making new regulations. As SBA administrator Philip Lader notes, "You will see increased concentration on our regulatory reform efforts."

For the small business community, the reshaping of the SBA, and its defense against the most vehement budget slashers, will mean a continual challenge. It is not only important to pressure Congressional leaders to keep the SBA fully funded but to be involved in policy shifts and structural changes that will inevitably occur over the next few years as the political fabric of Washington is rewoven.

FRIENDS OF BILL IN HIGH PLACES

Even the most cynical Washington insiders have to admit that the SBA is in the middle of a turnaround, and most of the credit is due to Erskine B. Bowles, the 50-year-old former Morgan Stanley banker who in late October 1994 left his position as the SBA's director to move directly into the White House as President Clinton's deputy chief of staff. Over his nearly 18-month tenure, Bowles took the SBA through some of its biggest changes since its founding more than forty years before.

Bowles, a "friend of Bill" who is a constant presence in the presidential golf foursome, is now considered to be the most influential figure in the determination of government policy toward small business. His elevation is a reward for what virtually all, including his most insistent critics, acknowledge to have been a superb achievement in running the SBA for the two years of his tenure. In particular, the Democrats credit him for using entrepreneurial programs in a job-creation plan that is widely viewed as the key to Clinton's reelection plan.

Around the SBA offices under Bowles you heard a lot of hefty target figures tossed around, but the one that still echoes throughout the corridors is 600,000—that's the number of jobs the SBA is hoping to create by the next presidential election. As long as the entrepreneurial lobby understands this priority and grasps its role in the plan, it can leverage this position to gain further support from the federal government. One of its main responsibilities will be seeing to it that Bowles continues to focus on small business and persists in presenting its agenda in the White House. This can be done directly by maintaining the open lines of communication with Bowles that developed during his time as SBA chief—which allowed the major trade associations representing small business, as well as individual entrepreneurs from across the land, to plead their case with him personally. If he hears from them often enough, he will be unable to ignore them.

The figure who will be most responsible for seeing that small business has support is Philip Lader, who was known inside the White House as one of Al Gore's chief cheerleaders in the "reinventing government" program by serving as chairman of the policy committee of the National Performance Review. He is also a veteran of the budget process. Before joining the White House staff, he was the deputy director for management at the Office of Management and Budget (OMB) and chaired the OMB's President's Management Council. Lader emphasized again and again during his confirmation hearings that he wanted to cut red tape and further streamline the SBA, which had already undergone heavy cuts and restructuring under Bowles. He made the SBA almost sound like a retailing operation:

> *The SBA, with the extensive field operation in place, is and must continue to be a customer-driven agency. I plan on combining my experience from the vice-president's 'reinventing government' initiative with the opinions of small business people and bankers across the country to build upon the progress the agency has made in the past two years.*

Lader and Bowles are the ultimate Washington insiders. Lader and his wife Linda are the founders of the "Renaissance Weekends" that have become an unofficial Clinton-circle think tank over the past decade. The 48-year-old Lader can use his Cabinet ties to carry out the other key plan, he told the Congressional committee members who confirmed him. He hopes to "rebuild bridges" between small businesses and the White House as well as other federal agencies—particularly those bridges that were badly damaged by the debate over health-care reform.

Despite the lofty position Lader holds, he is very much the product of an ordinary American upbringing. Raised at first in Queens, one of New York City's outer boroughs, he is the son of a short-order cook and an elementary school teacher. His family moved to St. Petersburg,

Florida, when he was 12, and he became active in high school politics. He earned a degree in public administration from the University of Michigan, went to Oxford on a Rotary Club fellowship, and then on to Harvard Law School.

Lader's business career has had a heavy social and political accent. He headed a development company, called Sea Pines, in Hilton Head, South Carolina, that was considered an exemplary environmentally conscious organization. Then he became involved in organizations that raised money for amateur American sports teams, including athletes preparing for the Olympics. His only bid for office was an unsuccessful attempt to become governor of South Carolina in 1986. Lader was chairman of the South Carolina Governor's Small and Minority Business Council, a director of the South Carolina Chamber of Commerce, and a director of First Union National Bank of South Carolina and First Carolina Bank. He has also been a professor of business and public policy at Winthrop University in South Carolina, as well as president of Australia's first private university.

Not everyone was happy when Erskine Bowles left the SBA to become deputy chief of staff at the White House, in charge of scheduling, operations, and personnel matters. "I'm angry and disappointed. He was just getting started," complained a senior bank official in Washington who was helping the SBA to streamline its credit programs. Bowles took a lot of heat from some factions in the small-business lobby—particularly the National Federation of Independent Business (NFIB)—for his support of President Clinton's health-care reform plan. One moment of hand-wringing came when the SBA under Bowles was investigated by the General Accounting Office for spending $93,000 on brochures explaining the Clinton health-care plan, including 10,000 given free to the Democratic National Committee, which eventually had to repay $5,000 for them.

As the NFIB's head Jack Faris, who is on record saying that Congress should "cut government wherever it can, and if that includes the SBA, so be it," comments on Bowles's role in the health-care debate: "The administration set up Erskine Bowles to lose credibility in the small business community."

In its critique of the SBA, the NFIB points out that the organization lacks focus. While supporting the move to elevate the SBA administrator to Cabinet status, the NFIB also wants the SBA out of the loan business, which they feel should be privatized and trimmed down to being a basic advocacy organization that offers limited management assistance. The NFIB's statement on the SBA in its official *Legislative Priorities* handbook reads:

> *All too often, SBA has been required to perform functions that are either too narrowly targeted to small segments of the small business community or are inappropriate activities, such as direct loans. Instead, SBA should do what it can do best—act as an advocate for all small businesses, provide appropriate types of assistance to small businesses, and serve as a link between the small business community and the federal government.*

Lader, Bowles, and other SBA supporters clearly have their hands full with a Republican-dominated Congress. Bowles weathered the attack by Republican watchdogs for his part in the campaign for health-care reform, but the call from House Republicans for a review of the SBA's programs in support of minority businesses was too strong for Congressional leaders like Newt Gingrich and Jan Meyers to evade. Meyers has promised a special investigation of the SBA to gauge the efficiency and cost-effectiveness of all its programs. In the meantime, the SBA will become the servant of two masters: the Democratic White House and the Republican Congress.

REVAMPING THE LOAN PROGRAM

For the most part, the legacy left by Bowles reflects some sound and rapid moves on his part to improve the SBA. He cut costs by 60 percent, and paperwork as well. One of the first steps Bowles took to try to move capital into small business—at a time when the bond and equities markets were looking pretty attractive to most banks and investors—was to double the budget for "micro-loans" under $25,000, pledging $65 million a year to the loans. In its first six months, the new "Low-Doc" program (including micro-loans), which simplifies the paperwork for loans of less than $100,000, had 12,000 customers for loans totaling $652 million.

In order to convince venture capitalists to participate, Bowles provided more than just loan guarantees for new businesses. Now long-term financing is also available. The SBA plans to guarantee over $9 billion in loans in fiscal 1995, up from $8 billion the year before. Its procurement assistance programs helped minority-run businesses win $2 billion in government contracts in 1994.

But not all the news was about expansion. Even before the Republicans took office in January 1995, the SBA had announced that it would withdraw from certain loan programs and put a $500,000 limit on the size of most loans. This was a dramatic turn of events, since 38 percent of the loans backed by the SBA in 1994 were for more than $500,000. There is pressure also to get out of the minority set-aside or 8(a) program that the SBA supervises, under which the government guarantees a share of federal contracts for socially disadvantaged small businesses. Since Congress passed a bill requiring all of the government to set goals for minority subcontracting through bid preferences, the SBA 8(a) program looks superfluous.

The expansion of the SBA loan programs during 1993 and 1994 had been so rapid, on the heels of the cutbacks in staff and funding, that some people wondered how the SBA was going to be able to administer the new loans. Even inside the agency there are worries that there are not enough supervisors to keep the loss rate on bad loans, currently at just 1.6 percent, down to reasonable levels. As Bowles explained, the key to expanding the loan program was actually cutting some of the overhead. "We were able to take the cost out and expand our services in this area. And, we have turned $155 million into $8 billion in loan funds."

In 1994, the first and only full year under Bowles, the SBA issued 37,000 loans totaling $8 billion, a jump from about 25,000 loans the year before. The total is expected to go up to 56,700 in 1995 and 95,000 the next year, when the SBA is expecting to lend $17 billion. In a move that was applauded by banks for its fiscal responsibility, the SBA is also using a $30 million appropriation to restructure extraordinarily high interest-rate loans to small businesses that borrowed in the early 1980s under the 503 Development Company loan program. All this is rolling despite Washington's pressure to keep SBA's spending to within 1 percent of last year's budget.

Part of the overhaul is a redeployment of personnel, which now number 3,400. Bowles moved 210 SBA administrators from the

Washington and other regional headquarters out into the 68 field offices in an effort to speed up loan applications. The emphasis on streamlining has cut the average loan guarantee review period to about a week, and the introduction of a new one-page application for borrowers requesting less than $50,000 has also helped the turnaround time. Before the changes, applications ran to 150 pages and were so convoluted that many owner-managers could not bear to fill them out. They still have to satisfy bankers with lengthy applications and collateral requirements, but the SBA step has been made drastically easier.

Two initiatives introduced in 1994, "Greenline" and "Low Doc," have made a big difference in the amount of traffic at SBA offices. The first is a radically easier revolving credit opportunity and the latter is a "low-documentation" loan application process. Although they sound to skeptics who view the SBA with disdain like typical government publicity ploys, both have had rave reviews among most bankers and entrepreneurs.

THE SMALL BUSINESS INVESTMENT COMPANY PROGRAM

The more important phase in the ambitious program begun by Bowles and now under the supervision of Lader is a reorganizing of the Small Business Investment Company (SBIC) program. This is one of the most controversial areas and a potential target for Republican budget cutters. These venture capital companies allow private investors to raise funds guaranteed by the SBA by raising debt and issuing equity that would be invested in start-ups. SBICs have been one of the principal concepts of the SBA since its founding. They invest in small business under the watchful eye of the SBA, which can revoke their licenses if they violate a stringent set of guidelines. They are audited by the SBA, which has the right to look at their books, send in examiners and accountants, review their correspondence, and respond to complaints from either small businesses or the public. The licenses are granted by the SBA to venture capital groups that agree to provide equity financing and management consulting services to eligible small businesses (where "small" is, for this program, defined as having assets of $7.5 million or less, a net worth of not more than $2.5 million, and profits of $250,000 or less).

While the SBIC must comply with the guidelines of the SBA, its involvement with any given business and the terms of the transactions are negotiated without the involvement of the SBA, but always with an eye on SBA regulations on eligibility. The SBA has pulled the plug on well over 500 licenses. There are legal parameters for the firms that an SBIC is permitted to back, and for the most part the businesses that manage to secure SBIC investment are fairly well established and inside the range stipulated by Congressional mandate.

A noble idea that has failed miserably in some cases while doing extremely well in other highly publicized cases, the SBIC program has left at least 200 firms still in the process of liquidation. And so the first thing Bowles decided to do was to enlist deeper pockets in the program. Under his orders, the capital requirements rose from a minimum of $2.5 million as a minimum investment to $10 million. The SBA assumes the outstanding debt of some SBICs until they are back in the black, then the companies repay the agency and turn over some of their profits. The SBA's associate administrator for investment notes that the new SBIC program has 56 investors ready to participate in the new phase of the program, representing an influx of $1 billion, and hopes to pull in $3 billion in new private capital over the next five years.

The SBIC program has helped companies such as Intel, Federal Express, and Cray Research get their start. Since its inception in 1958, in response to a Federal Reserve Board study that showed how hard it was for small business to get long-term loans and equity financing, the SBICs have invested over $10 billion in over 73,000 different businesses. The venture capital corporations had to pay interest on the SBA-guaranteed loans, and many of them, because they were poorly managed or backed ventures that took a long time getting off the ground, went into bankruptcy at the government's expense.

Bowles tried to reconfigure the way the SBIC shares are structured. Now they use a type of redeemable preferred stock, backed as before by the SBA, on which payment will be made only after the SBIC has retained earnings. For every dollar contributed by the private sector, the federal government chips in three dollars.

The SBA has targeted a return on investment of about 11 percent, and the private-sector capitalists generally set 20 percent as their target return. The small business owner is the one who benefits the most, as the cost of capital is drastically reduced and the availability of credit is considerably better. Congress gave the plan $550 million through the end of 1995, and experts agree that it will have to come up with an appropriation more in the order of $3 billion over the next five years to follow through on the full range of commitments, using the formula of three federal dollars to one private dollar. It will be up to the political voice of small business to ensure that Congress follows through, since a $3 billion commitment may be problematic in a Republican-controlled arena.

The new emphasis on SBICs has drawn a wide variety of interested venture capitalists. Among the most recent approved investors is Churchill Investment Partners (CIP) of Malvern, Pennsylvania, which is backing The Ben Franklin Technology Center of Southeastern Pennsylvania in a major project designed to promote start-up technology companies in the mid-Atlantic area. The new fund, launched in fall 1994 as the CIP–Ben Franklin Investment Fund, L.P., is expected to raise $25 million in private capital and will leverage additional funds through the SBA under the SBIC program. Churchill will be the general partner of the new fund and will also invest $500,000 as a limited partner. The Technology Center is coming up with an additional $1 million of seed money for the new SBIC. CIP, a well-known private-sector fund manager, already runs one of the most successful SBICs in the nation. With a proven track record in technology, the task of attracting investors is made that much easier.

As the SBA and its venture capitalists are discovering, in addition to finding new sources of funds the challenge is to channel them properly from investors who are experts in certain areas to companies that have bright prospects in those areas. Fred McClindon is president of Capital Resource Management Association Inc. in Kingsport, Tennessee, which has placed $600 million worth of investments in new firms and has had requests for capital injections in the $50,000 to $100,000 range. He views the relationship between venture capitalist and business as a matter of specialization. "It's a match-up situation—some fields, like those related to medicine, are stronger than others. And there are all types of venture capital companies. Basically, it's a match-up of the requirements of the guy seeking the funding placement and the funders that do the particular type of scenario he's looking for," he says. With the advent of computer databases, including the SBA's own that includes over 1,200 sources of capital, the challenge essentially begins with an online research project. An owner-manager with specific qualifications and needs has to troll the database for a source that matches those characteristics.

Help for Minority Business

Another SBA initiative is the Minority Enterprise Small Business Investment Company (MESBIC) program, which works in a similar way to SBICs but targets minority-owned business. Created in 1970 in response to several studies that showed how low the SBIC investment in minority enterprises actually was—less than 3 percent of SBIC dollars, or about $5 million a year went to minority firms through 1972—the MESBIC program started out with about 50 venture capital companies and less than $5 million in capital. Because the 330-odd firms they loaned money to were very small and had high ratios of debt to equity, the early efforts of the MESBICs were less investments than they were small loans.

In 1972, Congress moved again to authorize the SBA to buy preferred stock in MESBICs, which helped create more capital and also provided an interest subsidy on SBA loans and those purchases of stock. Most importantly, as a tax incentive to potential investors, Congress made the MESBICs nonprofit organizations, which also drew more funding because it meant that charitable organizations could contribute to them. The Ford Foundation alone has contributed about $100 million to MESBICs over the past 20 years.

The federal government has done more since the 1970s to promote minority-owned businesses, usually in the form of effective but fairly specialized regulatory exemptions and subsidies. For example, by guaranteeing surety bonds for small contractors, the government paved the way for about $50 million worth of contracts a year. In addition, the revolving line of credit extended to small firms that win government contracts lightens the capital expenditure burden on those firms. The most popular, and occasionally controversial, means of government support for minority enterprises remains the procurement assistance programs, most of which started in 1968 as part of an effort to develop larger minority businesses that have relationships with the government. By 1970, procurement programs included services and construction in addition to manufacturing, and have grown from about $22 million worth of contracts in the first years to over $100 million these days.

The clearinghouse for information about federal programs for minority enterprises is the Office of Minority Business Enterprise (OMBE), a part of the Department of Commerce. It is responsible for coordinating new initiatives on the part of both government and the private sector, but it has no substantial budget other than for administrative functions, so it does not play the same role in the financing of enterprise as the SBA.

This is a tough part to play in Washington. Other organizations, including the SBA, don't appreciate being told what to do by an outside agency, and, in an election year particularly, Congressional staffs do not relish the prospect of sharing control or credit for legislative ideas that involve job creation and enterprise development. It is occasionally a problem for the OMBE to be closely associated with the White House and the Executive branch, as well.

One hallmark of the OMBE has been its focus on the local level and the participation of trade associations, universities, churches, and volunteers in particular regions. Among the groups that it has pulled into its network are the American Bankers Association, the American Bar Association, the Advertising Council, the Menswear Retailers of America, the National Association of Purchasing Agents, the National Association of Accountants, and the American Institute of Certified Public Accountants. In conjunction with the Menswear Retailers of America, for example, the OMBE has helped set up a full-scale business packaging operation. Funded by the SBA, it provides lines of credit, training for candidates who receive a weekly stipend, and a "big-brother" mentoring program putting volunteer members together with rookie business owners for counseling. In recessionary times, these organizations often help out struggling members as well as start-ups.

In this way, the OMBE is something of a community planning office. Through a network of about fifty Business Resource Centers in target communities throughout the nation, the OMBE helps entrepreneurs find financing, prepare loan applications, and package business plans. They also provide grants to chambers of commerce and business associations that provide help to minority enterprise on the local level. The OMBE has sponsored local Construction Contractor Assistance Centers and has tried to set up rural centers that offer intensive small business training as well as sponsored local trade fairs. Through organizations like the Chicago Economic Development Corporation, a thirty-year-old SBA-supported organization that has targeted businesses with sales over $100,000, as well as smaller firms, and offered loans that average about $46,000, the OMBE has had a vital role in helping minority contractors get a start in a major market.

Also a key source of statistics and research for the public policy and enterprise advocates of Washington, the OMBE sponsored a very important Census Bureau study of minority-owned businesses in the early 1970s and administers grants for the study of minority business. It also studies the volume of commercial bank loans to minority-owned business, generally in conjunction with the American Bankers Association; keeps statistics on the ratio of minority owner-managers to other races and to total employment; and tracks the effectiveness of SBA loan programs and the "discontinuation" of minority-owned businesses either through bankruptcies or the sale of the company. By assessing the effectiveness of loans and investments of different sizes, the OMBE helps to determine what degree of assistance is sufficient to take the financial strain off minority-owned businesses without making them entirely dependent on the SBA and government.

All of the resources that the OMBE brings to the table are of tremendous help to the small business advocacy community, whether or not it is taking on issues that specifically pertain to minority businesses. But the OMBE is yet another budget battleground that has been threatened by House Republicans determined to trim back the official support mechanisms for small business. So the small business lobby is again faced with a decision: Should it go to bat on behalf of the OMBE with a letter-writing and public relations campaign, or should it stand by and let the organization try to survive on its own?

BRINGING IN THE BIG BANKS

Providing ammunition for small business advocates, specifically those trying to guarantee the survival of the SBA, success stories are already beginning to emerge from the Greenline and Low-Doc case files as well. In New York City, where cynicism outweighs enthusiasm continually, at least as far as government aid to business is concerned, the attraction of the SBA incentives is even drawing major banks back into the small business lending fray. A few years ago, the big SBA-backed lenders in New York were Banco Popular (which did a roaring trade in lending to taxi companies and drivers for the purchase of medallions), The Money Store (which specialized in second mortgages), Anchor Savings, and "ethnic" banks serving the Korean, Spanish, Chinese, and other communities. But now Citibank, Chemical Bank, and Chase Manhattan Bank are becoming far more aggressive in pitching the small business account, thanks in large part to the safety factor provided by the government guarantee.

These business partnerships should also be construed as political partnerships. Where win-win situations are created financially, there is bound to be a measure of loyalty that develops on the part of the banks when it comes to local as well as federal politics. Small business is giving these powerful banking forces reason to be protective of their mutual political and financial fate. The banks are also helping their own image in Albany and in Washington by coming to the aid of small business—and at no risk.

In 1994, the Consumer Bankers Association sat down at the conference table with the SBA to sort out ways to make it easier for commercial banks to qualify as preferred lenders. Under SBA regulations, banks must apply for preferred status in every SBA district where the bank has branches. If the SBA grants the commercial banks some leeway, then the banks could underwrite loans themselves and the SBA would go over the paperwork afterward.

At Chase Manhattan, for instance, Mark Alan Willis, president of Chase Community Development Corporation, is using SBA programs as the core of his $150 million annual mortgage and real estate business. While Chase has not traditionally been a big fan of the SBA, it is now finding that the reduced paperwork and faster turnaround, combined with the opportunity to bolster their federally regulated Community Reinvestment Act ratings, is irresistible as a package. For Willis, who likes what he sees at SBA headquarters, the time has come to pump up his organization's participation in the SBA programs. According to him,

"The SBA ought to be in the role of expanding business opportunities, of bringing access of funds to minorities. The new administration appears committed to this goal."

In the last quarter of 1993 and into the first quarter of 1994, Chase had loaned about $6 million using SBA-guaranteed funds, but that is still a tiny percentage of its overall small business loans. Internally, it is trying out a new policy permitting branch managers to approve "micro-loans" of $10,000 up to about $50,000 to low-income areas. The bank also made an initial contribution of $700,000 to the Small Business Investment Corp., an alliance of the office of former Governor Mario Cuomo, the New York State Bankers Association, and seven banks.

Willis offers several examples of how well the new SBA loan programs are working. From bodegas in the Bronx to drugstores in Brooklyn, it has meant that business owners who were dependent on loan sharks or family financing now have a "friend" at Chase Manhattan. One of the most memorable stories involves Millie Becker and her company, Westchester Air, an airplane taxi business in Purchase, New York, an upscale suburb of Manhattan. Becker's growing list of corporate clients made an upgrade in her fleet necessary, and she needed a loan to get the $700,000 turbo-prop, eight-passenger Beechcraft King Air craft she had her eye on for some time. With demand for her services climbing nicely, Becker was concerned that each time she hired another company's plane she was exposing clients to her competition. The bankers she contacted at first did not understand her business well enough to appreciate the need for having the Beechcraft. In the summer of 1993 she went to a Chase breakfast event in Tarrytown, New York, and the bank was drawn by her plan as well as the fact that she was born in Puerto Rico. Her next step? A Lear jet, which will cost $1.5 million.

The Government Comfort Zone

Without question, the decisive factor in getting Chase more involved in the small-business and low-income community banking business is the comfort zone created by SBA guarantees. As Willis points out, "When you feel comfortable with the borrower but his business doesn't fit the normal underwriting categories, the SBA guarantee gives you more freedom to make the loan. You can go into a situation that historically is riskier." There is greater incentive for the SBA itself these days, since Congress has reduced their reserve requirements from 5.5 percent to 2.5 percent of the value of a loan portfolio. This allows the SBA to have greater leverage on its money.

Other banks are following suit. Chemical is increasing its SBA lending by about one third, while Citicorp and European American are involved in both in-house plans to draw more small business customers and larger, city-wide schemes for enterprise development. This close cooperation of local government and major corporations on behalf of small business can be leveraged by small business advocates in a number of different ways when it comes to regulatory decisions. By enlisting public support of prominent government figures, both the banks and small business lobbyists are building up reserves of political credit.

New York City's Mayor Giuliani and the city's largest banks, under pressure from local trade associations and small business advocates, are hammering out a radical new plan to make capital available for the first time to some of the most needy areas in New York. During early fall 1994, the Mayor's office and bankers put together an SBIC, called the Community Investment Corporation, with $12 million in capital to help out start-ups in low-income neighborhoods in the outer boroughs. Among the banks participating are Citicorp, J.P. Morgan & Co., Republic New York, European American, and National Westminster.

One of the incentives for the banks is that it helps them to satisfy federal and local requirements under the Community Reinvestment Act. Each will contribute three dollars for every one dollar provided by the city—the initial idea is that New York will put up $3 million, although it is still a bit vague where the money is coming from, that will leverage a further $9 million from the banks—a reversal of the usual three-to-one ratio between government and private sector.

With a maximum loan of $500,000, the SBIC is patterned after the Community Preservation Corporation, a nonprofit organization involving 47 banks and a total of over $1 billion in capital that two decades before had its beginning in helping out the housing situation in the same areas. According to Ira Romoff, European American's head of small business lending, "The new SBIC is not the normal order of business. We're not here to finance someone's dreams, but we can help a viable New York City enterprise bloom, even if it might not have too much cash flow for the first two or three years."

Economic development projects funded by the Community Investment Corp.—the current plans call for shopping, senior citizen, and day care centers— would be sited near new low-income housing projects, as in South Jamaica, Queens, where 200 two-family homes are going up in an area where the nearest shopping is more than 10 blocks away. At the same time, an SBIC for high-tech start-ups for New York has put together $10 million in Economic Development Corporation (EDC) funds with up to $35 million from Prospect Street Investment Management, a Boston-based private venture capital firm. That $45 million is then leveraged up to $100 million with SBA money.

As EDC president Clay Lifflander points out, "It's an investment program, not a spending program. And it's proactive, not reactive— economic development that looks to capture a market we didn't have before." In addition to computers and software, the fund is targeting waste management, machine tools, and other industries in an effort to broaden the definition of "technology" and to ensure that these industries do not simply leave New York, where taxes and regulatory requirements are brutal.

The launch of the SBIC was marred by party politics, unfortunately. Since it started as a (former New York City Mayor) David Dinkins pet project about four years ago, Mayor Giuliani decided to skip the press conference and other hoopla surrounding the announcement of the SBIC; his office has been reluctant to provide support simply because it cannot take full credit for creating it.

A Secure Local Base

While the big banks grab headlines for jumping on the small business bandwagon, the continuous participation of community-based smaller banks is still the dominant mode of SBA lending. All across the nation, with the federal guarantee and a steady stream of funds, banks with assets generally under $50 million are continually advancing loans to area-based entrepreneurs. To take just one example, Citizens Bank in Elizabethton, Tennessee, is a mainstay of SBA activity in the southern part of the state. According to Mike Hill, its president, the basic formula for a start-up involves a solid business plan and demonstrated management ability and collateral, generally in the form of real estate. The interest rate is generally pegged to prime plus two and a half points—which is also the going interest rate for Greenline lines of credit—and the starting loans are between $100,000 and $1 million; most loans are on a 10- to 15-year schedule. Hill likes to see the owner-manager begin with a "cash injection" of about 20 percent as well.

While Hill prefers to go outside the SBA Greenline program for a revolving line of credit, he does note that the SBA 7(a) loan program, particularly under the new Low-Doc fast track, is fundamental to his business. Hill explains:

> *The Greenline program takes a lot of extra paperwork and tracking. We prefer to handle it ourselves. The government guarantee has been an incentive for us to participate in SBA loans. But that's not a reason to put together a loan that won't succeed. We want the borrower to succeed and have a long-term relationship with us.*

In New Mexico, where there are 17 "one-stop capital shops" under the auspices of the SBA, the number of businesses working with the SBA has gone up steadily from 182 in 1991 (for a total of $35.8 million) to more than 300 a year currently, for a total of nearly $100 million. As assistant district director for the New Mexico office of the SBA, Greg Devejian points out, "Contrary to what some people say, there is no big credit crunch."

The New Mexico innovations are among the most imaginative in the nation, and all have been put in place since mid-1993. In the area of fixed asset financing, which helps start-ups to buy buildings or heavy equipment and is viewed as a good way to keep business in the state, the local SBA has helped create The Enchantment Land Certified Development Corporation (CDC) under its 502 and 504 programs. The Microloan system for loans of $5,000 or less is administered by the Women's Economic Self-Sufficiency Corporation, and the Greenline provides revolving credit. The Enchanted Land CDC has already accounted for more than $40 million in projects using about $13 million in SBA loans, and SBA officials estimate that it has created about

800 jobs. The banks are encouraged by the fact that less than 10 percent of the more than 1,250 loans guaranteed by the SBA in New Mexico are considered to be "troubled."

NETWORKING IN THE GOVERNMENT

Both the current head of the SBA, Philip Lader, and former head Erskine Bowles are striving to improve the SBA's relationship with other agencies, including the Environmental Protection Agency (EPA) and Internal Revenue Service (IRS), and to study ways to help make the regulatory process more fair and more clear for entrepreneurs. By pooling information and coordinating their efforts, SBA and the other agencies can increase their efficiency. For entrepreneurs, this heightened emphasis on cooperation is especially good news because the SBA is by far the most accessible and entrepreneur-friendly agency and more likely to share information than the tax or environmental officials. If a particular trend in regulation is just starting, it is far more likely that small business will learn about it from the SBA.

Information flows two ways. Since Bowles and Lader are plugged into the White House and President Clinton's inner circle, their access means that not only will entrepreneurs who use the SBA eventually learn what the White House will do for them but that they will be able to pass along, far more directly and promptly than usual, what they can do for the White House and what they expect. Never underestimate the power of electronic mail and telecommunications when it comes to the possibility for feedback. The Clinton White House is the first in history to be accessible by e-mail, and the volume of faxes that concern small business issues that can reach the Cabinet is now many times greater than it ever was. Together with the public opinion machine generated by the NFIB, the likelihood of entrepreneurs being heard in Washington is now greater than ever.

THE SBA AND ACCESS TO CAPITAL

In many ways, the current debate over the status of the SBA is an echo of the circumstances surrounding its creation. Even before the Republicans seized Congress, the SBA wore many hats. It has served as a bank, a regulator, and an advocate. While the new Congressional leadership wants to place the SBA in a position where it helps small business gain access to political power, there remains a significant contingent, particularly inside the organization, who view its main role as one of providing access to capital. As in 1953, when the organization was founded, the relationship between government and business was undergoing a significant change, moving away from the close ties to major defense contractors that had grown up during wartime and progressing toward a more enterprise-reliant economy. Then as now, the federal government needed to step in on behalf of small business, politically and financially.

Parallel with the banking system, the SBA addresses the two basic problems for small businesses seeking funds in the financial markets: cost of capital and availability. Its main financial achievement over the years has been to reduce the risk, or perceived risk, of investing in start-ups. Nothing is more risky than the absolutely new, which is of course a hallmark of small business and its originality. By bearing part of this risk, through guarantees to banks and direct loans, the SBA has created an atmosphere in which the stigma of newness for the financial community has been removed and even created a sense, during periods of economic uncertainty such as the one we are going through now, that small business as an investment is on a par with other, big-business oriented vehicles.

The issue of risk is of vital importance. Small business is associated with services and lines of economic activity that have great variability in income, due to a number of factors in addition to capital and its cost. This means that the return on investment will vary widely, from the inevitable failures that the investors have to eat to the successes that pay off a hundredfold—the Silicon Valley stories are only the most dramatic examples. The extreme variance of return on investment associated with small business is often completely counter to the trends of the main equities markets, like the New York Stock Exchange and the Dow Jones Industrial Average.

With the growth in importance of the institutional investor in these major markets, however, the federal government had to find a way to lure the capital of pension funds and major banks to the private side of small business financing, and the picture of risk management had to be improved. Another problem for institutional investors involved the time it takes small ventures to bring a decent return. A five-year period is the usual measure of this, but in fact many small ventures take longer to bear fruit, and that is a difficult proposition for money managers who have to live quarter by quarter.

One of the economic factors that is likely to inhibit the flow of institutional capital into start-ups in our time is inflation. As during the 1970s, when spiralling inflation suffered by the economy as a whole inhibited the flow of capital into new ventures—because it increases the nominal cost of capital for businesses in all size categories—so too the prospects for inflation are worrying those who are already concerned about the availability of capital to small ventures today. The cost of equity capital and loans rise because interest rates tend to rise, and this leads us in a circle back to the monetary policies of Washington.

An aspect of risk that makes investors nervous is uncertainty, and a major factor in this dilemma is lack of information. If there is an area in which government assistance can make a difference it would be in research. Fundamentally, number crunchers like to have plenty of numbers to toy with and a consistent pattern of return for different types of investments. Research in business finance for the major corporations has become very sophisticated, allowing investment professionals to forecast and chart the stocks they are willing to bet on. If more data were gathered and available on small business and its performance, then it would attract the investment professionals that rely on a solid track record.

But research is expensive. Business schools, which prep their graduates for major firms, tend to invest in research about big business; it doesn't hurt that major corporations underwrite a lot of the research at places like Harvard and Stanford. The SBA and other government agencies ought to be urged to sponsor more research into small business issues to build up solid ground, in terms of data, for investors that require these data before even considering putting their money into SBICs.

As a regulator, one of the SBA's most important functions is to make sure that federal spending includes small business, so that a part of every federal dollar spent goes to small business. The enforcement of that is mainly undertaken by the SBA, which also helps to match the capacity of small businesses to government orders. This goes the other way, as well. When the government sells a valuable natural resource, the SBA makes sure that small business has the capacity to buy. For example, the SBA monitors the sale of timber in national forests to make sure small lumber firms get their fair share.

Beyond its regulatory and banking functions, the SBA offers indirect assistance to small business and communities through programs that include management and technical advising and special training for minority groups and communities that are struggling. Each year over 100,000 individuals go through training courses, conferences, workshops, and thousands of copies of publications go out.

One of the most active mechanisms through which federal assistance reaches small business on a day-to-day basis is the Small Business Development Center network. Generally funded in part by the SBA and in part by state universities and state appropriations, the SBDC specializes in counseling, with an accent on management and technical areas. In New York alone, there are eighteen such centers administered by the State University of New York. They pull together the resources of the university (including the library, and valuable office space), local private sector businesses and associations, and government in the form of both manpower and money. Women, veterans, the handicapped, and minority entrepreneurs are given special emphasis in their programs, and manufacturers, exporters, and technology oriented firms seem to get a warmer welcome than most retailers or service companies. Each center has an advisory board made up of individuals representing private and public organizations dedicated to helping small business grow and stay in New York, and through the board the entrepreneurs who use the center have an unsurpassed networking opportunity.

SBA'S REAL MOUTH IN WASHINGTON

While Philip Lader and Erskine Bowles get the headlines, in the shadows a potentially more important—even dangerous, in the eyes of some steadfast bureaucrats—figure quietly goes about transforming the SBA and the politics of small business. His name is Jere Glover, and he is the chief counsel for advocacy at the SBA. Nominated for the position by President Clinton, he was confirmed by the Senate in May

1994. Since then he has made an indelible impression on the various constituencies of the small business community—from owner-managers to legislators to trade associations.

A native of Lake County, Tennessee, Glover went through his undergraduate and law degrees at Memphis State University and then earned an advanced degree in administrative law and economic regulation from George Washington University. He ran his own law practice in Tennessee and was a trade association executive before moving to Washington in 1978 to take a position as counsel to the subcommittee on Antitrust, Consumers, and Employment for the House Small Business Committee under President Carter. From 1975 to 1977 Glover was director of the legal division of the Consumer Product Safety Commission. He was also an antitrust attorney with the Federal Trade Commission. To gear up for the 1980 White House Conference on Small Business, Glover was brought into the SBA as deputy chief counsel for advocacy; he moved up to the top spot fourteen years later.

Glover has a peculiar job, when you think about it. He is an SBA veteran whose stated enemy is bureaucracy. In his own words, "There needs to be a legal function to take on the rest of the government bureaucracy." Glover is responsible for serving as an independent voice for small business within the federal government. The small staff he commands studies the role of small business in the American economy and crafts policies and programs that will foster the growth of enterprise. The Office of Advocacy was created in 1976 to reduce the regulatory burden on small business and to encourage policies to support its growth. Day to day, it is the most effective voice inside government to let Congress, the White House, and federal regulatory agencies know when they have gone too far or are getting close to that point.

Glover is also in charge of the SBA's Office of Economic Research and Office of Information that maintains a vital database on American small business, from which the President's annual report on the state of small business, as well as several policy statements, are drawn. The research unit prepares economic indicators and conducts policy studies on issues such as the use of contingent workers, health care costs and coverage, pension plans, access to capital, federal procurement, and banking services. The Office of Information publishes issue profiles, the *Small Business Advocate* newsletter, and takes care of public relations.

Glover oversees 10 regional advocates throughout the country who identify new issues and problems and monitor the impact of regulation on local business communities. They work with state officials to develop legislation on behalf of small business. And on top of all this, he is head of the Office of Interagency Affairs, which pursues legislative and regulatory initiatives, recommends specific measures for helping small business compete effectively, and monitors and enforces government compliance with the Regulatory Flexibility Act, requiring federal agencies to scrutinize the potential impact of proposed rules and regulations.

Glover has obviously plunged the sharp point of his legal sword through a thick target of responsibilities. Beyond the energy and efficiency with which he dispatches a hectic agenda every month, meeting face to face with entrepreneurs who recognize instantly his ability to convey their message unabridged and undiluted to the highest levels of authority, is his talent for spotting unforeseen problems and finding a way to head them off before they have a destructive impact on small business. Everyone knows the main issues in Washington for small business, such as health-care reform, banking reform, taxes, labor laws, environmental regulation, minority enterprise, and access to capital. But Glover is in touch with entrepreneurs and so is attuned to patterns that extend past the ordinary agenda. For instance, he made an impassioned plea before Congress to address the problem of crime and the way in which it is eating up the profits and assets of entrepreneurs not just in the urban centers but in the suburbs. And he has addressed other peripheral issues like the regulation of utilities, drug abuse, and product liability—all of which are generally forgotten in the ordinary roll call of problems that small business faces.

If Glover is around long enough, he is likely to make a huge difference in the SBA and the way in which official Washington treats small business. He is the point man for entrepreneurs who want to express their dissatisfaction with federal policies of all kinds. Unlike most complaint bureaus, Glover's office has the legal and legislative teeth to make things happen in Washington.

THE SBA'S POLITICAL PROSPECTS

The SBA is still an underused and much maligned organization that, like all government, could use even more of an overhaul. The forces that face Washington in the years ahead, including new waves of dissatisfaction with government, will open doors for those who want to see change in the SBA and the way it works. In addition to the annual budget battle, the SBA is involved peripherally in a wide array of legislative areas where decisions are far from automatic from year to year. In the coming decade, chief among them will be the rearrangement of turf and oversight among the major agencies that regulate small business.

There are already signs that if Philip Lader and Erskine Bowles manage to hold on to their offices, they could be heavily involved in the cooperative aspect of interagency relations. This would include the Environmental Protection Agency, the Commerce Department, the Treasury, and, adding the most controversy, the departments that oversee Health, Housing, and Urban Development. To have small business represented in the restructuring of these agencies is key for the future of regulatory change in this country.

Banking regulation is a moving target, and small business has a very important role to play in the 1990s to ensure that new regulations do not squeeze credit in a way that favors major corporations. The SBA is involved in this and can help, on the state and federal levels, to shape policies that keep banking competitive and responsive to small business needs, but the main responsibility lies with entrepreneurs themselves. Inflation fears have led many finance experts to expect a return of the cyclical credit crunch. With a number of savings and loans and smaller banks either recently gobbled up by major banks or driven into bankruptcy by the crisis of the 1980s, the traditional picture, which matched small business with small banks, is changing. As in the late 1960s, when the cost of funds to commercial and small banks rose rapidly, so in the 1990s as interest rates rise the cost of loans to small business, which is already higher because of higher operating costs, is expected to go up.

With fewer alternatives to choose from in the way of banks, small businesses could get caught in a high-interest trap. As an advocacy group, the SBA can play an informed and active role in helping small business to avoid this. It oversees many of the regulations limiting the banks themselves on bidding for funds; allowing them to seek the lowest cost of capital has a direct impact on small business.

Small businesses are hit when the ultimate lender will not offer funds to banks that have deposit rate ceilings, set by state banking commissions, because it will mean that the commercial banks are no longer an attractive place for savers to keep their money. The money moves into stock markets, and small business is cut out. It is hard for banks to attract savers to certificates of deposit that are still way below the return offered a decade ago. As this source of funds dwindles, banks tend to "ration out" small business borrowers. Small business proponents have for more than a decade lobbied to remove the prohibition of interest payments on demand deposits as a way of reducing the cost of loans and making funds available. The danger can be a dual prime rate—one for big business and the other for smaller borrowers. Inevitably, banks would prefer to deal with the higher return on big business loans, and again the small business borrower would get a cold shoulder.

The hallmark of the early legislation that created the SBA and other types of assistance for enterprise is the way that it linked economic, political, and social goals to the health of a competitive and self-sufficient small business community. By making a cause of particular groups that are considered needy, Congressional leaders have linked small business development to a broader program of legislation on behalf of women, minorities, age groups like the elderly or teens, and the residents of particular regions or neighborhoods. The government bodies that become involved include not just the SBA, but the House and Senate Committees on Labor, Public Welfare, and of course Banking and Currency.

Over the years the stimulus packages and programs for small business fit into a broader agenda of social reform and empowerment. The Equal Opportunity Act of 1964, which established the Office of Economic Opportunity under the direction of the Executive Office, was part of the "war on poverty." Title IV of the Act focused on small business and the establishment of an Equal Opportunity Loan program that started off by providing loans of $25,000 or less for periods of up to 15 years. It was tested in Philadelphia, Harlem, and Washington, along with a special loan program that became known as "6 x 6" because it offered $6,000 for six years under soft credit criteria. The publicity surrounding the plan was tremendous. Since that time the programs for minorities have included procurement and investment measures on the federal, state, and local levels, and the appointment of special assistants to the president and most governors for minority enterprise.

By providing a conduit for private investment funds that would support long-term debt and equity capital for small business, Congress helped small business sidestep the high cost of the public sale of securities as well. It costs hundreds of thousands of dollars, particularly in investment bankers' fees, to float an issue. Beyond the cost in dollars, of course, is a genuine reluctance on the part of many owner–managers to carve up the ownership of their businesses before they or their families are ready to part with their share. Issues of shareholder control and the fundamental principles of self-determination in the running of the business come into play here. The best part of the SBICs is that they remove small businesses from the threat of government control and also keep aggressive investors from trying to take control over the company.

Rather than eliminate the SBA or dismantle its programs, its continuing reform should take into account the input of the small business lobby. While that influence has gained weight and recognition in the past year or so, much of the progress that has to be made on this front should be channeled through the SBA. A strong SBA, supported but watched as well by its constituents, is therefore an essential factor in the reshaping of federal policy on the role of small business in the economy. By helping the SBA to remain powerful, and making sure that legislators keep it at the top of their agendas, the small business community will be sure to have a good friend in Washington when they need one.

THE SMALL BUSINESS AGENDA FOR THE SBA

Faced with powerful forces calling for its demise, the SBA needs both support and constructive criticism. The small business community should stay involved by:

- Ensuring the survival of the SBA through a lobbying campaign that pressures the House to continue to fund it.
- Following through on the review of SBA programs to ensure the organization's integrity.
- Getting to know local SBA offices and finding a way to work with them locally on both political and fiscal issues.
- Pushing for greater access to SBA research and on-line database services through libraries and other public institutions, as well as the Internet.
- Expanding the role of the Office of Advocacy on the state and federal levels to make it even more active in regulatory issues.
- Increasing the tax incentives for investments in SBA investment programs.
- Supporting state and federal banking laws that encourage banks, both large and small, to work with the SBA.

7

GETTING IT TOGETHER
The Power of
Political Networks

Political power is the product of consensus. All political bodies work from the basis of a group, even if it means delays and compromises that often weaken an individual position. Beyond the dramatic schisms between parties, political culture is essentially a cooperative and team-oriented phenomenon. It puts the group first and individual concerns second. Moreover, political life always demands a strategy that aims at reaching the broadest possible group. And so the old cliché that small business meant "doing your own thing" just does not hold true in this context. In addition to being attuned to one's teammates, political life entails paying close attention to the opposition, and even to the referee and spectators. It is remarkable how quickly noncombatants can join the fray and neutral parties can turn partisan.

It is all very well to talk about what entrepreneurs should do politically, but nothing will happen unless at least some work together. Individually, very few can make much headway in policy matters. Many believe that in a world of political action committees and white-shoe law firms, only big money talks and that automatically excludes small business interests. But as long as they act in concert even a few entrepreneurs together can draw the attention of officials at the very highest level of government and set the machinery in motion to get things done.

Independent businesspeople are nothing if not independent, and it seems a contradiction in terms to call for consensus from a constituency that is so grounded in individuality. As those who devote a major part of their professional lives to speaking up for small business can attest, the problem of organizing is an immense one. There are 40,000 lobbyists for business in Washington, and all but about a dozen of them represent large companies. For that tight community of advocates, the major obstacle to advancing the small business agenda is holding together the fragile networks that come together in the face of a regulatory crisis. It's like herding cats.

SMALL BUSINESS AMERICA ONLINE

Help is on the way, however, partly in the form of technological advances that reduce the time and cost of reaching a geographically and politically wide-ranging constituency. What used to involve the nightmare of the mailing list—with all the time and money it ate—is now an automated process bringing together computers and telecommunications at a surprisingly low cost. By means of fax broadcasts and fax-back reply systems, for example, a more rapid turnaround on requests for information lets a trade association check its members' position on an issue before taking up a cause, or supply advocates with the kind of statistical ammunition they need to attract official attention.

The best of the lobbying organizations, like the National Federation of Independent Businesses (NFIB), have their own sophisticated telephone polling and voice messaging systems, as well as an automated way to get a "heads-up" from members and record the kind of feedback that they can use in Congressional hearings and other testimony. Even the federal government is getting in on the act with electronic filing and regulatory procedures that make it easier for entrepreneurs or their trade associations to become involved in the process of regulation. The expanded powers of the laptop computer are tailor-made to help small business both economically and politically. By combining the most common office equipment—phones and copiers— with the most advanced computer peripherals and software, political networks can confer more easily.

The electronic town meeting has revolutionized the political campaign business. But because it relies on satellite or television cable transmission, it is still technically and financially beyond the means of most small business activists in their networking and lobbying activities. But teleconferencing through the personal computer is on its way. Datapoint has already devised a way to put teleconferencing on the desktop with a point-to-point system that integrates the personal computer, monitor, speaker, microphone, and camera in a video network that costs less than $40,000, which is well within the budget of most trade associations. Using new developments in the compression of data and the use of fiber optics, Datapoint's MINX system can bring together multiple users locally or around the globe. Its potential as a political tool for small business is enormous.

So much has changed in the last decade with regard not only to the technical capabilities of communications media but also the business community's attitude toward communications. Suddenly high-tech networks are hot and the executive who spends his or her time and money getting into the information loop is no longer considered to be an eccentric nerd. It is a necessity to be online, and that extends to the political as well as business dimension.

More important than high technology is the emergence of a new kind of entrepreneur who is willing to be politically active and knows that this means joining forces with others. Intrigued by the prospect of being heard, and less intimidated by the idea of sharing ideas and information with other businesses, the new, engaged small business activist is prepared to use high-tech means to mobilize a network. As the most successful small business lobbying groups are finding, there are signs of a change of attitude and priorities among entrepreneurs. Instead of remaining independently apolitical, they are increasingly aware of the need for working together and are willing to find time in their busy schedules for advocacy and networking. With government officials paying more attention to what they have to say, and organized political advocacy groups providing the formal means of communication to allow them to get their message across, these politically active entrepreneurs are delivering their opinion personally.

Using the Power of the Net

The key to small business flexing its political muscle is, then, access. There have to be channels of communication linking the decision makers and the entrepreneurial community and as an equally important factor in this equation, there have to be open lines of communication linking the community itself. A decade ago, small business leaders hoping to form some sort of coalition faced obstacles of cost and inconvenience that were far more formidable than they are now. To get together meant organizing conferences, trying to connect by phone, and sending out fliers and newsletters by mail.

One startling indication of the difference electronic media can make in the common ground linking business and politics is the sudden growth in power of the Internet as a forum for dissent and political activism. In 1995 the House of Representatives decided to provide access to its documents online, providing people with the sort of inside information that was previously the province of top lobbyists and government insiders. As House Speaker Newt Gingrich, who pushed for the online text service for House business, notes:

> If you really want to weaken the Washington lobbyists, there is no single device that weakens them better than to simply disseminate the information in real time so that the people who are paying them to lobby are reading the same documents that they've got and there's no longer any great advantage to being an insider.

In the first few days that the House documents were available on the Internet, 175,000 documents appeared on the service and 30,000 users tapped into them.

The specialized bulletin boards of the Internet have what has been described by Michael Wolff, author of several books on computer networks, as a "lynch mentality." More specifically, the sophisticated but subversive tenor of Internet discussions is proving to be the equalizer between small business and large corporations. To the extent that these discussions are picked up by politicians (following the example of Al Gore) or journalists looking for stories, they have resonance. As Wolff comments, "The culture of this thing is so much to take to task the big guys."

When the Microsoft antitrust case was in the headlines during the spring and summer of 1994, the Internet was ablaze with highly charged political commentary on the role of antitrust law in the computer industry. More recently, and more devastating in its effect, the Internet wolf pack showed how powerful it can become in the consumer area through the crucial effect of a network "news group" of 130,000 Intel customers. They were instrumental in forcing the recall of the Pentium chip, driving down Intel stock, and creating a major dispute between IBM and Intel that itself was partly fought out on the Internet, since IBM challenged Intel's defense of the chip in part by posting its own research findings on the Internet. One of the major issues raised by the Intel and Microsoft affairs was the persistent shadow of cartels and flagrant violations of antitrust laws in the computer industry. Many of those attacking Microsoft and Intel, usually anonymously, were independent software developers and small businesses involved in the industry. As an article on the Intel phenomenon in *The Wall Street Journal* in December 1994 observed, "It illustrates how the online medium allows consumers to align, organize, and focus their activities."

If it works in the computer industries, why can't it bring together small businesses in other industries as well? The posting of a notice regarding a potential regulatory change draws a few comments and responses. As other users pick up on the issue they add their own suggestions and opinions. The government officials are identified and their e-mail addresses are provided. A call for letters or other political action arises. These are exactly the steps that entrepreneurs need to take if they want to make their political causes known. By giving the users the capacity to broadcast or publish their views at a tiny cost and minimum of trouble, the Internet confers on them a real position of influence.

Becoming Media-Savvy

Flying solo is an entrepreneurial tradition of sorts according to the model of the maverick or nonconformist who sets out to start an independent business to avoid being part of large institutions. But in political circles, where information that is available from other businesses or from the government or trade associations is of such value, the stubborn individualist is left out of the loop.

The rise of talk radio and television, and the more issue-oriented approach many of the best programs are taking, has opened up a more direct way in which entrepreneurs can shape policy. From the campaign tactic of televised town hall meetings to the massive and lucrative empire of Rush Limbaugh, the momentous shift toward offering the microphone to a politically charged up, vocal "man in the street" has turned audiences into activists and linked that individualistic man in the street with interest groups that have real power.

Talk radio and television have also brought regional issues, including many that directly involve the problems of small business, on to the national stage. Coupled with the rise of C-Span and even Court TV, which bring some of the day-to-day workings of the legislative and judicial branches of government into the average living room, these suddenly popular media have opened up channels of access. They have broken down the old division between the traditional opinion molders and policymakers and those who used to wait passively for their decrees. Now the opinion molders can include the proprietors of the store on Main Street or other members of the community who pick up the phone while they are listening to a political discussion and chime in on a problem one of their neighbors may be having with local government or the lack of action taken by Washington on a pressing concern. When others with a similar plight listen in, you already have the beginnings of a network. This is just one way allies are identified out of the faceless sea of anonymous businesses that are connected to one another by the fact that they share a common difficulty or motive for political collaboration.

The most common and still most potent means for owner-managers to reach one another is through industry associations and trade groups. These organizations, which should already be using the Internet and new technology to efficiently unite their forces, are the most trusted of media through which small business owner-managers let their elected officials know what bothers them most. By whatever mechanism or medium the contacts are made, the importance of breaking down the barriers that ordinarily separate one owner-manager from another is vital. Political power in the end depends on this process. It involves networks and interbusiness communication. While the conventional wisdom may dictate that competitors should be kept at arm's length, the advantages of open and active communication can offset the need to maintain a proprietary distance.

BRINGING IN THE NUMBERS

We generally think of networks as systems for disseminating information—getting the word out. But getting the word back in is a key component of an effective political network. The best of them work continually to devise new and better ways to collect data from their membership. It may be somewhat more complicated than simply publishing a newsletter and holding an annual conference, but the ongoing surveys and data collection from members can serve several functions. Most important, it helps the organization's leadership stay in touch with the needs and views of the members, so that the organization does not go off on its own tangent and express political views that do not reflect those of its constituency or pour resources into issues that are removed from their immediate needs.

Statistics have always had a tremendous effect in Washington, and it is generally the case that if you can appear before a Congressional subcommittee at a hearing armed to the teeth with volumes of verifiable statistics that dramatically illustrate the view you are advancing, then you are going to stand a far better chance of gaining your objective than if you presented anecdotal or general support for your point. The power of statistical evidence and polls in Washington can never be underestimated. As Georgia Falkenberg of Amoco's regulatory affairs department and author of the best available handbook on interacting with the government for independent businesses, *Participating in the Rulemaking Process*, notes vis-à-vis the comment procedure on a new rule:

> *When buying a house, the advice is often location, location, location. When commenting, it is data, data, data. Experiential, historical, and*

anecdotal information gives the agency specifics on how your industry or facility will be affected by the proposed rule. It is not enough to say the rule is too expensive or won't work.

That is why the National Federation of Independent Businesses (NFIB) invested so much in its computer system and its membership surveys. Its regular stream of poll results is put to constant use during testimony as proof of how America's entrepreneur's feel about certain issues. By quantifying these undercurrents, the NFIB and other lobbying groups can appeal to the bureaucratic instinct that values numbers over any other kind of evidence.

POLITICS IN ACTION: THE REGULATORY PROCESS

There are plenty of opportunities for trade associations or individual entrepreneurs to become involved in the shaping of policy. Most of the official occasions for action involve what is called the comment process. Once the arcane, behind-the-scenes specialty of bureaucrats, the comment process is being opened up to what insiders call the "stakeholders" (businesses that will be substantially affected by the rule changes) in a way that promises to make the whole regulatory machine far more accessible. The comment process continues until the closure of the docket just before the rule is signed into law. This chance to sound off on how regulations are shaped, from the moment of their birth to their implementation, should be seized by the small business community as a time to exercise political power in a direct way.

For federal regulations, the guide to the comment process is a schedule of published notices that indicates where the new rule or regulation stands in the progress from its first stages as a proposal to its enactment. The first indications of a new rule, even before the published Request for Information (RFI) makes its status as a proposal official, can occur in an official's speech or committee meeting at one of the regulatory agencies. Technically, however, the published RFI sounds the opening gun on the comment process.

After that, the government posts the Advance Notice of Proposed Rulemaking, followed by the Notice of Proposed Rulemaking. Since government bodies treat a lack of comments as disinterest, and occasionally as support for what they are proposing, the official notices are crucial tests pinpointing the need for businesses that will suffer hardship under the new rule to seize the chance to fight back. These notices are generally the signal for the heaviest action on the part of businesses and lobbyists who are commenting. The regulatory agency receives letters from individuals and organizations. These organizations or entrepreneurs can arrange meetings with regulators. If the volume and intensity of comments warrants it, the government may schedule public hearings and other opportunities for business to weigh in.

In addition to approaching the regulation-proposing agency itself, individuals and associations that strongly disagree with a new rule also have recourse to judicial review. This is usually more expensive because it involves legal fees and more time. Some trade associations could try an end-run to bypass an agency by going to the Office of Management and Budget (OMB). As insiders realize, the OMB must approve any Information Collection Request by an agency that is proposing a new rule.

Within the OMB, the Office of Information and Regulatory Affairs (OIRA) is the main source of information and expertise on regulatory issues, including the way new rules are likely to involve more than one agency. For entrepreneurs who are serious about becoming involved in the regulatory process, the OIRA is a very important gear in the regulatory machine and one of the few departments in government that is likely to be on the side of small business. The OIRA can stop a new rule cold if it has a strong case for showing that it duplicates or overlaps with other existing regulations from other agencies that are already in place. For small business advocates, this power, together with the cost analyses mandated by the Regulatory Flexibility Act, constitutes one of the most significant tools in questioning the need for new and more stringent regulations of all kinds.

One of the side benefits of the comment process for individual companies is that it provides a written basis to establish one's legal standing, which is necessary for future litigation. Once a company's objection to a proposed regulation is on the record, then it can file a lawsuit against the government. If a trade association submits a comment, a company can follow up with a suit, but the legal road is much more smoothly paved if the company itself has voiced its concern on the record before legal action is taken.

In its ideal incarnation, the process unfolds as a dialogue. The agency, in its request for information as well as the notices for rulemaking, asks specific questions. The organization of the document presenting the rule very often becomes the model for a comment letter from a company or trade association, which answers the rule point by point. In other words, the questions posed in the notice for rulemaking become a guide to the entrepreneur or organization that is organizing the information it intends to present in a comment.

In addition to studying the government notices for rulemaking, it is important for the entrepreneur or trade association to understand the rather strict legal limitations—including the stilted language of statutory texts—under which an agency operates when policy is not just created by it, but imposed upon it by legal forces beyond its control, such as the courts or Congress. That is one of the reasons that seasoned lobbyists who are in a hurry to get action do not send copies of comment letters to members of Congress, since agencies have to respond to inquiries from Congressional staffers and that can delay the process.

The dialogue becomes face to face when the agency and company or association meet in hearings, conferences, or special sessions. Public hearings are held for the most important rulemaking situations, and they require written testimony submitted in advance as well as post-hearing written comments. Although they are difficult to schedule, because government officials and their lawyers are reluctant to accede to them, private meetings offer one other way for a business and the agency to discuss proposed rulemaking.

Government representatives point out that meetings of this kind should be held at company facilities rather than at the agency (which is unlikely, as offices are genuinely overcrowded) or in the offices of an association, which are not as neutral as they seem. The written records of these meetings and even telephone calls with agency officials are prepared in summary form and are called "ex parte" communications. Nothing is completely off the record, no matter how informal the conversation seems.

The Final Rule is only published by the agency after several opportunities for comment have been offered to small business and trade associations between each published request for information and notice. In the eyes of some small business advocates, the forty-five- to sixty-day comment period is insufficient time for small businesses to read, comprehend, and respond to official notices, especially if they do not have the help of trade associations. Even if, as has been proposed, the comment period was extended to 120 days, the paperwork and possibilities for documents to go astray are obstacles to gaining success in the process.

The basic calendar was established in President Clinton's executive order on Regulatory Planning and Review of September 1993. Each agency is responsible for preparing a regulatory plan that will become part of a consolidated Unified Regulatory Agenda for the actions that the agencies reasonably expect to issue in proposed or final form for the year and published in October of each year. In order to leave time for the comment process, the agencies submit their plans to OIRA by June 1 of each year, and within ten days they must be circulated to other affected agencies and the vice president. The same executive order also set up Regulatory Policy Officers in each agency to monitor each stage of the process, with the specific marching orders to foster effective, innovative, and most importantly less burdensome regulations.

Playing the Comment Game

As any lobbyist can attest, there is a friendly way to play the comment game, or one can go kicking and screaming through the process. Since federal agencies often need the information that companies and trade associations bring to the table in order to write policy and, what can be more tricky, to find a way to enforce it, the interdependence of business and its regulators is greater than many first expect. By presenting alternative solutions to a regulatory problem, and by speaking the language of the agency, a business has a chance to build credibility and gain a hearing, at which more documents should be presented to build up the official record of a comment procedure.

Whether an open attack or a friendly gesture of cooperation, a comment letter or document from an entrepreneur or trade association that is weighing in on a new regulation is judged on its detail—

particularly in the area of cost estimates where the main argument is that a regulation places an undue burden on a business—as well as its ability to persuade.

The regulation-proposing agency is responsible for carefully tracking comments, which are entered into the docket and numbered upon receipt and sometimes contracted out for summary and review if they are technically complex or long. Within the agencies, the comment is sent out to research and development, the general counsel, and other departments for their analysis, and eventually the agency responds. At OSHA, copies of comments are sent to the project solicitor, the standards office and the regulatory impact assessment office, which subsequently meet to formulate a response on the staff level, unless there is controversy and the comment is bumped up the administrative ladder. The agency's response becomes part of the public record of the final rule. To take one example, the Clean Air Act operating permit rule drew more than five hundred comments, and each had its separate response.

When the Small Business Administration (SBA) and Office of Information and Regulatory Affairs brought together top level officers from the Environmental Protection Agency, Internal Revenue Service, Food and Drug Administration, Food Safety Inspection Service, and Departments of Justice, Transportation, and Labor for a forum on small business in July 1994, an extremely valuable idea to improve access to the mechanism of regulation for individual entrepreneurs as well as trade associations was proposed: the development of electronic dockets and more advanced notices of rulemaking through online services. Opening an electronic docket for each proposed regulation at the moment when an agency decides to draft it would allow individual entrepreneurs and trade associations the chance to participate fully in the discussion of whether or not to proceed with it. Since some of the agencies had already experimented with electronic filing systems that were also used to engage in online notice and rulemaking, and most agencies track the progress of proposed rules by computer networks in-house, it made sense to many to extend the capability to those stakeholders who would be involved in the comment process.

For some years now, trade associations have found that submitting comments on disk, usually in WordPerfect, is a good way to expedite

COMMENT PROCESS STRATEGIES

- The earlier you start, the better. Once the rule is in writing, it is tougher to change it.
- Spell out the cost/benefit consequences of the rule to your business and include the data as an appendix to the comment letter.
- Find out the lines of division, if any, inside the agency if the proposed rule is under debate.
- Cover the bases of how the new rule will present a hardship, including not only financial or cost problems but also constraints regarding manpower and scheduling, inconsistencies with other regulations, and other technical and legal issues.
- Look for hidden side effects, such as the risk to workers or neighborhoods of transporting pollutants.
- Find something to like in the regulation, and show your support for any possible positive outcome from it.
- Be ready to compromise, or offer alternatives and reasons for using them. When looking for alternatives, consult existing voluntary consensus standards, state, local, or industry association requirements, or overlapping agency jurisdictions.

the process when dealing with the EPA and OSHA, for example. However, as the official record of the forum records, many were not so sure that the electronic docket was in the best interests of the agencies:

Much discussion and deliberation took place in the work groups regarding the earliest date at which input should or could be solicited from stakeholders affected by a proposed regulation. At any given moment in time, there may be hundreds of ideas and concepts afloat in an agency. To solicit input at the very inception of an idea would impose too much of a burden upon the agency and the small business community.

In addition to the electronic docket, the forum also proposed the creation of an electronic regulatory information center (ERIC), yet another "one-stop shop" for small businesses, that would be a comprehensive information and filing center. Following Vice President Gore's suggestion to use information technology to help small business, the regulating agencies at the forum vowed to expand their current use of bulletin boards and other databases (such as SBA On-Line, the Hazardous Materials Information Exchange, and the FedWorld system, which has 139 different bulletin boards dealing with the federal government) to establish, possibly on the Internet, an ERIC that would primarily be maintained by the SBA.

In the not-too-distant future, these services and the Internet could be the medium for everything from comment to compliance. In addition to the cost savings, it would make it far easier to search an industry-specific, issue-specific, or region-specific online regulatory profile for any small business that would bring together in one coherent form all the federal, state, and local rules. As government agencies add ombudsmen and service personnel to help small business, these contacts could be more accessible through e-mail, as would speeches, talking papers, educational and training materials, electronic forms and applications, calendars of seminars and workshops, and newsletters and press releases having to do with breaking news about regulation. Putting the ERIC system into public and university libraries, and ensuring that it maintained plain-English explanations and how-to directions, it would go a long way toward clearing up the great FOG surrounding the federal regulatory process.

A MODEL OF SMALL BUSINESS ADVOCACY

An outstanding example of the way in which the small business community can become organized is the National Association of Women Business Owners (NAWBO). In a glowing tribute, *Inc.* magazine in May 1994 called NAWBO "the best little advocacy group in America" and praised its success in terms of the ideals the magazine continually touts, namely the way NAWBO made itself look much bigger and stronger than it is by, as *Inc.* commented, "assertively behaving like the tough-minded, relentless crowd it represented— chiefly, owners of small companies."

With an annual budget of only $450,000 and a full-time staff of only three people headquartered in donated office space in the

Washington suburb of Silver Spring, Maryland, NAWBO is scarcely what you would call a massive operation. The organization has less than 10,000 members, but its clout in Washington is dramatically disproportionate to the number of dues-paying members it represents. But policy makers realize that NAWBO symbolically stands for the 5.4 million woman-owned businesses in the country—approximately 28 percent of all American businesses—that employ more people than all of the Fortune 500. That makes NAWBO impossible to ignore.

Its public policy division is very active, holding "issues retreats" in locations across the country, surveying members, and most importantly, grooming representatives for the state White House conferences on small business, as well as the all-important national White House Conference on Small Business (WHCSB). At the last national WHCSB in 1986, NAWBO surprised, and even infuriated, the entrenched small business advocacy groups of Washington by snaring 200 of a possible 300-odd elected and appointed delegates. With that kind of voting power, NAWBO won resolution after resolution.

The momentum continued after the WHCSB was adjourned. Two years later, Congress passed the Women's Business Ownership Act, which helped open up access to credit markets and created a $10 million, three-year training and technical support initiative and a National Women's Business Council. The White House briefs NAWBO's president, along with other top business advocates, on an almost daily basis, and since 1992 the organization's top leaders have had three meetings with President Clinton and members of his Cabinet, including a special event on the White House lawn.

The organization prepares its members for breakout discussions at the White House conferences on capital formation, community development, environmental policy, human capital, international trade, procurement, regulation and paperwork, taxation, and information technology. More than a year before the state White House conferences began in late 1994, NAWBO was gearing up for them (and the 1995 White House Conference), urging each chapter to appoint a committee chair and have members participate in the state as well as national conference. By sewing up the delegate spots on the state level, NAWBO secures its continuing power for the next six years.

The mastermind behind all this is a remarkable individual whose Powerbook is equally devoted to treatises on the global future of business and children's fiction. Virginia Littlejohn, who was head of NAWBO for a term and is now a consultant to the organization in charge of its political programs, is a strategist by profession. The name of her consulting firm, which is based in Chevy Chase, Maryland, is Global Strategies, and her lecture topics tend toward futurist trends in the international economy. She uses terms like "breakthrough thinking," "transformational leadership," and "tidal wave of change" with conviction. The press loves it—she is a frequent guest on radio and television, as well as a source for the *The Wall Street Journal*, *The New York Times*, *Washington Post*, and other publications. *The Washington Business Journal* named her one of the city's Top 50 Power Brokers in 1994. She was president of NAWBO in 1984-85 and vice president of a 33-country international organization called Les Femmes Chefs d'Entreprises Mondiales from 1992 to 1994; that organization along with the United Nations has asked her to chair a special conference on women in small business in Beijing in September 1995.

Littlejohn's career as an activist began in the late 1970s in San Francisco. She served as the president of Women Entrepreneurs in San Francisco and helped NAWBO and other organizations devoted to the cause of women in business get together. She has been involved in the White House Conference on Small Business since 1980 and won the SBA's first National Women in Business Advocate of the Year Award. She is an adviser to the U.S. Chamber of Commerce and serves on the Department of Commerce's Industry Sector Advisory Committee on Services as well as the board of the Small Business Legislative Council.

More than her domestic triumphs, Littlejohn is renowned for her international experience. She has been president of six trade associations, including the Professional Services Council, which represents the $200-billion-a-year professional and technical services industry. Her column, "Going Global," appeared in *Association Trends* from 1991 to early 1994, and she lectures on international trade, focusing on what American trade associations are doing to help their members penetrate international markets.

Littlejohn's expertise comes from years of experience abroad. She lived in Germany for three years, Tokyo for three years, and spent her sophomore year in college in Mexico. In an immense stroke of good timing, she found herself working as a business consultant in Prague during 1968 and 1969, during the epochal Prague Spring and subsequent Soviet crackdown. She went on to Vienna, Yugoslavia, Hungary, Bulgaria, and Romania, and then went off to travel for a year throughout Turkey, Iran, Afghanistan, Pakistan, India, Kashmir, and Nepal. In the mid-1980s she helped Philippine entrepreneurs reach Western markets.

While so many entrepreneurs have to move directly from college (or even high school) into their family business, staying in their hometown like poor old George Bailey in the movie "It's a Wonderful Life," Littlejohn has had a splendid opportunity to get to know firsthand many of the world's hot spots for business and change. In most cases she has turned it to her professional advantage, helping companies and government development agencies through the transformation to a market economy in Central Europe in 1990, organizing entrepreneurial training and management development, and assisting Russian business organizations in creating joint ventures and licensing agreements, and advising the state television studio in Russia. Her emphasis throughout remains the need to develop advocacy skills and the ability to seize the opportunities offered by a market economy.

Under Littlejohn's stewardship, NAWBO keeps political activism on the front burner of a nationwide network of women entrepreneurs. Their rallying cry is a variation on the theme of civic responsibility. As Littlejohn says:

> *Big business is already entrenched as a force in Washington for themselves and their industries. Individual entrepreneurs need to take much more responsibility and be much more active as their own advocates—you can't roll over and play dead. It is extremely important to have organized, very aggressive grassroots groups championing the cause of small business.*

Guerrilla Tactics

The organization's secret is maintaining a tight focus on the issues where progress is possible. "To be effective in the cacophonous symphony of lobbyists you have to have a very targeted message. You have to personalize it and make it real not only for members of Congress and the Executive branch but their staffs as well," Littlejohn points out. However tightly she focuses on the issues she chooses, when it comes to presenting them to policy makers she works on incorporating the big picture. Like a good journalist, she looks for an angle. As Littlejohn suggests:

> *Your policy idea has to be positioned as having fundamental or transcendental importance to the American economy for its role in job creation or export expansion, which also creates jobs. I usually try to come up with an angle that involves job creation, the quality of the American workforce, or enhanced national competitiveness so that you are not doing it as a lowest-common-denominator issue but something that policy makers will feel passionately about.*

NAWBO has been praised for its ability to focus on a handful of vital issues rather than take a shotgun approach to several at once. "We pick our fights—and we focus a lot of resources on them. You try to come up with a few important issues that people care about rather than trying to do a hundred issues," Littlejohn says. Among the issues NAWBO has scored major successes with are access to capital, liability insurance regulations, and foreign trade bills including NAFTA and GATT. By organizing their own town hall meetings around the country, holding press conferences, and flying women entrepreneurs to Washington from all over the country to testify before Congressional hearings, NAWBO works like many other advocacy groups, but because they are better organized and represent a special sector of the voting public that Washington is trying to court, their events end up as White House lawn events, get exposure and press coverage, and generally gain a lot more mileage than most other groups can attain.

The organization's triumph at the 1986 White House Conference, where 25 of NAWBO's 27-item wish list of proposals were adopted for the conference's final resolutions, was the first opportunity for Littlejohn's tactics to be showcased. As she recalls, "We were totally invisible at the time and decided that we wanted to catapult ourselves onto the national stage. It was a guerrilla campaign that made us the 900-pound gorilla of the conference."

Littlejohn and a handful of policy experts picked the issues and trained candidates from ten individual chapters on how to get elected, who in turn trained other women across the country. Then they waged an all-out national campaign for delegate positions as well as top spots such as the chair and co-chair of state delegations. As each state held its WHCSB, they would follow it with conference calls to share input and improve their techniques.

In addition to running a tight ship, NAWBO succeeds because they stay ahead of the curve. It seems hard to believe this when in 1995 we are virtually deluged with exhortations for small business to go global, but at the 1986 WHCSB for the session on international trade the room was nearly empty except for NAWBO's members, who had chosen the issue for in-depth research and preparation. "We owned the issue of getting small businesses more involved in international trade that year," Littlejohn recollects. Together with NAWBO members who were Mexican by origin or involved in trade with Mexico, Littlejohn mapped her events strategy during the NAFTA campaign according to the Congressional districts that would have a strong interest in trade with Mexico, particularly in California, Texas, and Florida.

For their encore at the June 1995 White House Conference, Littlejohn wrote a special training manual for the conference delegates and sent it to each chapter to be reproduced for potential delegates, as well as a training tape that Martin Marietta helped to reproduce, and a series of ten issue papers. In fall 1994, the wisdom of this meticulous preparation was abundantly clear when eight of the sixteen delegates chosen to represent the state of Kentucky at the 1995 White House Conference on Small Business were NAWBO members. A week before the White House state conference in Louisville, Littlejohn was there to meet with the media, government and economic development officials, and bankers to prepare the ground for her candidates, with whom she met one-on-one to discuss the issues and approaches that NAWBO expects from its candidates.

NAWBO also convened a think tank in February (sponsored by MetLife and IBM) to work on what Littlejohn calls "very forward-looking public policy ideas" with futurists and experts in such big-ticket areas as diversity, social responsibility, information technology, and the changes in the workforce. Littlejohn explains the agenda:

"We are looking at how issues cluster together to come up with a real value-added slate, not a reiteration of the same boring old issues in which people have been treading water for ten years."

The High-Tech Edge

For the trade bill endorsing the General Agreement on Tariffs and Trade (GATT) that ran into rough sailing in 1994, NAWBO's special international committee of the public policy council also made a commitment to supporting free trade, but not without going through a complex review process to ensure that the membership supported that position. As Littlejohn and her committee recognized, not everything in the trade bill ratifying GATT was in the interests of all her members, and there were some rather serious questions raised by inventors regarding intellectual property laws.

Using the most advanced communications equipment they could afford, NAWBO under Littlejohn's direction set up a high-speed policy clearance process. To get feedback, the organization uses a proprietary voice-messaging system called VoiceTel, packaged by Barbara Kasof, a Detroit-based member. Through VoiceTel, NAWBO's top leadership can reach a core group of 300 chapter heads and committee members within seconds. They "broadcast" the call for comments by fax and audio message, and within 24 hours they know where membership stands. The response rate and cooperation among members is phenomenal, by comparison with other lobbying organizations. Rank-and-file members can also use the Voice-Tel numbers to leave their own comments or respond to polls with a simple local call.

This high-tech edge is of paramount importance to NAWBO's ability to mobilize. Through October and November 1994 they conducted a campaign that used an 800 number to automatically generate letters to Congressional leaders, pushing for the ratification of GATT. As Littlejohn notes, "More and more advanced communications technology will be the focus of the whole government affairs and responsible citizenship in the very near future."

Littlejohn manages to balance NAWBO's long-range and global vision with pinpoint issues and constituencies:

I don't think you can focus on any one level. We are working in a global village, though it's a cliché, and you need to be looking at a tiered approach to things, on the local, state, regional, national, and international levels. What allows you to do that is technology, with the merger of telephones and computers and e-mail and the growth of the Internet. As more firms learn how to surf the Internet they will have the opportunity to operate politically on multiple levels in real time, hopefully without drowning in a deluge of information and contacts.

This is all about strategy, of course. As Washington insiders, Littlejohn and her top staffers pick their targets and deploy their forces in a way that will achieve their aims. Since they run a national organization, with ties to international sister groups, they have a broad range of potential speakers from which to choose when presenting a case. Often the coast-to-coast chorus of testimony is the most compelling, but on occasion it helps to identify a particular industry or region in addressing certain types of legislative proposals.

HELP FROM BIG BUSINESS

It is highly unusual to see big business put real money into political organizations that represent small business, partly because the two are on different sides of so many issues, but NAWBO has proved a remarkable exception to that rule. They have managed to attract corporate sponsorships from AT&T, Chrysler, Continental Airlines, Federal Express, IBM, Nordstrom, and *Working Woman* magazine, each of which has provided $25,000 or more of support to the organization. Its brochures, newsletter, and other publications are underwritten by special arrangement with American Speedy printing centers. By means of other deals they've managed to keep their own expenses down and provide special discounts for members. For example, FedEx allows NAWBO members to enroll in a special discount program that reduces the cost of overnight letters from the $15.50 retail price to $9.85. If members send one FedEX letter a month the savings covers the cost of membership in NAWBO. In the case of Chrysler, the company offered to distribute NAWBO's Corporate Partner membership packages free to its dealerships.

While NAWBO is not entirely alone in working with major corporations (the Council of Growing Companies gets funding from IBM and Price Waterhouse), its unique "win-win" strategy should be more widely copied. It helps to have a growth sector going for you. Women have been going into entrepreneurship at a rate twice that of men, and the market is too enticing for major corporations, especially banks, telephone companies and other service firms, to overlook. When NAWBO courts a big company the trick is to find common ground for both organizations, such as the experimental marketing device using reduced rates for selected nonprofit clients that FedEx wanted to test out. At this point, NAWBO can afford to be selective. As Littlejohn comments:

> *We try to ally ourselves with companies that are in advanced areas of technology and international trade, because we want to educate our members in those areas, especially where a major corporation will allow small firms to move into international markets by piggybacking on their initiatives and using second tier exporting strategies or providing training and consulting services that might be necessary as part of the large corporation's export plan.*

Looking Bigger to Win Bigger

With just over 10,000 members, NAWBO is not by any means large enough to be the most feared lobbying group in Washington. Yet it manages to gain a hearing through an organizational genius that makes it seem a great deal larger than it is. In interviews with several members, an interesting pattern began to develop. Many of them had been in business for years before they felt the urge to become more politically aware and involved, and in most cases it was the guidance of the organization itself that enabled them to understand both the legislative process and what their role in it could be.

Like many entrepreneurs throughout the country, they felt that politics and all its rhetoric was either completely irrelevant to their concerns, or even a bit ridiculous and beneath them. Some of the NAWBO members I interviewed were carried across the line separating the apolitical from the politically conscious by the pro-choice movement. Others were alerted by the effects of government on their business, along the lines of the recent college graduate who stares in dismay and disbelief at the net pay on his or her first paycheck stub and realizes that the state and the IRS have already scarfed down a good chunk of it. When taxes or export/import restrictions began to impinge on their business, they realized that, rather than fight individually in court, they had to do something.

Take the case of Terri Boekhoff, who edits NAWBO's newsletter, *NAWBOtime*, a solid eight-page monthly with a column set aside for updating the VoiceTel list, a calendar of the organization's meetings and elections, and a very savvy section of short-takes covering new regulations. It reaches 10,000 businesses coast to coast. Boekhoff had never been very interested or active in politics. As she explains, "I was certainly not politically active before NAWBO showed me the importance of having a voice, and I think the biggest problem in getting people organized is helping them understand the importance of activism." She attributes all her political education to the organization. She is also a firm believer in its impact.

Boekhoff joined NAWBO in 1986 and was immediately pressed into service, chosen by Iowa's governor as a delegate to the White House conference in Washington that June. In Washington she was struck by the degree of sophistication of the delegates and the unexpected degree to which her voice would be heard: "It showed me what this kind of mobilization can do if it is done through an association that helps you take action. It would be very difficult for an individual to do this much on her own."

As a political activist Boekhoff makes the most of her communications skills. She is assiduous about returning calls and answering faxes from NAWBO members or addressing the organization's needs, often ahead of her own. She claims, "I don't spend a lot of my time in Washington, but you can do anything from anywhere now with computers, fax machines, the phone, and express mail. Lots and lots of express mail!"

Boekhoff runs her own publishing firm with just three employees in San Francisco. She recently started another branch to begin publishing trade books under the imprint of Rudi Books, which has a list of four titles every year. While politics has become a more and more important part of her life since the 1986 White House conference—she was just elected president of the International Association of Literary Publishers and hopes to reshape that organization into a more proactive, NAWBO-like group—she is not utterly devoted to one cause or another. "It was not a particular issue that drew me into politics but a general awareness that one should do something and I felt that NAWBO needed me. So I got myself to be in the position of being a political player," she observes. It is precisely this kind of awareness that helps a grassroots movement take root. Experts in political activism would perceive Boekhoff, and the thousands of others like her who are willing to embrace an organization's agenda as their own, a potent force.

Another NAWBO member, who serves as the group's resident tax policy expert, is Chicago-based Debra Lessin. A fast-talking, supereffi-cient CPA who is so devoted to NAWBO that she closed her office four days before the tax deadline just to attend the 1995 Illinois White House conference, Lessin was also a political latecomer. She paid no attention to politics in college but through friends became involved in local issues and also started to write a regular column for a local newspaper on tax policy. Journalism gave her a creative outlet for her thoughts on policy, and she found herself inextricably involved. As she recounts, "It's not my life, but as I wrote the column I found out that I could have a forum. I'd also have to say that the pro-choice movement was a defining experience for many of us who had been apolitical in college and later."

As an indispensable member of NAWBO's policy team, Lessin writes position papers and alerts members to upcoming rule changes. Since the analysis of tax bills and rules is her profession, she knows the nitty-gritty details and is completely current on what is coming down the pipeline. The tax issue that finally drove her to get involved with NAWBO was the home-office deduction question. As she recalls, "I was sitting home on a Sunday reading the papers and watching football and the more I read about the new home office deduction rules the more I went ballistic. NAWBO reached me and I figured that small business has so few lobbyists, because we don't have the money behind us, that I should do something."

Lessin has decided views about what should or should not be done by Washington. She also has a basic distrust of government: "I'm nervous; I need to see what Congress is doing," she says. As head of her own accounting business, she has cut the number of staffers in half in the last year and views her decision to "stay small" as symbolic of how a lot of other entrepreneurs feel. She perceives a kind of discrimination against service businesses that are the size of her own:

> *Most political groups and events address what seem to be huge businesses in the eyes of us little babies. But I don't like the term micro-enterprises. It's insulting. The dictionary definition of 'micro' is 'abnormally small' but we're not abnormal—we're where it is."*

Running a Tight Ship

One of NAWBO's strengths becomes apparent very early in one's acquaintance with the organization: It is very closely knit together. At the conclusion of my first interview with just one of their members—once my agenda had been thoroughly checked out during the interview—I was offered the names of a series of highly placed associates in Oklahoma, California, Washington, and Maryland whose telephone numbers were at the ready. The members of NAWBO know how to work a Rolodex, and when they refer you to their colleagues they are happy for you to use their names and the introductions are always good. This gives them access to highly placed political and business figures from coast to coast, all of whom will take the call, answer the fax, or follow through. That kind of solidarity is essential for an organization with an ambitious political agenda.

Another of NAWBO's great sources of power is its ability to commit members to research and to produce the kind of statistical evidence that legislators love. As Boekhoff explains:

> *The organization has been instrumental in doing a lot of the statistical research that has been used to illustrate for Congress the inequities involving women in business. They have made the effort to gather these statistics for the purpose of political action.*

By working together with Dun & Bradstreet on obtaining the numbers nationally on women-owned business, they have established themselves as the principal source of statistics on businesses owned by women in this country.

The success of NAWBO can be measured in many different ways. If increased profits are the ultimate yardstick in business, then NAWBO's members have clearly benefited from their political association. While the organization primarily exists as a lobbying group and a springboard for political projects, its benefits for members range well beyond the satisfaction of winning legislative battles. For NAWBO members who regularly attend the monthly get-togethers, the networking possibilities and deal-making are clearly a major return on the modest investment of their dues. At special meetings, such as the Women Business Owners' 1995 Economic Summit in Raleigh, North Carolina, one of the main drawing attractions is the opportunity to meet with government and industry procurement officers, in addition to attending workshops on such subjects as finance and technology. In other words, real business gets done at these meetings, and members go home with real contacts and contracts.

FIRST-STRIKE CAPACITY

One of the main arguments for a politically attuned trade association is that it serves as a welcome defense mechanism. When entrepreneurs create networks, they are setting up an early-warning system that passes on the news when a bill or campaign promise threatens to bring unwelcome change. Like a blip on the radar horizon, the early detection of a regulation gives the members of the association time to do their research, estimate the damage the regulation can do, devise a strategy, contact one another for support, and finally present their case in the crucial, formative stages of the legislative process.

There is no such thing as being too early in matters of this kind. The later one waits to kill legislation, the more difficult it becomes, no matter what level one is working on. That is partly because so many bills only advance through a state assembly or Congress by virtue of the elaborate deals that are made among voting members.

Bearing this in mind, it is obvious that the best way to stop an idea from becoming law is to nip it in the bud. In that way, the complex web of payback has less to do with it, and the idea can be addressed more directly. But early intervention is demanding. It happens only to an organization that is really plugged in to the political process. It depends on a sensitive reading of the political language of the moment and the subtle changes it goes through almost day by day.

Political activity is not always about stopping a law, however, and this is where a network is necessary. A deeper commitment is often needed for those who want to *introduce* their own policy initiatives and see them through to implementation. While there have been famous examples of individuals pushing their own bills through to legislation, it is unquestionably true that having a strong organization, representing community leaders, voters, and influential entrepreneurs, is an aid to convincing a state assembly member or representative from Congress that they ought to sponsor legislation.

Include the Government in the Loop

In addition to communicating with one another, small business has to learn to include the government and its agencies in their networks. In particular, the linkup with the SBA is vital. This may sound a bit backward, since government is supposed to be working at bringing small business into its loop. But the shortcomings of government have to be compensated for by a small business community that builds its own bridges to the government resources it needs.

In its typical bureaucratic way, the federal government's effort to reach small business by computer networking is hampered by incompetence and low budgets. Practically nobody knows it, but the SBA has several online services that are available via modem or on the Internet; the most important of these is SBA On-Line. In October 1994, the SBA started a regular program of teleconferences to reach businesses on new laws governing government procurement. Covering 23,000 miles by satellite teleconferencing methods, they conducted an hour-and-a-half nationwide seminar on ways in which small firms can benefit from the recently streamlined federal acquisition process. Businesses were invited, free of charge, to attend broadcasts at sites such as community colleges and public libraries, and the seminar could be downlinked anywhere by using satellite dishes. The seminar was interactive, and extensive question-and-answer sessions helped businesses understand in more precise terms how $200 billion in goods and services would be bought by the government every year. The new reform measure on government procurement was the subject of many questions even before President Clinton signed it into law.

The SBA viewed the satellite teleconference as the best way to reach the most small businesses simultaneously. In addition to Philip Lader and Jere Glover, the seminar featured Robert Neal, Associate

Deputy Administrator for Government Contracting and Minority Enterprise Development, and Betsy Myers, Assistant Administrator for the office of Women's Business Ownership. One of the new services explained during the seminar is the way in which procurement briefings and other training information can be obtained through SBA On-Line, Internet, and other computer bulletin boards. In order to help businesses with their own satellite technology to get the broadcast, the SBA sent out notices and released on the wires the particulars about the satellite, transponder, downlink, and audio frequencies. The Department of Commerce also runs a free computer network, called the National Technical Information Service, which is part of the U.S. Government Computer Network. Of course, the grandfather of all government-sponsored network projects is the Internet, and its low monthly fees remain one of the best buys in the computer services industry for small business.

THE WHITE HOUSE CONFERENCES

Probably the biggest network—loosely defined, of course—has been created by the White House through its state and national conferences on small business. With 50,000 participants from all 50 states—representing companies employing 500 employees or less—the conferences have become focal events in the small business activists' calendar every six to eight years. In 1986, the main conference brought together 4,000 people, including 1,813 official delegates, and the statewide conferences had about 20,000 participants. Delegates are elected or appointed by each state's governor or member of Congress, and even the president is allowed to make some appointments. A little more than one third of the delegates for the national conference are women, and nearly 20 percent are minorities.

As NAWBO's relentless effort at training and promoting potential delegates shows, there is a lot more to becoming one than just showing up at the conference with a good volunteer attitude. The competition can be intense and the commitment to boning up on the issues can be considerable.

The White House conferences target particular issues, starting with access to capital, procurement information, and the need to make government more user-friendly. The national conference prepares recommendations and resolutions for both Congress and the White House regarding taxes, the budget, regulatory reform, liability insurance, and other matters.

As professional advocates of small business know, the state-by-state versions of the White House Conference on Small Business are where the action is. By setting the agenda and picking the delegates for the 1995 White House Conference on Small Business in each of the states, the groundwork is laid for what has turned out to be a broad-ranging program of legislation. Half of the issues brought up by the two previous White House Conferences ultimately resulted in new laws, including provisions for a graduated corporate income tax, protection for small businesses sued by the government, paperwork reduction efforts, and a program for small business research. They all had their start at the statewide conferences in the form of position papers or ideas offered in discussion. As Jere Glover of the SBA observes, "Not one single piece of legislation positive to small businesses has been enacted that didn't come out of the conferences."

The state conferences are content-packed, with daylong sessions divided between formulating proposals for new regulation and position papers electing a slate of delegates to the national conference. Each state is permitted to send to Washington as delegates twice the number of its senators and representatives, with a minimum of ten delegates in smaller states.

Many state conferences begin with a morning "capital formation breakout group" devoted to ideas about access to capital and other financial topics. The plenary session meets through the first part of the morning, followed by more breakout groups that meet most of the day on such issues as international trade, human capital, technology, and procurement. In between sessions, candidates for the delegate positions do their stumping for support. Balloting for delegates takes place between lunch and mid-afternoon; a closing session reports on the results. Attendance at these meetings tends to be heavily tilted toward delegate candidates rather than onlookers, noncandidates, or entrepreneurs just interested in learning more about the political process.

GETTING STARTED IN THE
POLITICAL SPHERE

While NAWBO, the NFIB, and the White House conferences all represent well-established, well-oiled political machines by now, it is interesting to check in on groups that are still in the process of putting their political game plan together. Some of them are ad hoc organizations drawn from diverse sources to combat a certain legislative move that will drastically affect their businesses. Once united for the purpose of addressing that issue, they find it practical and mutually beneficial to stay together. Even as the initial threat to their businesses is met and handled, new possibilities become evident and the need to push on as a group is recognized.

Some industries only realize the need for political action once disaster hits and it is nearly too late. Blitzed by a sudden change in leadership or an unexpected regulation, they try to strike back furiously. There is nothing like a regulatory bombshell to rouse a group of entrepreneurs to political action. That is precisely what happened to the country's real estate appraisers. Formed in 1991 in response to the news that the Federal Reserve Board was contemplating the change in the *de minimis* level at which property has to be appraised, the Appraisers Institute pulled together 2,000 members and a small budget. In 1994 the Appraisers Institute headed to Washington when the Fed announced in March that it was raising the *de minimis* level to $250,000. This would exempt between 90 and 95 percent of all real estate from appraisals.

The appraisal industry started up after the Great Depression as a way of valuing real property after the banking collapse. It was never regulated by any government institution, rather by trade groups that conferred official status on different levels of expertise. As Dominic Pompeio, an activist and residential appraiser who is spearheading a new drive to change the *de minimis* laws, explains:

Because we were never regulated or had any interaction with the government until the S&L debacle, our members found it abhorrent. When we tried to get them involved as far as contributing to PACs, they refused and saw it as a legal bribe and were strongly opposed to it. The membership was and is extremely naive about the political process

and PACs and industry groups and even how legislation is formulated,
so we've been a virtual punching bag for the other industries.

The Institute struck out in its first time at bat. As Douglas C. Brown, its president, notes, "We started making a name for ourselves on Capitol Hill. Now I realize just what an important role recognition plays in trying to get legislators to listen to your cause. Even if you lose the first round, you can always continue to fight."

The historic moment of the appraisers' quest is important, of course. Just after the savings and loan debacle of the late 1980s, there was a cry for more rigorous scrutiny up and down the lending ladder. About 50 percent of all losses were attributed to fraudulent appraisals. Although most saw it as shutting the barn door well after the horse was loose, a whole regulatory infrastructure grew up around real estate and lending. It was the appraisers' first brush with federal authority, but it also directly benefited the appraisers by institutionalizing the need for their services and boosting the values of those services.

Within a few years, the backlash started as banks and other businesses began to complain about the high cost of overregulation and its tendency to slow business to a crawl. Paradoxically, while the Appraisers Institute represents more than 2,000 small businesses—little firms with two or three senior appraisers, generally a couple of trainees and a small support staff—its aims are antithetical to the interests and aims of many groups looking for regulatory reform, since in effect the appraisers want to keep the regulations in place that require their services. Unfortunately, the same regulations impose added cost and compliance requirements upon other small businesses.

In its first attempt to change the *de minimis* rule, the Institute decided to close ranks with a few other lobbying groups that had been often adversarial—principally, the banking lobbies, including the American Bankers Association (ABA) and the Savings and Community Bankers of America, which had pushed for the new rulings because they were tired of paying high fees for appraisals. It enlisted both liberal and conservative groups, such as the Consumer Federation of America and the United Taxpayers Union, to bring back the old requirements and standardize licensing. But some of these industry groups quickly assumed the opposite position from that of the Institute when it came to the *de minimis* rule. Specifically, the much larger, and better funded, ABA decided to oppose the Appraisers Institute, so that the appraisers did not just have to deal with the government alone but with a big business lobby, too. They were not powerful enough to defeat the American Bankers Association. As Pompeio recounts:

> *We tried to fight it but couldn't get our membership motivated because of this reluctance to engage government. They beat the crap out of us. It was a disgrace, because we're a nonentity politically.*

The Institute drew Congressional attention by pointing out that its cause was not just to save its own business but to help lenders, home buyers, and others connected with real estate. The appraisers took their cause to Housing and Urban Development and FDIC officials, testified at House subcommittee meetings, drafted position papers, conducted letter-writing campaigns, and spread themselves out across Washington as well as they could.

The letter-writing campaign centered on a letter drafted with the Mortgage Insurance Companies of America, the American Society of Farm Managers and Rural Appraisers, and the American Society of Appraisers, which was hand delivered to the House Banking Committee's members. Letters of support also were pulled together from consumer interest groups, such as the Consumer Federation of America and the law firm Manatt, Phelps, and Phillips, which provided a letter of opinion giving a detailed argument on behalf of the appraisers.

The General Accounting Office (GAO) prepared a report for Congress on regulatory issues in real estate that seemed to support the Institute's position. By stressing the lack of qualifications of financial regulators, the report suggested that financial institutions needed the guidance of evaluations prepared by trained and accredited professionals. It also suggested that the evaluations required by financial institutions were not reliable enough. As the GAO report stated, "Without the proper guidance and procedures, regulators cannot adequately ensure that financial institutions use evaluations in a manner that will ensure safe and sound real estate lending practices while reducing regulatory burden."

At a Congressional hearing on March 1, 1994, House members took to the floor. Floyd H. Flake, a Democrat from New York, spoke on behalf of the role of professional appraisers in the lending process, and Charles Schumer, also a Democrat from New York, stressed that the independence of the appraiser is important to the consumer. Peter Deutsch, a Democrat from Florida, used his own experience as a land-use attorney to stress the importance of professional appraisers in the lending and management decisions affecting real property. They followed up the Congressional hearing by scheduling several meetings with the House Banking Committee (of which Flake is a member) and their staff.

As a result, Representative Flake and other members of the House Banking Committee sponsored an appraisal amendment to the 1994 housing bill, HR 3838, that would require the use of a licensed or certified appraiser for federally related real estate transactions no matter how large or small, which would effectively override the *de minimis* rule. The amendment was supported by Banking Committee chairman Henry B. Gonzalez, a Democrat from Texas who has since been replaced, but others, all of them Republicans, including Spencer Bachus from Alabama, tried to block it by making a point of order that the amendment was not germane to the bill. The Republicans also argued that the use of a licensed appraiser would raise the cost to consumers and pose an undue regulatory burden on lending institutions. They also denied that real estate transactions under the $250,000 threshold played a major part in the savings and loan disaster of the 1980s. Despite all the Institute's efforts, the amendment was defeated in June at the conclusion of a marathon twelve-hour session of the Banking committee.

At the end of the day, Douglas Brown observed, "The actions we have taken help the Appraisers Institute and our membership build a base of support with Congress for the integrity of the appraisal process."

The Retreat to State Level

Dominic Pompeio realized that on the federal level he can't beat the bank lobby, so he is working on mandatory licensing on the state level. Way out ahead of the Institute, Pompeio and a small group of New York–based appraisers are advancing their own regional agenda.

Pompeio figures that in states like Connecticut and Maine, 96.7 percent and 98 percent of all real estate, respectively, do not need appraisal for sales now. He predicts that 25 percent of appraisers will be out of the industry before the end of 1995, and eventually 40 percent will be driven out of business. The result? According to Pompeio:

The only positive aspect is that this is the first time that appraisers, who see that government has affected their lives, realize now that they have to be involved. It took being hurt for us to get any sort of motivation or cohesiveness. Our typical members are conservative, Republican, accountant-types with pocket protectors—your basic nerds. We're not exactly activists, but now we are forced to be.

Pompeio himself was a community activist in Brooklyn, trying unsuccessfully to save his old neighborhood, and is a persuasive, shrewd political player on the local scene. As he points out:

You don't have to be a big PAC to defeat bad legislation; you just have to raise your voice. The big boys have a lot of power, but they have a lot of issues and a lot of baggage. To satisfy us on one issue is easier than to satisfy them on the other 99. We don't carry a lot of the baggage that the large organizations carry.

There are both consumer and discrimination issues at stake; the law obviously reads differently for low-income individuals and small-capitalization firms. As Pompeio notes:

We work on behalf of the people buying their first homes—their largest single investment in their lives. We're the only ones watching out for the consumer and now, through politics, the banks are effectively taking us out of the system. We want the de minimis restored or for the law to specify that the appraisal has to be done by someone who is trained for it, subject to uniform standards, and subject to sanctions if they take a bribe, are negligent, or incompetent. Right now the only requirement is that the individual be knowledgeable about real estate—whatever that means!

You would think that these factors would weigh in the appraisers' favor, but as a small group they have not been able to leverage them into much political recognition. The prevailing force became the banks, which were fighting to regain control over loans from start to finish. One of the main problems is simply getting the appraisers to work together. As Pompeio jokes, "You can't get two appraisers in a room to agree on whether it's raining outside."

Pompeio's blunt manner offers one approach to the grassroots style of politicking. At a meeting with Congresswoman Marge Roukema in New Jersey, he knew that the ranking Republican on the house banking committee was initially against him. Leaning across the table he said in the most casual manner, "Marge, look at it this way. If you were driving in a cab would you say the cab driver needed to be licensed only to drive above 50 mph?" She answered that she had never thought of it that way, and became the only Republican that supported the appraisers. Pompeio also adds that at first only her staff would meet with him "and they were extremely arrogant. We were so upset that we had appraisers who lived in her district call her office and start kicking and screaming and threatening to picket her office. She called up and said, 'Hold them off, hold them off please.'" Now the appraisers attend her fund-raisers. As Pompeio concludes, "We're learning."

For the average appraiser, working in the trenches against bank deadlines and trying to grind out a living, these issues can seem fairly distant. A typical firm is Michael Axler and Associates of Manhattan, who specialize in commercial real estate but do some residential projects as well as hotels and motels. Axler, an affable and tremendously hard-working entrepreneur in his fifties, split off on his own from a larger appraisal group that was running into financial difficulties. He took with him one of the best appraisers in the group. Setting up shop in a modest office in midtown Manhattan, Axler worked his Rolodex and established a thriving business that ranges across the country but is concentrated in the greater New York area. Under his tutelage, his son as well as another intern is also on board as he builds his staff. Axler follows politics as a matter of course and is a staunch Republican.

At the end of a long day, Axler considers for a moment what Pompeio and the Appraisal Institute are trying to do politically. "It's worth it because it's a pressing issue," he says reflectively. Then he adds, with a shrug of the shoulders that tells it all: "But you know, it's not exactly going to ruin the economy, and I don't feel the need or urgency day to day to worry about this kind of issue." Then he reaches for his coat and he and his son make a dash for their commuter train and the two-hour ride home.

That slice of life, the glimpse of the entrepreneur wrapped up in his own busy world, is more devastating to activists like Dominic Pompeio than all the bank lobbyists in Washington combined.

THE SMALL BUSINESS AGENDA FOR GETTING ORGANIZED

With the rewards of networking so high, the means to get together—online or in person—have to be pursued. This is how small business can make it possible.

- Press Congress and federal agencies to institute electronic dockets for all proposed legislation and rule changes.
- Urge federal and state governments to expand the legislative information available on computer databases.
- Lobby for more funding and government support for federal and state computer networks linking government and small business at low cost.
- Lobby Congress to support the expansion of access to the Internet and other nongovernment computer networks that can give small business advocates a means of organizing.
- Urge the SBA to increase the frequency of the White House Conferences on Small Business to keep up with the pace of legislative change.
- Work with trade associations and other political entities that have an established political track record on the state or federal level.
- Start up new lobbying groups to address specific issues.
- Review legislation on political contributions to lobbying groups to make it possible for small businesses to have professional interest groups in Washington that can compete with those of major industries.

8

FACE TO FACE
When All Else Fails,
The Case for Fighting
Government

When you get an audience with your government, every little detail counts. Sometimes the civic-spirited, cooperative attitude with which entrepreneurs approach local or federal institutions is simply not enough. However it happens, the moment arrives when an entrepreneur's interaction with the government shifts from the comments and suggestions of a "stakeholder" to the dreaded adversarial role, from a participant in the regulatory process to the target of a regulatory inquiry. An official asks the questions; the owner-manager hopes to have the right answers. We are too late for policy debates and advocacy. The time to fight arrives.

GOING IT ALONE

It is 8:15 on a sunny May morning and the entire top management team of Arts and Events Inc. is packed into a shiny new hunter green Lexus parked on Lexington Avenue around the corner from 42nd Street in New York City. The two founding partners of the specialized tour and event management company, Lisa Hahn and Ellen Sax, with their silent partner Bill Kulok at the wheel of his car, are going over strategy for a 9:30 meeting with the New York State Bureau of Labor. The encounter has them so worried that they are considering throwing in the towel on their eleven-year-old business. Ostensibly, all that is at stake is a tax assessment for $7,000 based on the nonexempt status of freelance lecturers they hire to address the corporate and museum groups who sign up for their tours of private art collections, artists' studios, and galleries in Manhattan and around the world. But if they lose this first battle, new fronts open up: workmen's compensation, benefits, Social Security, the Internal Revenue Service. The downside risk is high.

With a tiny staff of two assistants, Sax and Hahn also have managed to arrange tours for as many as a thousand people who attend conferences in New York as well as Laguna Beach, California; Aspen, Colorado; and other locations that they scout out in advance and create special programs for. Their profits come from the service fees that they charge. Many of their best customers are museums that bring groups of patrons or "friends" on tours that include a donation to the museum as part of the package tour deal. Because the museum takes a donation on top of the costs of travel, the added cost of Arts and Events in terms of service fees has to be kept down, and the travel business, which is highly competitive, does not allow for much in the way of a profit margin.

The total amount in back taxes that Arts and Events may owe is not overwhelming by most standards, but that $7,000 is also the difference between profitability and another year in the red. For Hahn and Sax the anxiety over money may be the last straw in a partnership that, like many others, has its stress points. When they first joined forces, Hahn and Sax viewed their partnership as a perfect blend of complementaries. Sax, at 51, is older, well-connected in the entertainment industry (particularly television), and experienced in the ins and outs of corporate entertaining on a grand scale, having organized client conferences for massive trade groups like the American Council of Shopping Centers as well as corporate giants like the Scudder Funds, Morgan Grenfell Bank, American Express, Xerox, and Gerber. Hahn, Sax's junior by about fifteen years but more sophisticated in terms of her art history training (in archaeology, her major at Princeton, and museum management, which she studied at the master's level at New York University), is attuned to the needs of a young, more intellectual clientele interested in specialized art study programs.

Between them, they figured, they could bring in high-end business among corporate clients looking for events management as well as smaller museum groups of affluent patrons who would enjoy brief guided study tours combining art museums, galleries, private collections, and artists' studios. Sax and Hahn quickly built a client list that included many of the most powerful museums in America and Europe, including New York's Museum of Modern Art, the Metropolitan Museum, and the Guggenheim Museum; the Art Institute of Chicago; and the Royal Academy in London—and added a number of big-name corporate clients. But expenses are bound to remain high when you want to impress top-end patrons, and the constant struggle to make it into the black took its toll on their friendship as well as their business. This incursion of the government into their business could, they both realized, be the ax head that split them in two.

The three partners think they have studied the law and precedents as far as they can and have been busy devising a list of questions they anticipate they will be asked. Unfortunately, their understanding of what is about to happen, shaped as it is by their experiences with the Internal Revenue Service (IRS) audits, is distorted. Their information on the law regarding employees and independent contractors is incomplete and out of date, and six months after this they will learn that a batch of letters and documents sent by the Bureau of Labor to an address that Arts and Events has not used for two years never reached them. Nervous, prepared in all but the ways they should be, they are heading into the unknown. By common consent, they have elected to leave their attorney behind, in the belief that his presence would only serve to alienate the government interviewer. According to sources at the Bureau of Labor as well as small business activists, this was the right move.

To help bolster their contention that the lecturers they hire are independent contractors and not employees, they have brought along Elinor Perry, an assistant professor of art history at Hunter College and one of the lecturers they use regularly on the art study programs. Right from the beginning, Perry is showing signs of nervousness regarding her own tax status. As the morning unfolds, we see a textbook example of the tension-filled relationship between small business and government when they come together face to face. Nerves are frayed. Paranoia is inevitable. Misunderstandings rule the day.

As Bill Kulok gingerly pulls into traffic and heads to the Brooklyn Bridge, the others continue to pore over trick questions and earlier cases. The problem is that the state is cracking down on tour companies that do not deduct taxes from their payments to guides. The challenge is to prove that their lecturers are not tour guides but freelance contractors who are not under the day-to-day direction of Arts and Events. The key to determining whether or not they are employees, and subject to withholdings both for tax and Social Security, or freelancers working for a fee, lies in finding out if the employer exercises a certain degree of supervision and control over them.

According to the IRS, the degree of control is measured by a set of 20 guidelines that includes such factors as whether the employee is trained by the company, is providing services that are integrated into the company's business, is assisted by the company's employees, has a continuing working relationship with the company, has to follow a set work schedule and is paid regularly, works on the premises, has travel and business expenses reimbursed, relies on the company for tools and materials, must submit reports, and can be fired by the company or can quit at any time without incurring liability.

Lost in Transition

More philosophically, the focus of the problem becomes the definition of an employee. One point of division between cutting-edge businesses run according to the latest ideas in management and the government agencies assigned to police them is a type of generation gap between them. In the eyes of many entrepreneurs, the government's official concept of what an employee is, or how business ought to be conducted, is hopelessly out of date. The IRS and Bureau of Labor have one particular view of what an employee is—a view that has been on the books for more than a decade under the Unemployment Insurance Law. But the concept of an employee has changed in most industries, so that different companies, and even workers themselves, have their own view of what an employee is. (In September 1994, a *Fortune* magazine cover story under the headline "The End of the Job?" took a hard look at the rapidly changing nature of the job.)

Despite the evolution of labor relations during the past few years, the government holds on to its old definitions and interpretations. Consider also the way in which government employees view their jobs—secure, by-the-clock, and old-fashioned relationships in a highly structured framework that resembles American corporate life in the 1950s. It is no wonder that the government auditors and examiners have difficulty, from a personal perspective, in seeing the changes that are occurring out there in the real workforce.

So far, the major advocacy groups have not been much help to small businesses like Arts and Events when it comes to issues involving labor. The National Federation of Independent Businesses (NFIB), for example, is noted for its conservative stance regarding all labor legislation. It has taken a firm stand against increasing or indexing the federal minimum wage, against mandating parental and medical leave, against mandatory safety committees and the expansion of employer criminal penalties for violations of OSHA standards, against giving more power to the unions, against legislation that bars teenagers from the workplace. While the NFIB and other small business lobbying groups have their solid and well-reasoned arguments for the tough positions they have taken, the result is that the atmosphere surrounding small business and the Department of Labor is very tense indeed.

That is the kind of adversarial situation facing Arts and Events. It all started with a state tax audit at their offices in March 1993. As the auditor examined the books, he was looking for subcontractors who are paid on a noncontract, nonhourly basis. His report flagged a group of about one hundred payments to lecturers, musicians, and other services—like a calligrapher—that the state is looking into. The meeting at the Labor Department is a prehearing investigation by the auditor's supervisor to determine whether the lecturers ought to be considered tour guides. If the supervisor feels that the lecturers and others are indeed freelancers, the investigation can be dismissed. If he feels that they are under a sufficient degree of control from Sax and Hahn, he will pass their file to an administrative law judge for a formal hearing.

Close Encounters of the Worst Kind

The Arts and Events team arrive at the Bureau of Labor building early. In the lobby, a guard's head is just visible over a massive mahogany desk, framed by the state and American flags. Two guards challenge them for identification and bruskly tell them there is no waiting in the lobby. They are directed at first to the wrong floor, where rows of metal chairs are set up for formal hearings. Joking Labor Department officers in ties and short-sleeve shirts hang around the elevators. There is no laughter among the people sitting quietly in the rows of chairs waiting for their hearings. At one point Kulok, glancing through an open doorway into a large common office space where among a sea of empty desks a few Bureau examiners worked in silence, articulates the feelings of distance and distaste shared by each visitor: "It's a whole other world from ours."

At last, visibly nervous and confused, the Arts and Events team find the correct floor and stand awkwardly in the doorway of a large open office while an administrative assistant goes to find the supervisor they are scheduled to meet. Ushered into a tiny windowless room to wait, in hushed voices they continue to plot their strategy. On the bulletin board hanging on the scuffed white walls with beige plastic trim are official notices, such as "NYS Department of Labor Policy Statement on Sexual Harassment."

The case supervisor enters. A balding, heavyset man in his forties, he is soft-spoken, initially cheerless, and attentive. He wears the unofficial summer uniform of the supervisors seen elsewhere in the building, with his collar unbuttoned, gray polyester pants, patterned tie, a striped short-sleeved shirt. His name is Matthew Rothbaum, and he is the supervisor of James Walkins, who nearly a year before prepared the audit forms. Not terribly well-organized, it takes Rothbaum at least fifteen minutes to find the right documents in his immense manila folder. The paperwork in the manila folder in front of him became gradually more and more disordered as the meeting progresses.

At first Rothbaum refers to a blue carbon copy of the report of audit filed by Walkins—its columns of numbers telling a three-year story of tiny payments to subcontractors, of as little as $25 and $75 in many cases, that had been flagged as possible tour guides. A batch paid to people in Brazil have captured the supervisor's attention. Thirty minutes into the meeting and his brow is beaded with sweat. The pace of the questions picks up. He asks whether the lectures are advertised. He wants to know if Hahn is a partner or the vice president. Every catch in the voice, every contradiction is noticed. He levels his stare at each speaker and pauses a moment before responding. But he also chuckles at the jokes.

Explaining her role in the business, Perry inadvertently uses the word "tour." Rothbaum pounces: "Did you say tour? So these are tours?" The word is quickly corrected. "Actually, it is more like a seminar on the art of a certain region or period," Hahn volunteers, trying to take the heat off. At this point, Rothbaum leaves the room momentarily to make a photocopy. "I hate this," Hahn gasps. "I always flunked the trick questions on the SATs, even though I know they are in there." Implicitly, there are trick questions. "Why did he dig that stuff up about the musicians and the people in Brazil?" she asks. "He was fishing," Kulok points out. They chug down their little conical paper cups of water under the rush of the air conditioning.

Rothbaum returns with the photocopies and asks them to make a list of the lecturers drawn from the payments. He flips through case papers while he waits for them to finish the list. Perry is asked for her résumé, but suddenly she takes it back and puts it in her briefcase, worried that it indicates she works for Arts and Events. Rothbaum leaves the room again to make more copies and the tension mounts. "He was concerned that we didn't show it," Kulok points out. Right away they decide Perry should give him her résumé, but a lingering doubt persists that the damage to their credibility has already been done.

Kulok, sotto voce, points out, "We're not under oath here." They have been asked by Rothbaum to sort out the lecturers from other contractors, and they have to decide what to call a few scarcely remembered subcontractors, who are about to become computer experts rather than tour guides. When Rothbaum returns he takes Perry's résumé, expressionless. The questioning has petered out, but there is no indication that the Arts and Events team has provided all the answers he needs. He notes that the interpretation of the service category is "very vague." There are hints that the decision the company is hoping for today, at this meeting, will have to be postponed. He will have to get the file out and study the cases some more before he can proceed. The machine has ground to a halt. "The individuals we picked up in the audit could be dropped, but I'd like you to go over the audit and I have to be one hundred percent sure that these people are lecturers."

That phrase—one hundred percent sure—is the key to the whole experience. You have to give the official the sense of one hundred percent assurance or he will not move in your favor. It is also worth noting the phrase "picked up" and all its connotations—caught, pulled over as though by a police cruiser.

Mr. Rothbaum is clearly running out of steam and disinclined to weigh in on either side of the issue. He states with some degree of regret that he cannot do anything but pass on his recommendation to the powers that be in Albany. He draws a deep breath and summarizes: "I have to call Albany. I don't know if it will be today. There's one case, with about two sentences in it, that could help me." He needs a precedent. A squeaky chair outside grates on the nerves. There may be a hearing. With a smile, Kulok asks, "And will we have the pleasure of your company at the hearing?" It is greeted with a smile, but his auditor will probably handle the case.

At this stage, the Arts and Events team, who have been hoping for a conclusive indication of where they stand, are visibly disappointed. They do not know who in Albany will be considering their case, or when it will be handled. Kulok asks if they can expect an answer by the end of the week, but it is clear from Mr. Rothbaum's facial expression that the idea of such swift justice is way overoptimistic.

The Postmortem Begins

Arts and Events has been caught in an issue. They are not just one case that is to be handled on its own merits. If the government decides to target a particular category or classification, then it's vital for a business like Art and Events to get out of the cul-de-sac by redefining itself in the eyes of the government. The less they referred to "tourism" and the more distance they place between themselves and the tourism industry, the better off they are going to be.

Arts and Events made many mistakes. The partners erred in not providing their own photocopies of materials and in not handing over the lecturer's résumé right away when Rothbaum asked for it. They also failed to make a dramatic enough distinction between their lecturers and ordinary tour guides. Rothbaum is also to blame for some of the problems during the meeting. He erred in not fully understanding the nature of their business, particularly its more serious educational aspect, and the type of lecturing that the company does to prepare its clients for art exhibitions in museums. This is not to say that by association with art or education a business can be whitewashed of all its liability and responsibilities to the government, but the difference between Manhattan's thousands of tour packagers and Arts and Events is far more pronounced than Rothbaum grasped. Because of his hazy sense of what they do and how many people it takes to do it, Rothbaum was unable to make a firm decision on the basis of the information provided.

As any owner-manager knows, delay is costly. Without a timely decision, Arts and Events had to put its plans for expansion and its budget on hold. The delay also guaranteed that more time would be spent on dealing with the problem, and for a business that does not have an in-house legal staff or the money for outside counsel, this meant that valuable time had to be spent on detail-oriented problem-solving activities that are outside of the revenue stream. Dealing with the government does not bring in new clients, nor does it add to sales. The entire top level of Arts and Events had been out of the office at least half a day for an indecisive prehearing meeting.

"It could affect so many aspects of what we do," Sax complains. She is less and less eager to drum up new business, while Hahn is disenchanted with the corporate clients and wants to forge ahead with the museum groups and arts-oriented work she prefers. The old synergy they used to have is giving way to a creeping awareness of their differences and the likelihood that they will part ways. More than the financial blow, the damage to morale and their sense of enjoying the business has taken its toll.

More than four months later, the letter arrives from the Department of Labor in Albany. Arts and Events, despite a valiant effort, has lost. "We find we must adhere to our original determination that the lecturers, calligrapher, musicians, and songwriter were your employees," the letter opens. Beyond noting that the company had a "sufficient degree of supervision, direction, and control to establish an employee relationship," the letter, signed by an Unemployment Insurance division reviewing examiner named Audrey Branion, also pointed out that many of the other freelancers were employees based on the Unemployment Insurance Law, part of which is quoted at length. As if to highlight the disparity between the high-brow, perfectionist style of Arts and Events, which carefully edits all the literature it hands out to its participants, and the slovenly style of the Labor Department, the letter is full of misspellings and typographical errors—addressed to Ms. Ellen Sax, its salutation reads, "Dear Mr. Sax," and ends "The case file has been forarded..." After a four-month delay, a sloppy, half-literate notification in bureaucratese is not exactly the way for the government to command respect or cheerful cooperation.

The hearing before an administrative law judge is the next step in the case. It occurs in January 1995 and takes two and a half gruelling hours of taped interrogation by a judge who fires a rapid series of questions about the lecturers at Hahn and then adjourns the session without a decision. The outlook does not seem bright—but after a second three-hour hearing in February, the judge rules in favor of Arts and Events. However, the damage has already been done.

At the end of 1994, Hahn, Sax, and Kulok had dissolved the company. The breakup was bitter. Kulok decided to take a tax write-off on his loss and move to Florida. Hahn incorporated a new company called Art Horizons under her own name and pressed on with a reduced client list and one assistant. Sax went into semiretirement. In their eyes, the Bureau of Labor had essentially driven them out of business. From a sympathetic standpoint it looks like just another case of "you can't fight City Hall."

PUTTING UP A BETTER FIGHT

Even if it is late in the game in terms of regulatory action, an individual case like that of Arts and Events can have an impact on an industry and other small businesses. The issue of whether workers are independent contractors or employees is a burning topic in the legal field, and it is particularly important to the small business community. In a feature story on the problem as it relates to the messenger industry that appeared in *Inc.* magazine in September 1994, the application of the law to bicycle messengers is used as a focal point for the discussion of how widespread the ramifications are likely to be if businesses like Arts and Events lose their legal battles about the definition of contractors.

As the *Inc.* feature makes clear, the first level of inquiry is not the last possible point of vulnerability for a business, since a redefinition of contractors that makes them employees can touch off a domino-like progression of other problems. Once the Labor Department has ruled on the contractors, the case goes back to the IRS and a determination of back taxes, albeit within limits set for small business (generally $15,000). Then the Labor Department may have to inquire into whether any overtime is owed to retroactive employees, and an employee benefits package worked out. As the messenger companies are learning, the problems can go even further. In addition to being suddenly responsible for benefit programs, they could also face unionization among drivers and messengers, which would push wages through the roof.

The history of the recent crackdown extends back to the early 1970s, when the IRS went after the classification question until lobbying groups fought back. In 1973, Congress passed a very liberal safe-harbor provision, called Section 530, that was designed especially for small businesses. They qualified for a break on payroll taxes if they could meet a number of tests, including continuous and accurate 1099 records, "consistent use" of independent contractors rather than a mix of contractors and employees, and something the IRS called "reasonable basis," which meant that the use of freelancers was in line with industry practice or their own traditional way of doing business.

Although that provision kept the IRS at bay for a period of time, by 1985 they were back again test-auditing independent contractors in seven districts. When the agency learned that there were widespread abuses, involving nonpayment of taxes that they now calculate to be about $2 billion in lost revenues every year, they decided to make the Section 530 provisions more stringent. Audits are way up; after all, it is easier to go after a company that employs fifty or so messengers or lecturers or accountants or construction workers than it is to hunt down those fifty who are likely, the IRS maintains, to underreport their income from freelance contracting. The IRS points out that the official tally of independent contractors went from 12 million in 1985 to 15 million by 1990.

The jump in numbers is mainly thanks to three disparate trends: outsourcing, the vitality of start-ups, and a fear on the part of all businesses to face the costs in benefits as well as workplace litigation when having employees rather than contractors. All three trends have shown surprising longevity. Outsourcing became a buzzword in 1990 when the back office operations of major banks and investment concerns—as well as the support manufacturing needed by major appliance, car, and computer companies—were farmed out to smaller, more specialized firms that worked on a contract basis. For the large corporations that took advantage of the idea, the savings were considerable. It wasn't long before small businesses saw the positive impact of outsourcing on their bottom lines.

The Government Picks a Moving Target

But outsourcing and the economic benefits of contractors became a balloon that finally rose high enough for the government to notice it and take aim. While small businesses like Arts and Events put up only token resistance to the state's aggressive attempts to recategorize workers, others have elected to fight tooth and nail. As the story in *Inc.* relates it, Kevin Gallagher and George Hraha, owner-managers of Quicksilver Messenger Service in Chicago, have taken on the state Department of Employment Security and the IRS with lawyers, accountants, industry associations on the local and national level, and obviously the press. They have invested months of their own time and thousands of dollars on the reclassification challenge, which threatens to virtually close down their $1.2-million-a-year business, which just celebrated its tenth anniversary. For Gallagher, that means about 20 percent of his time is spent proving that his 30 car and 15 bike messengers are freelancers.

As even the pro–small business magazine has to admit, it looks like Gallagher is headed to martyrdom. Since the industry standard is to use contractors, Gallagher is fighting the battle for his competitors as well. Quicksilver was audited by the IRS for the first time in 1989 after his office manager applied for unemployment and the words "courier service" on his application alerted the state labor board. The company was audited for every year from 1987 through 1990 on taxes, and Gallagher spent the last two years in audits, hearings, and appeals at the state and federal levels.

Gallagher was first assessed $15,000 in back taxes, which cost him $25,000 in legal fees to fight. Then he got a letter of liability from the IRS stating that he owed $80,729 in back taxes. In order to survive the nine hours of testimony before the State Department of Employment Security, Gallagher has hired lawyers, accountants, and a consultant who once worked for the state in the same department. As with Arts and Events, Gallagher is caught in an issue, and the category is not one that the state or federal agencies is likely to let go of now that their bulldog grip is on it. After two appeals, Gallagher told *Inc.*, "We'll take it as far as I can financially afford to take it."

Gallagher did not shy away from political activism. Back in 1992, to push for a state exemption he worked together with his lawyer and a former Illinois state representative to write and file a House bill specifically letting courier companies off the hook from penalties for using contractors. The lobbyist cost him $3,500 for the first four months, after which he raised another $20,000 for the lobbyist's services through a group of messenger services. If the bill passed, the lobbyist would get another $20,000 from the group. The main obstacle to the bill is getting the unions to sign off on it, which has to happen before it goes to a vote. Even the state Department of Employment has signed off on it, but the problem of getting labor to settle has held it up.

Gallagher has also gone to the federal level for one of the weapons he has brought to the fray. He is hoping to benefit from the political clout of his national lobbying group, the Expedited Package

Independent Contractors Council (EPIC), which is pressing for exemptions for the messenger industry on the federal level. The executive director of EPIC is Joe Morris, who told *Inc.* that he does not see the issue being resolved in favor of the messenger companies anytime soon. The cause was not warmly received at the usually pro–small business White House, because it interferes with President Clinton's health-care agenda, which relies on employees rather than contractors, and it is antiunion.

Gallagher's other strategy is to grow big enough to spread out the overhead of having employees and generate sufficient revenue to survive reclassification. He recently bought out another messenger service and is hoping to push sales to $5 million a year. Reasoning that it takes a bigger and more structured organization to comply with state and federal rules, Gallagher is ready to invest in a growth program to protect himself rather than pouring more money down the rathole of a lobbying campaign that has the odds against it.

Gallagher was still mired in the appeals process in February 1995; his bill, still alive, was held up by a reshuffling of the Illinois state House and Senate, both of which have a Republican majority. Although he is not betting the farm on its passage, Gallagher remains guardedly optimistic: "With the Republicans in office, it could be better, but I'm not too excited one way or another—it just depends on which way the winds blow politically." The *Inc.* article about his crusade brought supportive letters from a whole range of small business people, from the owners of nail salons to accountants, who are similarly affected by the independent contractor issue. Reflecting on his struggle with both state and federal authorities, Gallagher has become philosophical about the need for cooperation between government and small business: "Basically the problem could be resolved if both parties worked together. After all, the IRS could make better use of their time and money by targeting the 1099s that don't match with tax returns, and there's no reason they couldn't ask the companies to help locate the independent contractors. That way we could preserve the independent contractor classification, save companies from going out of business, hold on to jobs, and the IRS would get the revenues."

TURNING ON THE POLITICAL POWER

Between the quiet compliance of Arts and Events and the feisty defiance of Quicksilver Messenger Service, the solution to how one deals with a basic regulatory challenge must be found. In both cases, highly intelligent business minds were confounded by a government snare that cut deeply into their ability to work and into their budgets. Their ability to strategically plot the course of their business in the coming years is now impaired by uncertainties arising from what the government is doing. How could all this have been avoided?

A little political radar detection would have helped. Both companies were surprised to be "picked up" in a government audit. If you are bombing down the highway as fast as you can go in a red Ferrari and are nevertheless astonished to see flashing lights suddenly appear behind you, then you don't know the road and the mentality of state troopers who are trained to spot a certain type of vehicle from miles away. It would have been far better for both companies if they had realized their businesses were in a category that was attracting special attention from the state labor and tax officials. An early warning of the coming crackdown would have given them the chance to fight on the outside for exemptions or legislative change, and reconfigure on the inside to avoid the classification that is under scrutiny.

Although the solid work ethic of minding one's own business and pushing hard to build up an organization and clientele is admirable, both companies should have been paying attention to what was going on not just in their industries but in the service field in general, where regulators have been circling for more than six years looking for cases that they can use to make examples. The logic of using one highly publicized case against a minor entity to deter larger and more numerous companies from testing the law is captured in an ancient Chinese proverb that states, "Kill the chicken to scare the monkeys."

By learning about the thinking behind the crackdown, Arts and Events, for example, could have changed some of the wording on business cards and brochures and built up the paperwork that would have allowed it to slip out of the tour company classification. There might also have been time to work, through industry associations and individually, on legislation in Albany or even Washington to exempt educational tourism from being targeted along with all other kinds.

While Hahn and Sax were reluctant to join a tourism association just before their audit for fear of being lumped together with others and confirming the state's suspicions, the political savvy and information from an industry association could have helped.

The trouble for both companies is that they reacted to government moves against them. They never worked proactively before the government arrived. Giving the state auditors the first move in the tick-tack-toe game is the same as placing your company in the position of automatically coming out with a draw, or losing. The first move is so much more valuable. If Gallagher had launched his legislative drive for an exemption before the audits had started he could have stood a chance, even if it did mean spending $40,000 for a lobbyist.

Once the battle was engaged, both companies could have maneuvered more skillfully. The all-out confrontational approach taken by Gallagher probably drew more attention and a more concerted effort from the state. By contrast, the confused and uncertain demeanor of Arts and Events may have cost them their opportunity to escape classification because they did not present their case clearly or effectively when they were given the chance to do so. With the right legal counsel and a sense of what the government agenda is, the owner-manager has a fighting chance against being swept up in an issue like this one. Failing to define what the auditors want or need in terms of assurance and information, both companies ended up on the losing side.

For its part, the government agencies that pressed these cases are also prone to mistakes. They are behind the times when it comes to the new compact between business and its employees. The government also struggles to understand the highly individualized nature of many small businesses, such as the ways in which Arts and Events is different from most tour operations. By insistently attempting to fit a niche business into a broader category, the state sometimes loses touch with what that business really does. There is little or no effort at educating or consulting with small businesses to give them a sense of the law and how it works. Before agencies such as the Bureau of Labor haul in a victim or send out an inspection or auditing team, they ought to balance this kind of enforcement with technical guidance. That is the key to voluntary compliance. Finally, the protracted period it takes for bureaucrats to conclude an investigation and hand down a ruling is crippling for business. While the excuse of heavy caseloads is a common one, in a time of computerization and rapid communication it should not take four months for a decision to filter back to a company on a matter as simple as this.

These are not just tales of woe; they are stories about misunderstanding, cultural clashes, and the fundamental division between government and small business on the most basic level. When the two meet face to face, they scarcely know each other. It may have been too late for these entrepreneurs to learn who and what they were dealing with, but we can only hope that those who follow in their footsteps will have a far better idea of where they are going inside the government labyrinth.

WHEN FIGHTING MEANS WINNING

Not every journey into the labyrinth has to turn out this way, however. Many small businesses have not only survived close encounters of the political kind but have managed to turn around entrenched policies for their own benefit and that of the industry they represent. With confidence, skill, a knowledge of the laws, and as always, a bit of good timing and luck, the politically savvy entrepreneur can fight City Hall and win.

As a dramatic illustration of how small business can carry the day, consider the ongoing, nationwide battle between small business advocates and state governments over changes in zoning and environmental laws that allow so-called "big box retailers" to move into regions with the threat of driving out local small retailers. This proved to be one of the most fascinating socio-political developments in the business world during 1994, because in many instances the small business forces, with the help of local political activists, were able to keep the Wal-Mart and Kmart and Tops outlets out of town.

In legal and political moves, and even pickets and protest marches, that have so far been targeted mainly at Wal-Mart, the small business forces and 40 local organized groups have fought the expansion of Wal-Mart into places like Lake Placid, New York; Oceanside, California; Gaithersburg, Maryland; Quincy, Massachusetts; Gallatin, Tennessee; and Norwich, Vermont. Wal-Mart gave up on plans to put stores in three other Massachusetts towns, as well as Bath, Maine; Simi

Valley, California; and Ross and West Hempfield, Pennsylvania—although Wal-Mart adds more than a hundred stores a year to its more than 2,000 outlets. In the other locations, Wal-Mart's real estate management team is trying to cool the movement by promising "green store" environmentally friendly policies.

The coalition of small businesses and local activists uses town meetings, advertisements, letter-writing and faxes, and full-blown press campaigns, including articles and editorials, to push its case with town supervisors and state assemblies. The colorful composition of the coalition forces was a blessing for nationally syndicated columnists and business journalists covering the story. It brought together the typically conservative owner-managers of the community with former Vietnam War–era protestors and environmentalists—"hippies" or "aging activists," in the words of The Wall Street Journal's October 1994 front-page story that covered the phenomenon. That exposure and other articles in Time, Newsweek, and many newspapers—as well as a two-week series of "Doonesbury" comic strips on the fight against Wal-Mart—started a six-month slide in Wal-Mart's stock that cut its price in half.

More importantly, the veteran activists brought their expertise regarding protests and media campaigns to the aid of the small business community and showed owner-managers how to turn around government policy through the manipulation of public opinion. For small businesses nationwide, the encouraging news was not simply that a few towns were saved from "colonization" by Wal-Mart, but that state and local policies that were devised to raise tax revenues at the expense of small businesses, many of which were doomed by the policy changes, could be reversed by the mobilization of an activist community. It was also significant to note how rapidly a few local brushfires turned into a national issue. The forty different activist groups arose individually in disparate communities, but the success of a few helped the others both morally and politically, building pressure through precedents and media attention.

Making All the Right Moves

Sometimes, taking on the federal government depends on finding a very focused issue and approaching it when the right people are in office. At least, that is what the nation's independent booksellers found when they decided to overturn a seemingly minor rule regarding the kinds of businesses that are eligible for Small Business Administration (SBA) loans. In this case, the small business forces successfully won a decision to allow media-related businesses, for the first time, to participate in the loan programs.

For over forty years, businesses such as bookstores, publishing companies, movie theaters, and advertising agencies have been unable to obtain SBA loan guarantees under an "opinion molder" restriction, which kept government apart from businesses that influence public opinion. The law was originally designed to safeguard the general populace against propaganda and government control of the media. Paradoxically, by cutting off an important source of support for independent bookstores and others it has turned out to be a means for administrations that are nervous about opposing points of view to simply repress them. What started as a noble gesture toward maintaining the independence of the media ended up as a menace to the First Amendment. But it roused a previously disengaged—you could even say dormant—part of the small business community to political action, and their success offers a textbook case of how entrepreneurs can shape public policy.

The change in SBA rules did not come about overnight or on its own. It stemmed from an articulate and determined lobbying effort that engaged many of the nation's independent booksellers, who had previously, despite their leadership role in many communities, been strangers to politics. The nonpolitical history of booksellers may seem strange given the fact that for small towns they are a principal source of information on public policy through their offerings in politics, biography, business, history, and periodical sections and are gathering places for the intellectually active members of a community. While some bookstores have a decidedly political angle and cater to sympathetic customers, a good general bookstore pleases a wide spectrum of readers by remaining objective.

But sitting by passively while others have the assistance of the federal government does not make sense. That is why the American Booksellers Association (ABA) stepped in to challenge the opinion molder rule. A trade association founded in 1900 and representing

4,552 retail bookstores (with more than 7,000 locations nationwide), the ABA is headquartered in Tarrytown, New York, just north of Manhattan. Among the sharpest arrows in the ABA's quill are its combined size and its ability to say that it speaks for the very small enterprise. Bookstores make up a significant part of the national retail economy, accounting for $8.8 billion in sales in 1992, according to the Bureau of the Census Current Retail Trade Branch of the Department of Commerce. They employ 72,000 people and pay them about $600 million a year. But most of the ABA's members do $125,000 a year or less in annual sales and employ fewer than five people.

The ABA's director of government affairs is Oren Teicher, who was even a bit surprised at how politically charged up his members became in changing the SBA rule. As Teicher recalls, the early going was pretty rough:

> We tried to get the rule changed during the Bush years and got nowhere with the SBA, which did not have an iota of interest. The senior staff of the SBA were intransigently opposed to the change because they perceived it as a way to have another excuse to deny folks access to loans to people who had different political views than their own. It was an unspoken way for them to frown on the First Amendment.

The turning point was the 1992 election, and Teicher suddenly found that the White House and the SBA were far more receptive. "We got a hearing! At the very beginning there was a difference between their willingness to deal with us. At least with Erskine Bowles we had a forum and there was a willingness to hear us out. For all our members, that was a breath of fresh air," says Teicher, with a touch of wonder still in his voice. Among the other issues he and his organization are addressing are antitrust matters involving trade publishers and a perpetual string of First Amendment infringements that are the meat and potatoes of his work. Teicher's successful campaign to change one specific aspect of SBA policy, however, stands as a paradigm for the effect that small business owner-managers can have in Washington if they play their cards right.

Win or lose, small businesses have to address the need to fight and have to know that they have the right to fight. As long as official Washington claims that it is on their side, small business activists can expect a break or two, but the opposition inside the bureaucratic machine can be solid and intimidating. Since the cycle of public opinion and public policy is currently in the favor of small business activists, the time to wage these fights—and lay the groundwork for an even more favorable regulatory environment—is now.

THE SMALL BUSINESS AGENDA FOR EFFECTING POLITICAL CHANGE

Although it is far from ideal, the situation does arrive when you have to fight government. To improve your chances in the contest, it's important to:

- Pick your spots. The more focused and detail-specific the campaign the better its chances for success.
- Pick your friends. Small business is finding an unlikely variety of allies in the activist community who are helping to get positive results.
- Know the enemy, by taking the time to find out who the local and federal government officials are and what their agenda is.
- Do your homework regarding the most up-to-date versions of the applicable laws as well as the recent legislative history so you know the direction regulation is taking before arguing your case.
- Start on the local level and build toward bigger issues.
- Enlist the press, and use the editorial and op/ed pages of local newspapers, as well as talk radio and local television, to get the point across.
- Keep the courts as a backup, since successful lawsuits against the government are not quick or cheap.
- Play to the heart as well as the pocketbook of public opinion, which tends to idealize small-town life and the family values that small business epitomizes.

FOR FURTHER

READING

For Further Reading

Batra, Ravi, *The Myth of Free Trade: A Plan for America's Economic Revival* (New York: Scribner's 1993).

Bennett, Steven J., Richard Freierman and Stephen George, *Corporate Realities and Environmental Truths: Strategies for Leading Your Business in the Environmental Era* (New York: Wiley, 1993).

Breaking Into the Trade Game: A Small Business Guide to Exporting (AT&T and Small Business Administration, 1994, available from the Small Business Administration).

Falkenberg, Georgia and Ann McCabe, *Participating in the Rulemaking Process: A Comment Preparation Guide* (Amoco Corporation, Regulatory Affairs Department, Chicago, 1993).

Edwards, Paul and Sarah, *Working from Home* (New York: Jeremy P. Tarcher, 1994).

Federal Register, Semiannual Regulatory Agenda, available from the Department of Commerce.

Harrison, Bennett, *Lean and Mean: The Changing Landscape of Corporate Power in the Age of Flexibility* (New York: Basic Books, 1994).

Howard, Philip K., *The Death of Common Sense: How Law is Suffocating America* (New York: Random House, 1995).

Kohlmeier, Louis M., *The Regulators: Watchdog Agencies and the Public Interest* (New York: Harper & Row, 1969).

Legislative Priorities, an annual publication of the National Federation of Independent Business.

Maynard, Herman Bryant and Susan E. Mehrtens, *The Fourth Wave: Business in the 21st Century* (San Francisco: Berrett-Koehler, 1993).

Small Business Forum on Regulatory Reform: Findings and Recommendation of the Industry Working Groups (Washington: July 1994, available from the Small Business Administration and Office of Management and Budget).

Tax Guide for Small Business, available annually from the Internal Revenue Service.

PART FIVE

DIRECTORY OF

RESOURCES

Directory of Resources

American Booksellers Association
828 South Broadway
Tarrytown, NY 10591
Tel: 914-591-2665; 800-637-0037;
    914-591-2720
Director of Government Affairs:
    Oren J. Teicher

American Small Business Association
1800 North Kent St.
Arlington, VA 22209
Tel: 800-235-3298

European Council of American
    Chambers of Commerce
21 Ave. George V
F 75008
Paris, France
Tel: 33-1-472-38026

Independent Small Business
    Employers of America
520 South Pierce St., Suite 224
Mason City, IA 50401
Tel: 515-424-3187

International Council for Small
    Business
Saint Louis University
3674 Lindell Blvd.
St. Louis, MO 63108
Tel: 314-658-3896

National Association of Private
    Enterprise
Box 612147
Dallas, TX 75261-2147
Tel: 817-428-4236

National Association of Small
Business Investment Companies
1199 North Fairfax St., Suite 200
Alexandria, VA 22314
Tel: 703-683-1601

National Association of the Self-
Employed
Box 612067
Dallas, TX 75261-2067
Tel: 800-551-4446

National Association of Women
Business Owners (NAWBO)
1377 K St., NW, Suite 637
Washington, DC 20005
Tel: 301-608-2590
Fax: 301-608-2596
Executive Director: Judith S.
Johnson

National Chamber of Commerce for
Women
10 Waterside Plaza
New York, NY 10010
Tel: 212-685-3454

National Family Business Council
1640 West Kennedy Rd.
Lake Forest, IL 60045
Tel: 708-295-1040

National Family Farm Coalition
110 Maryland Ave.
Washington, DC 20002
Tel: 202-543-5675

National Federation of Business and
Professional Women's Clubs
2012 Massachusetts Ave., NW
Washington, DC 20036
Tel: 202-293-1100

National Federation of Independent
Businesses (NFIB)
600 Maryland Ave., SW, Suite 700
Washington, DC 20024
Tel: 202-554-9000; 800-634-2669
President: S. Jackson Faris

National Minority Business Council
235 E. 42 St.
New York, NY 10017
Tel: 212-573-2385

National Small Business United
1155 15th St., NW, Suite 710
Washington, DC 20005
Tel: 202-293-8830

Small Business Coalition for
Health-Care Reform
413 North Lee St.
Alexandria, VA 22314
Tel: 703-836-7900
Fax: 703-549-0771

Small Business Council of America
4800 Hampden Lane
Bethesda, MD 20814
Tel: 301-656-7603

Small Business Foundation of
America
1155 15th St., NW
Washington, DC 20005
Tel: 202-223-1103

Small Business Legislative Council
1156 15th St., NW, Suite 510
Washington, DC 20005
Tel: 202-639-8500

GOVERNMENT OFFICES AND REGULATORY AGENCIES

Department of Commerce (DOC)
14th St. & Constitution Ave., NW
Washington, DC 20230
Tel: 202-219-3605
Secretary: Ron Brown

DOC Minority Business
Development
Tel: 202-482-5011
Director: Michael Rogers

DOC National Technical
Information Service
5285 Port Royal Rd.
Springfield, VA 22161
Tel: 703-487-4650

Department of Energy (DOE)
Forrestal Building
1000 Independent Ave., SW
Washington, DC 20585
Tel: 202-586-6210
Secretary: Hazel R. O'Leary

DOE Office of Small and
Disadvantaged Business
Tel: 202-254-5583

Department of Justice
Office of Small Business and
Minority Affairs
Tenth St. & Constitution Ave., NW
Washington, DC 20530
Tel: 202-616-0521
Director: Joseph Bryan

Department of Labor (DOL)
200 Constitution Ave., NW
Washington, DC 20210
Secretary: Robert Reich

DOL Office of Small Business and
Minority Affairs
Tel: 202-219-9148
Fax: 202-219-9167
Director: June Robinson

DOL Occupational Safety and
Health Administration (OSHA)
Tel: 202-219-8021; 202-219-8055
Director of Policy: Michael
Silverstein
Legislative Affairs: Lorraine Colbert

Department of Transportation
(DOT)
400 Seventh St., SW
Washington, DC 20590
Secretary: Federico Pena

DOT Office of Small and
Disadvantaged Business
Tel: 800-532-1169
Fax: 202-366-7228
Director: Luz Hopewell

DOT Minority Business Resource
Center
Tel: 202-366-1930
Director: Joe Capuano

Environmental Protection Agency
(EPA)
401 M St., SW
Washington, DC 20460
Tel: 800-368-5888
Fax: 703-305-6462
Ombudsman: Karen V. Brown

EPA Small Business Assistance
Program
Control Technology Center
OAQPS (MD-13)
Research Triangle Park, NC 27711
Tel: 919-541-5437

257

EPA Regulatory Flexibility Officer:
Paul Lapsley
Tel: 202-260-5323

Food and Drug Administration
Office of Small and Disadvantaged
Businesses
200 Independence Ave., SW
Washington, DC 20201
Tel: 301-443-6776
Director: Mary Ann Danello

General Services Administration
Office of Small and Disadvantaged
Businesses
18th & F St., NW
Washington, DC 20405
Tel: 202-501-1021
Fax: 202-219-1243
Director: Joan Parrott

Internal Revenue Service
111 Constitution Ave., NW
Washington, DC 20224
Tel: 202-622-3359; 800-829-1040
Fax: 202-622-8393
Small Business Ombudsman: Barbara
Jenkins

International Development
Cooperation Agency
Department of State Building 320
21st St., NW
Washington, DC 20523
Tel: 703-875-1551
Fax: 703-875-1498
Director: Joan Ashley

National Economic Council
Office of Policy Development
Executive Office of the President
1600 Pennsylvania Ave., NW
Washington, DC 20500
Tel: 202-456-1414
Fax: 202-456-9280
Director: Robert Fauver

Office of United States Trade
Representative
Winden Building 600
17th St., NW
Washington, DC 20506
Tel: 202-395-3204
Fax 202-395-3911
Representative: Mickey Kantor

Small Business Administration (SBA)
409 Third St., SW
Washington, DC 20416
Tel: 202-205-6583; 800-827-5722
Fax: 202-205-6928
Administrator: Philip Lader
Chief Counsel: Jere Glover

SBA Export Legal Assistance
Network
New York District Office
26 Federal Plaza, Suite 3100
New York, NY 10287
Tel: 212-264-9487
Director: Herb Austin

SBA Office of Advocacy
Tel: 202-205-7064
Fax: 202-205-7064
Assistant Chief Counsel for
Environmental Policy: Gregory
Koontz
Tel: 202-205-6949

SBA Office of Interagency Affairs
Tel: 202-205-6532

SBA Office of Economic Research
Tel: 202-205-6530

SBA Office of Information
Tel: 202-205-6531

SBA Small Business Answer Desk
Tel: 800-8-ASK-SBA

Small Business Hotline
Tel: 800-321-6742

United States Customs Service
Office of Regulations
1301 Constitution Ave., NW
Washington, DC 20229
Tel: 202-927-1000; 202-482-6900
Fax: 202-927-1380
Director: Harvey Fox

The White House Conference on
  Small Business
1800 G St., NW, Suite 1233
Washington, DC 20006-4407
Tel: 202 724 0891
Fax: 202 724 0903

NONPROFIT ORGANIZATIONS AND SERVICES

Environmental Technology
  Network
PO Box 21390
Washington, DC 20009
Tel: 202-342-9050
Fax: 202-328-3001

The Ford Foundation
320 E. 43 St.
New York, NY 10017
Tel: 212-573-5000
Secretary: Barron M. Jenny

MIT Enterprise Forum
201 Vassar St.
Cambridge, MA 02139-4310
Tel: 617-253-0015
Fax: 617-258-7264
Director: Joan Sonderburg

National Center for Public Policy
  Research
300 Eye St., NE, Suite 3
Washington, DC 20002
Tel: 202-543-1286

Small Business Assistance Center
554 Main St.
Box 1441
Worcester, MA 01601
Tel: 508-756-3513

Small Business Exporters Association
4603 John Tyler Ct., Suite 203
Annandale, VA 22003
Tel: 703-642-2490

Small Business Network
Box 30149
Baltimore, MD 21270
Tel: 410-581-1373

Small Business Science Bureau
554 Main St.
Worcester, MA 01601-1441
Tel: 508-756-3513

Soros Foundations
888 Seventh Ave.
New York, NY 10106
Tel: 212-757-2323
Director: Jody Spiro

Index

W

The Wall Street Journal, 110–11, 195, 244
Wal-Mart, 19, 243–44
Washington. See Federal government
The Washington Business Journal, 206
Watkins, James, 232, 233
Weidman, Jim, 115
Weiss, Howard, 69–70
Westchester Air, 177
WHCSB, 205, 208–9, 218–19
White House Conference on Small Business, 205, 208–9, 218–19
Willis, Mark Alan, 176, 177

Wolff, Michael, 194, 195
Women-owned small businesses, 5
Women's Business Ownership Act, 205
Women's Economic Self-Sufficiency Corp., 180
Working Woman, 211
World Bank, 141, 142
World trade. See International trade
World Trade Organization (WTO), 108, 110, 111, 113, 114, 115
Wyden, Ron, 91, 94

Z

Zierler, Sidney, 142